Mothers of the Nations

Indigenous Mothering as Global Resistance, Reclaiming and Recovery

Edited by

D. Memee Lavell-Harvard and Kim Anderson

Demeter Press logo based on the sculpture "Demeter" by Maria-Luise Bodirsky <www.keramik-atelier.bodirsky.de>

Cover Photograph by Patrick Chondon Photography
Cover and Book Design by Lyndsay Kirkham
Printed and Bound in Canada.

Library and Archives Canada Cataloguing in Publication

Mothers of the nations : indigenous mothering as global resistance, reclaiming and recovering / edited by D. Memee Lavell-Harvard and Kim Anderson. Includes bibliographical references.

ISBN 978-1-927335-45-1 (pbk.)

1. Motherhood. 2. Mothers–Social conditions. 3. Indigenous women– Social conditions. I. Anderson, Kim, 1964-, editor II. Lavell-Harvard, D. Memee (Dawn Memee), 1974-, editor

HQ759.M928 2014   306.874'3089   C2014-906022-X

Demeter Press
140 Holland Street West
P. O. Box 13022
Bradford, ON L3Z 2Y5
Tel: (905) 775-9089
Email: info@demeterpress.org
Website: www.demeterpress.org

Table of Contents

TABLE OF CONTENTS

IV: Building on the Past to Create a Future

Acknowledgements

For Indigenous mothers around the world, though your arms may be tired from holding up each new generation, and your throats raw from demanding to be heard, know that your efforts have not been in vain. Without your strength, your resilience, and your many sacrifices, we would not be able to maintain our faith in the promise of each new dawn—the hope for a better future.

For our own mothers, Jeannette Corbiere Lavell and Jocelyn Anderson, you have set the standards by which our own lives are measured. Without you we would not be where we are today, as your strength, courage, and sheer persistence in the face of adversity have inspired a belief that together we can overcome most anything.

We would like to thank our children Denia and Rajan, Autumn, Eva and Brianna, for being our greatest teachers. You have modelled patience, as you waited for us to "finish just one more page," and you were optimism personified when you actually believed it would be "just one more," but most of all you taught us about compassion when you forgave us for turning one more page into another few hours of work. Without you, our homes might be cleaner and our lives less chaotic, but we wouldn't have it any other way.

As we labored to bring forth this volume on Indigenous Mothering (and yes the allusion is intentional) we find ourselves owing a tremendous debt to David Lavell and Jo-Anne Lawless for their ongoing moral and editorial support. You truly went above and beyond the call of duty. Without you, all would be lost.

Introduction

Indigenous Mothering Perspectives

D. MEMEE LAVELL-HARVARD AND KIM ANDERSON

After centuries of persecution and oppression, the simple fact that we are still here, as proud Indigenous mothers, at the heart of our families, communities, and nations, signifies the strength of our resistance. Whether this resistance has been overt, as our sisters engage in constitutional challenges or human rights demonstrations, or covert, as we silently reconnect with the land and teach our children the ways of our ancestors, our efforts have ensured the continued survival of our people.

Our traditions remind us of the power of motherhood. In the Indigenous nations that we (Lavell-Harvard and Anderson) come from, we are taught that the women are the water carriers; they carry the waters of life and, therefore, water represents the female element. It is this belief in one's own ability—that like the water we can adapt to and eventually overcome any obstacle—that inspires resilience and persistence in the face of adversity. Sylvia Maracle (Mohawk) explains:

> The other thing to remember about the water is that it is the strongest force on the earth...Even the wind can't do what the water can do...that is our role in terms of tradition; we have the capacity as women to take those shapes, but also to make those shapes. We recognize that we don't have the kind of power where you bang your fist on the table, but that we have the power of the water—that sort of every day going

against something that ultimately changes the shape of the thing (quoted in Anderson, *A Recognition of Being* 185).

Indeed, like the waves that eventually wear away the rocks on our shores, the strength of our women is subtle but relentless. Such characteristics are unquestionably powerful tools in both the everyday struggles for survival as Indigenous mothers, as well as the larger struggles to challenge, subvert, deconstruct, and eventually break free from the oppressive structures of the racist, sexist, patriarchal society in which we find ourselves.

Although we set out to achieve the impossible, since "writing about an 'Indigenous ideology of motherhood' is, of course, an exercise in making generalizations about peoples who are extremely diverse" (Anderson, "Giving Life to the People" 761), we have, within this collection, found some common themes within the experiences of Indigenous mothering across the globe. While we can never claim to adequately represent the extremely nuanced diversity of Indigenous maternal experience, Indigenous peoples do share many values, epistemologies, and worldviews, including a belief in the centrality of strong powerful women, as demonstrated by the stories told herein. Unfortunately, as a graduate student recently reminded Lavell-Harvard when she glibly called out "the White Man" when asked to identify our greatest enemy, the one thing that we all have in common is a history of resistance; the experiences of colonization, oppression, and marginalization have been all too similar the world over. While this shared experience may determine the field upon which we must choose our battles, it does not define who we are at heart as Indigenous mothers since Indigenous mothering is, in essence, about something much larger, and much older, and much more empowering.

Interestingly, it is our shared experience of exclusion from society that provides a fertile ground for the revitalization and maintenance of empowering mothering practices. In the Canadian context, many of our mothers, grandmothers, and great-grandmothers before us found that an "Indian" or "half-breed" woman could never be assimilated enough to be accepted by colonial society (Van Kirk). As a result, the large scale inability (or more likely the conscious refusal) of Indigenous women to adapt to the western institution of motherhood instigated the apprehension of generations of Indigenous children and subsequent placement into residential schools or foster care where they could be isolated from the influence of their "backward" mothers. Despite the concerted and often brutal efforts of both church and state to erase Indigeneity, it became apparent that our cultures, the very essence of who we are, could neither be overcome, nor beaten out.

Traditionally, our women were respected and valued within our communities. Arising out of our role as mothers, as the givers of life, the role of Indigenous women is to care for and nurture life once it is brought into the world and, by extension, to care for and nurture our nations (Anderson, *A Recognition of Being*). Referencing the teachings of the Dakota nation, Anderson has explained that according to our traditions Indigenous women not only literally "birth the people" they are also given a "lifetime responsibility to nurture the people:"

> It's not just women's responsibility to the children—we have a responsibility to all of the people. We have to. We are the life givers. We are the life force of the nation. Our responsibility is to everyone; male and female, young or old, because we are that place from which life emanates. And there is nothing greater than that. (Ivy Chaske, quoted in Anderson, *A Recognition of Being* 169)

Bringing forth and nurturing new life is understood to be the basis of the creation of our nation. Thus, unlike western ideologies that denied women decision-making power in the family and positioned them in a role equivalent to a family servant, Indigenous mothers historically had responsibility for the life they created and, by extension, for the whole family and the entire community. With such responsibility came authority and the "right to make decisions on behalf of the children, the community and the nation" (Anderson, "Giving Life to the People" 171).

Unfortunately for our people, a fundamental belief in the equality and interdependence of all people, and the resulting egalitarian social structures found in many Indigenous societies, as well as the empowered women therein, were seen as a threat to the patriarchal order of the colonizers. In the North American context, Indigenous women not only birthed each new generation, they were simultaneously "bearers of a counter-imperial order," and so their subjugation was "critical to the success of the economic, cultural and political colonization" of the "new world" (Smith 15). The very existence of women who were subject to the authority of neither fathers nor husbands had the potential to throw into question the supposed natural order of patriarchal hierarchies and could therefore not be tolerated. As Andrea Smith has argued, the subsequent and continued "demonization of

Native women can be seen as a strategy of white men to maintain control over white women" (21) thereby reinforcing patriarchy, and simultaneously destroying the social structures of Indigenous nations. In Canada and the United States, Eurowestern "matrons" were sent to Indigenous communities to train the women, in a largely unsuccessful attempt to encourage acceptance of a more acceptable role as docile and subservient housewives and mothers in patriarchal nuclear families (Rutherdale, Jacobs).

Dua, Stevenson, Smith, and Monture-Angus have all described the many ways in which the colonial imagination constructed the "myth" of the Indigenous woman in North America in order to denigrate, disempower, and dehumanize her, thereby serving a racist and sexist colonial agenda. According to Dua, departures from the traditional patriarchal nuclear family model were seen as a danger to the social order and fears of miscegenation were intimately mixed with fear of "degeneration" into so-called "primitive patterns of social and family practices" in North America (254). Through their missions, the early French colonizers actively worked to replace the functional gender, sexual, and familial relations in Indigenous communities with patriarchal relationships based on monogamy, discipline, and dependency for women. While such attempts were generally resisted (as the dismayed accounts of missionaries attest), they were not without effect, as familial relationships that had served the Indigenous people well since time immemorial were disrupted.

Indeed, even when Indigenous ceremonies, dances, or gatherings were outlawed, and our very survival was dependent upon compliance with the dictates of colonial society, our grandmothers learned how to effectively hide any indicators of adherence to our traditions by actively cultivating the outward appearance of conformity. We have been persecuted for as long as we can remember, not only because we were different in a society with very little tolerance for diversity, but because society deemed our differences, our heathen legacies, as a threat to the maintenance of social order. It is therefore not surprising that many of us learned at a very young age the importance of deception. Thus began a long tradition of "keeping up appearances" as a strategic form of resistance, and as a result many of us find ourselves living a double life as we construct and work to maintain a façade of normalcy in order to evade the always vigilant gaze of the larger society.

In retrospect, it was a blessing in disguise that Indigenous women were never completely or effectively assimilated enough to become the kind of wife and mother idealized in western patriarchal society. While non-

Indigenous women are struggling to break free from the constraints of the patriarchal family and the oppression of motherhood, many of our women have resisted (or been excluded) and, as a result, have always existed outside these particular paradigms. Andrea O'Reilly explains that feminist mothering functions as a counter narrative or "oppositional discourse: its meaning is constructed as a negation of patriarchal motherhood" (797). In this context, as it is defined in oppositional ways, feminist mothering is still responding to, and therefore structurally and conceptually influenced by, the parameters and definitions of patriarchal mothering. In this manner, the revolutionary power of feminist mothering is hobbled as the terms of the debate and the field of battle are already set by the traditions of patriarchal society. However, generations of resistance and resilience means those Indigenous women do not necessarily face the same dilemma as we work instead to reclaim and revitalize the more empowering cultural beliefs, traditions, and practices of our ancestors.

Indigenous women have had to become practiced at resistance in order to survive in a system that functions globally to subjugate and oppress both Indigenous peoples and women generally, and, therefore, Indigenous women particularly. Generations of strong women have provided the foundation for such resistance, for, as Anderson explains, the "guidance that women receive from their mothers, aunts and grandmothers, shapes the way they learn to understand themselves and their positions in the world" ("Giving Life to the People" 123). Having had to learn how to resist subjugation and how to survive under the weight of oppression, previous generations of Indigenous mothers have maintained a definition of womanhood and mothering premised upon strength and capability that was distinctly different from the negative images and subservient female role offered by mainstream society. Indeed, according to the definition of womanhood cultivated by Western society, the so-called "true woman is self-contained within her nuclear family, with specific and separate roles for men and women and with an economic dependence on men, in such a way that motherhood is one's true occupation" (Snorton 57). In contrast, for Indigenous women, the role of wife and mother did not historically preclude working outside the home and was certainly not defined by dependency.

In land-based communities, given that the men were often away from the community for long periods, women were not only encouraged, but expected to be independent and self-reliant. Women were therefore neither prevented, nor discouraged from learning tasks that were traditionally seen to be men's work and, moreover, engaging in such work was not seen to take away from one's femininity (Anderson, Berkin, Brown, Landes). The provision of foodstuffs and resources for the family often relied heavily upon tasks traditionally performed by women, thereby negating any possibility of women being dependent upon their husbands and creating, instead, relationships characterized by interdependence and equality (Anderson, "Giving Life to the People"). For centuries, strength, independence, and self-reliance have defined our mothers, and interdependent supportive networks of kin have shaped Indigenous motherhood; the legacy of which continues to influence our collective experience today. We see evidence of the power and strength of traditional Indigenous motherhood in the stories told within the chapters of this volume, which we have divided into four sections to demonstrate the many aspects of resistance, reclaiming and recovery.

We begin with a section (I) on "Healthy Beginnings;" opening with Malika Grasshoff/ MAKILAM's description of mothering practices among the Kabyle, the "oldest people of Northern Africa" (Chapter 1). Grasshoff starts with the proclamation that "the womb of the mother is the source of human life, and, respectively, human civilization." She goes on to demonstrate how Indigenous mothering practices among her people challenge patriarchal norms and even notions like gender complementarity—a theory and practice we work with in other Indigenous contexts. As such, her work encourages us to begin by re-situating our thinking about gender roles and the place of mothering, which, as we have described earlier, is a significant purpose of this book. Hannah Neufeld's chapter (2) follows by bringing us back to the original mother/beginning (land); she makes the connection between land and mothering bodies. Writing about the disruption to land-based food acquisition and the accompanying traditional knowledge among Saulteaux women in Manitoba, Canada, Neufeld prompts us to reflect on Indigenous approaches to healthy beginnings, which include food intake during pregnancy. This chapter encourages us to see how healthy beginnings involve re-connecting to mother earth.

"Healthy beginnings" for Indigenous peoples ultimately leads to reclaiming pre-natal, birth and post natal care, the subject of the next two chapters. Kadetz (Chapter 3) writes about colonial biomedical interference with traditional birth attendants (*hilots*) among Indigenous people in the Philippines. Drawing from interviews with almost 200 Indigenous Filipino women about their experiences with childbirth, he documents a preference to have *hilots* continue their work supporting home delivery. In spite of this, *hilots* and home births were sidelined by a 2008 Department of Health Administrative Order requiring in-facility birthing with "skilled" birth attendants—a vivid demonstration of contemporary colonial policy and the disregard for choice in Indigenous women's childbirth experiences. As Kadetz asks "Can maternal child health policies formulated at international and global levels ever be truly appropriate or safe for Indigenous women by continuing to dictate rather than to listen?" Chapter 4, by Tabobondung et al., provides an example of moving forward with the listening, as it describes reclaiming Indigenous centered care and the resurgence of Indigenous midwifery through the establishment of an Indigenous-grounded birth centre in Toronto, Canada. Framed by the personal stories of five women who were involved in the visioning and establishment of the birth centre, this chapter is a heartening example of how the circle comes around, for here we have Indigenous women reclaiming an Indigenous vision of healthy beginnings in a modern urban context.

In Section II, "Voicing Resilience," we offer more powerful examples of how Indigenous mothers envision themselves through the oppressive colonial practices that have lead to poverty, poor health, child welfare intervention and sexual violence. This section allows us to hear the voices of Indigenous mothers in Kenya (Van Tyler), Toronto, Canada (Baskin et al.), Guatemala (Jayakumar), and Saskatoon (Anderson). In Van Tyler's chapter (5), we hear from nine mothers living with HIV/AIDS in the mega slum of Kiberia, Kenya. All widowed, these women must navigate through experiences of "being up, feeling down and stress up" as they steadfastly work to raise their children without adequate support. The chapter by Baskin et al. (6) highlights the voices of Indigenous women navigating the child welfare system in Toronto, Canada while simultaneously working to address alcohol and drug substance misuse. Baskin and her co-authors conclude that more time is needed to allow the mothers to heal, build partnerships with and between service providers, implement holistic approaches and learn from each other.

Nation building can be a fractious place for mothers, and Jayakumar's chapter (7) addresses how Indigenous mothers become centered within the battleground. This chapter draws on testimony to depict the sexual violence experienced by Mayan mothers during, and following, the Guatemalan Civil War. The resilience required of these mothers is almost unfathomable; yet they continue to find ways to mother in the face of colonial, state and community violence. In Chapter 8, Anderson begins with a visual study of mothers in Saskatoon, Canada, presenting a heartening show of resilience and self-definition through the beautiful photographic portraits that they shared with the city where they reside.

In section III, featuring "Othermothering Spaces and Multiple Moms," "othermoms" are an integral part of alternate "families of the heart" (Castellano) that urban Indigenous people create in the wake of disruption to extended and land based family systems. The theme of learning from each other, and providing support within a community of mothers also comes through in Chapter 9, where Charbonneau et al. write about Indigenous mothers engaged in street sex work in Winnipeg, Regina, Edmonton, and Calgary, Canada. The authors of Chapter 9 begin by making public the "disavowed" point that "most street sex workers are mothers." This mothering work includes not only mothering biological children, grandchildren, nieces, nephews and siblings, but mothering each other within communities and taking on the necessary leadership roles for keeping families and nations together.

The chapters by Proverbs and Sellers (10 & 11) depict "multiple moms" through stories of birth and adoptive mothers. Proverbs envisions a conversation that might have happened between her Kasa-Dena birth mother and her adoptive settler-Canadian mother. Her chapter (10) gives personal expression to the legacy of colonial interference in Indigenous family systems in Canada, and, in particular, residential schooling and the child welfare system, yet shows how the multiple moms who find themselves caught up in these systems can come together around healing. For Sellers (Chapter 11), the healing came through moving from her Jewish birth mother toward adoptive Indigenous grandmothers among her father's people. Sellers contrasts patriarchal Judeo-Christian creation stories with women-centered creation stories of the Haudenosaunee to contextualize the impact on mother-daughter relations in her own life. Whereas adoption is usually framed in a negative manner in writing about Indigenous experiences, these two chapters (10 & 11) highlight transformative and healing adoptive practices—it's about what we adopt. Finally, multiple moms can come in many forms, and Jennifer Brant's chapter (12) on "Finding Empowerment through Indigenous Literature" shows us that we always have our Indigenous literary moms standing by when we need them. Brant writes of her experience teaching Indigenous women's literature to Indigenous mothers at Brock University in southern Ontario, Canada. As one of Brant's students reported after studying these authors: "It's like coming home."

The final section (IV) of the book, "Building on the Past to Create a Future," depicts how Indigenous mothers are drawing from distinct Indigenous histories and traditions to rebuild sacred and powerful mothering experiences and practices. Earlier in this introduction, we wrote about finding common practices and values among Indigenous peoples worldwide, in spite of our distinct cultures and traditions. As Indigenous scholars living in the territory now called Canada, we can see similarities across the globe in Helen Connor's depiction of Māori mothering in Aotearoa/New Zealand (Chapter 13). Connor describes traditional Māori mothering practices, colonial interference and the reclaiming of traditional mothering practices through the Māori Renaissance. Having been invaded by the same Anglo-settler culture that came to Canada, it is not surprising to see similarities in colonial policy and its consequences, but there are also similarities in the traditions that pre-date colonial practices, starting with female-centered creation stories, connections between land, new life and spirituality, the significance of extended family and kin-centric societies, and the sacredness of the maternal body. These are the histories and traditions that, as Indigenous mothers worldwide, we share in reclaiming. The chapter by Fontaine et al. (15) then offers a model for reclaiming, and a refreshing lens on the Canadian residential school story. It documents Indigenous mothering recovery among daughters of residential school survivors/mothers. Using the tools of digital storytelling, this new generation of mothers is re-imagining their way out of a colonial legacy and healing themselves and their mothers as part of the process.

In the second last chapter (15), Dawn Marsden offers a provocative exploration of how one might incorporate traditional Indigenous mothering practices in a modern context (and even into space!). She walks the reader through a series of principles that she has applied as an Indigenous single mother living in mostly urban contexts, including spiritual based living, integrating interconnectedness, environment centered thinking, self-sufficiency and self-discovery, recognizing and nurturing gifts, apprenticeship training, self-determination, working with communal food and water, nurturing relationships, employing free trade and gifting, working with restorative justice, restoring public rites of passage, employing circle talk, working with consensus, and leadership from below. As editors of the collection, we (Lavell-Harvard and Anderson) then end the book (Chapter 16) with words on our own unique experiences, drawing attention to the attempts of Indigenous mothers to negotiate our positions in contemporary society while engaging in our various and distinct mothering traditions.

As we finish putting this book together, we take heart that these chapters have collectively reinforced that we are not alone in our communities, territories and nations—that there is a global context of resistance, reclaiming, and recovery among Indigenous mothers and their allies. We hope that the book will similarly inspire Indigenous mothers and allies around the world to continue mothering the nations into a healthy future.

WORKS CITED

Anderson, Kim. "Giving Life to the People: An Indigenous Ideology of Motherhood." Ed. Andrea O'Reilly. *Maternal Theory: Essential Readings*. Toronto, ON: Demeter Press, 2007. 761–781. Print.

—. *A Recognition of Being*. Toronto, ON: Sumach/Canadian Scholars' Press, 2000. Print

Berkin, Carol. *First Generations: Women in Colonial America*. New York: Farrar, Straus, and Giroux, 1996. Print.

Brown, Judith. "Economic Organization and the Position of Women Among the Iroquois." *Iroquois Women: An Anthology*. Ed. Wm. G. Spittal. Oshweken, ON: Iroquois Printing and Craft Supplies, 1990. 151–187. Print.

Castellano, Marlene Brant. *Aboriginal Family Trends: Extended Families, Nuclear Families, Families of the Heart*. Ottawa, ON: Vanier Institute, 2002. Print.

Dua, Enakshi. "Beyond Diversity: Exploring the Ways in which the Discourse of Race has Shaped the Institution of the Nuclear Family." *Scratching the Surface: Canadian Anti-Racist Feminist Thought*. Eds. Enakshi Dua and Angela Robertson. Toronto, ON: Women's Press, 1999. 237–260. Print.

Jacobs, Margaret. *White Mother to a Dark Race: Settler Colonialism, Maternalism, and the Removal of Indigenous Children in the American West and Australia, 1880–1940*. Lincoln: University of Nebraska Press, 2009. Print.

—. "Working on the Domestic Frontier: American Indian Domestic Servants in White Women's Households in the San Francisco Bay Area, 1920–1940." *Frontiers: A Journal of Women's Studies* 1 and 2 (2006): 127–161. Print.

Landes, Ruth. *The Ojibwa Woman*. 1971. New York: Norton and Company. 1974. Print.

Monture-Angus, Patricia, and Mary Ellen Turpel. *Thunder in my Soul: A*

Mohawk Woman Speaks. Halifax: Fernwood Publishing. 1995. Print.

O'Reilly, Andrea. "Feminist Mothering." *Maternal Theory: Essential Readings*. Ed. Andrea O'Reilly. Toronto, ON: Demeter Press, 2008. 792–821. Print.

Rich, Adrienne. *Of Woman Born: Motherhood as Experience and Institution*. New York: Norton, 1976. Print.

Rutherdale, Myra. "Mothers of the Empire: Maternal Metaphors in the Northern Canadian Mission Field." *Canadian Missionaries, Indigenous Peoples: Representing Religion at Home and Abroad*. Eds. Alvyn Austin and Jamie S. Scott. Toronto: University of Toronto Press, 2005. Print.

Smith, Andrea. *Conquest: Sexual Violence and American Indian Genocide*. Cambridge, MA: South End Press, 2005. Print.

Snorton, Teresa E. "The Legacy of the African-American Matriarch: New Perspectives for Pastoral Care." *Through the Eyes of Women*. Ed. Jeanne Stevenson Moessner. Minneapolis: Fortress Press, 1996. 50–65. Print.

Stevenson, Winona. "Colonialism and First Nations Women in Canada." *Scratching the surface: Canadian anti-racist feminist thought*. Eds. Enakshi Dua and Angela Robertson. Toronto, ON: Women's Press, 1999. 49–80. Print.

Van Kirk, Sylvia. "Colonized lives: The Native Wives and Daughters of Five Founding Families of Victoria." *In the Days of our Grandmothers: A Reader in Aboriginal Women's History in Canada*. Eds. Mary Ellen Kelm and Lorna Townsend. Toronto, ON: University of Toronto Press, 2006. 170–199. Print.

I: Healthy Beginnings

1.

The Meaning of Motherhood Among the Kabyle Berber, Indigenous People of North Africa

MALIKA GRASSHOFF/MAKILAM

The Berbers are known as the oldest people of Northern Africa today still living in Algeria, Tunisia, and Morocco. In Algeria, the two most important groups of the Berbers are the Tuareg—famous all over the world as the People of the Desert (they are nomads)—and the Kabyle, who are sedentary. For a certain time, they were Christians, but later became Muslims, due to the conquest by the Arabs. However, the Berbers of Kabylia in Algeria have retained many of their pre-Islamic customs.

I come from the Kabyle, a Berber tribe in Algeria, and I learned very early about the central position of mothers in this society. The best way of explaining motherhood is by telling you of my own experience in my mother clan. In the first part of my explanation, I outline the basics, the patterns of Kabyle motherhood, and in the second part I present photos illustrating how mothers lived their independent female potency, which is expressed in artistic drawings during the daily chores of women, such as pottery, weaving, and murals.

PART I: THE KABYLE WOMAN AS THE MOTHER OF CHILDREN AND NATURE

The history of every man and every woman has a concrete beginning in the womb of a mother. Still today, the birthing rites by Berbers, the secrets surrounding birth and labor, are exclusively reserved for women alone. As in some societies, the Kabyle prohibit the presence of a man at birth, for the beginning of a new life is something only the women can share together. As the religious historian and philosopher Mircea Eliade wrote: "the secret of delivery is a religious experience which can't be translated into the vocabulary of male experience" (Eliade 165).

The womb of the mother is the source of human life, and, respectively, human civilization. It's very important to understand and to accept this, because, as a mother, a woman can give birth to a new woman and she can also give birth to a man, whereas a man cannot give birth to a new man and even less to a new woman. My mother taught me that the best world would be a world where men could produce men and women could produce women, because "an apple tree produces an apple and not a pear." In the same way, it would be better if a man gave birth to a man and a woman gave birth to a woman. She had learned that it is evident that by giving birth to a woman a mother reproduces her own self. But to produce another body—a man's body—inside a woman body is more. To give birth to a man is even better, as men are physically different to women. It is the reason why the mothers in Kabylia always say "Mothers are the mothers of women and also the mothers of all men." A man cannot be born without a woman.

In Kabylia, mothering is considered a social constant throughout time. The girl becomes a woman—a potential mother—with the onset of menstruation, and the grandmother remains a mother until her death. The veneration of mothers is strongly supported by songs, poems, texts, and in the arts, in praise of the mother. This mother veneration is also supported by men, for men in Kabylia say: "The woman carries the life of the man in her womb—either a husband, a brother or a father—as a man, he is the defender of her *honor*." This saying demonstrates that Kabyle men acknowledge that they come from a woman's body. The life of each man depends on a woman, because women are the mothers of their sons. Without a woman, none of the men could exist—so the male community would disappear. Our understanding is that man needs a woman to continue his life. All this underpins the notion that each man has to protect and to defend women, and his responsibility consists in supporting all mothers. In the Berber society, men can't commit a murder in front of a woman. If a man kills or rapes a woman, the group will kill him.

Generally, in patriarchal western societies, we speak about an egalitarian form of society as being harmonious and balanced among the genders and the genders are traditionally seen as complementary. In Europe, for example, we refer to the theory of the Greek philosopher Plato (428/427–348/347 B.C.), which describes man and woman as two parts that originally formed a whole Sphere. This concept of two parts that are complementary has many regrettable consequences on all levels. With this theory of complementary, a man is incomplete without a woman and a woman is incomplete without a man. In this way, a human being is incomplete or "unfinished" and he always search his other half (Makilam 137–138). This theory of complementarity is inherent to patriarchy, and is strange to the Kabyle understanding of gender. Kabyle women and men are seen as complete entities in their own rights, though of the same nature. This explains why a Kabyle woman is never compared to a man. She feels as a part of the female community, which is distinguished from the men's community. The representation of the human society in the Kabyle mind consists of two communities, but not with complementary gender logic.

Indeed, it is typical for the mother-centered Berber society that women and men work in different fields and different tasks. Like in Native and Mesoamerican societies, the genders in Kabylia have their separate economic sphere and authority—and these do not interfere with one another. Each group works separately, but for the same goal: the continuity of the mother's line.

Women in traditional Berber society do not want to be men or to take over masculine values, as in patriarchal western societies. A Kabyle woman does not want to be complementary to a man and, we will see later—as a mother—she teaches their daughters an artistic secret script, which is the proof of the honor to be born as a woman.

THE SOCIAL PATTERN: FAMILY AND CLAN

Birthing among the Kabyle today is still a collective opportunity inside the female clan, wherein the old women help to give life. In this way, birthing represents the foundation of the whole society. What is family for you? In modern societies, the mythical "normal" family consists of the father, the mother, and the children. Traditionally, in the Kabyle society, family is understood as a vertical line from the old mothers to the offspring. First come the grandmothers, then the next generation of women, who are mothers of the following generation of daughters. The mother represents the link between old mothers and children. We can see that the family organization is not primarily aligned to the male community, as it is in patriarchal societies. My mother always tells us that a mother is unique because we can have a new man or a new child, but never a new mother. The definition of the mothering at the center of a community encompasses one grandmother-mother-daughter relationship.

The women's clan consists of grandmothers, mothers, the children (daughters and sons), and the children of the children (granddaughters and grandsons). They all live in close relation within the same house, and children experience that they are a part of the chain that descends from their mother and ancestral mothers. The concept of Kabyle family is the clan of our mothers with her brothers, sisters and children. That is why the words "brother" or "sister" don't exist in Kabyle language. Instead, we speak of the son of the mother or the daughter of the mother. This means that, for us, each person is always connected to the maternal line. If a woman has problems, she does not go to her "husband," but asks help from the son or the daughter of her mother. If we have a problem, we do not ask the relatives of our father but of our mother. In fact, in a mother-centred society, the woman (or the man) is not the property of her husband or her father. She remains a member of her grandmother-mother clan. Kabyle mothers are the founders of families, of the clan, and therefore of the village. In Berber society, even today, it is not the woman who looks for a husband, but the man who must accept the wife his mother has chosen for him. Assisted by daughters and sisters, mothers choose the future daughter-in-law and become mediators of human life in organizing their son's marriages.

THE VALUES OF MOTHERING: GIFT-ECONOMY WITH NURTURING, HELPING AND LIFE-GIVING VALUES

Nourishing characterizes motherhood, and, in the Kabyle tradition, milk contains such power that the end of the world is predicted on the day when milk won't be available. What's more, we observe that, in Kabylia, the woman becomes a mother, not only with the birth of a child who is hers by blood connection; there are other means to becoming a mother. For example, the symbolic gesture of offering a breast to someone constitutes an adoption rite, which carries the prohibition to marry someone from the clan. The bonds built by breast-feeding are as strong as the blood bonds.

Mothering is life-giving. Immediately after birth, the Berber mother and the newborn have to retreat for forty days. These forty days are also known in other cultures all over the world, as described by Rahmani: "The Israelis generally keep to the tradition of the 40 days. Catholics still celebrate Candlemas on the 2nd of February. This festival commemorates the purification of the Virgin Mary forty days after Christmas" (Rahmani III). This ritual is intended to support what is regarded as the most dangerous phase in a mother's life. We say the woman is like a tomb because she is now—after these forty days—out of danger, reborn to life (Rahmani 110 & Makilam 2007/2). We can note that this forty-day retreat of a mother after birth will also be observed after the death of a person. The visit to the cemetery must be conducted on the 3rd and also on the 40th day after death. Within those days, the straying soul of the deceased is hovering over the threshold of the house, and will return after forty days. The magical ritual of forty days after life and death underlines the importance of mothering as life-giving and also the connection with life and death.

The culture of mothering is gifting. These values of mothering, like helping, giving and nurturing, are kept by women and also by men. The Kabyle sociologist Mohand Khellil has described the importance of motherhood values and underlines what it means for a man to be a part of a mother's clan: "The supreme qualities that define a Kabyle man (his honor, his bravery, and dignity) are found in the same word which designates a Kabyle woman and Kabyle language: *taqbaylit*" (Khellil 61). We can observe how the Berber men's community support the values of maternity and, also, that the distinction of two genders around the mother clan create an egalitarian form of society. In contrast, the complementarity of genders in the modern western society create opposition or violence between the genders, because the women do not have their own sphere and have to turn down their female and maternal values for patriarchal values.

The economy is connected to the values of helping, as expressed in mutual aid, called *tiwizi* or *Touiza* in Kabyle language. This principle requires relatives to accept responsibilities for each other. In all traditional activities, like the construction of a new house, or the events of life, like birth and marriage, the clan has to help the others and to receive help from the other clan members no matter if they are poor or rich. This giving and taking of aid to support the group, this reciprocity of aid, creates equality between all the members. Therefore, economy is not only a relationship of selling and buying between two persons, but is based on the relationship of the whole group. Economy is life logic with rituals as a form of sociability and responsibility, and the difference between genders and their different tasks and roles do not result in a relationship of power between men and women.

RELIGIOUS AND SPIRITUAL PATTERN: THE WOMAN AS THE MOTHER OF LIVING NATURE

If the womb of the pregnant mother is the source of human life, then the origin of human being must be understood as coming from the body of a mother and not from God. The nature and the life flowing through the body of men and women are sacral and they come from a divine origin, which gives the same life to flora and fauna. Planet Earth is an organic system, animated by invisible forces of life. Like a woman, the earth has life inside, and this life is sacral. Therefore, maternal activities among the Kabyle are not restricted to giving birth and to nursing. Women are mothers of the earth and also of all life, guaranteeing the survival of nature in the macrocosm. For example, when a plant in a vegetable garden sprouts, the woman passing has to untie her belt in ritual silence and contemplation, not to hamper the growth of the plants. She acts in the same way when she gives life to a new baby. These practices apply to interactions with the animal kingdom as well.

Berber women live the religious and spiritual dimension in union with nature, which is considered women's support of mothering. For generations, in all traditional Berber societies, mothers have passed their knowledge and skills onto their daughters through the every-day ritual contact with nature. Moreover, they confide the secrets of nature to the next generation of mothers in accordance with female nature. In my first book, I described how the rituals of pottery-making and weaving—the sacred practices given from our ancestors—reproduce exactly the physical union between a man and a woman. For example, by the ancestral ritual of pottery-making, the Kabyle woman potter must always begin from a flattened base which reproduces the female sex. To this, she adds a shaped piece of clay similar to the male phallus. These gestures, which have never changed, are ritualized and practiced in all of Grand Kabylia. For an indigenous Kabyle, transforming the clay in a new pottery is like a human birth. This rite of practice is seen as magic. In the same way, the woman potter creates an object with the spirit of her own creation and birth. All traditional activities, like pottery, food-making and weaving, are always accompanied with blood rituals through the sacrifice of animals. With the example of pottery-making, the woman potter transforms the clay in a human being.

THE COSMIC DIMENSION OF MOTHERING

Among the Kabyle, motherhood is a collective event attended by all women in the clan; the birth of a child also affects the whole village. Even more, birthing is a sacred activity depending on the forces of the sky and especially the moon. Motherhood is subjected to cosmic laws and is connected to the fertility of the fields and the animals. For example, during all the time of pregnancy, it is prohibited to take fire out of the house. This same rule applies to the birth of a calf, during the time of marriage, and during harvesting. The cosmic dimension of mothering can be seen in all daily chores like pottery, food-making and weaving (Makilam 2007/1).

THE CULTURE OF HUMANITY

Mothers are the founders of human culture because they teach the Kabyle language. Without a Kabyle mother, one cannot get the Kabyle identity. Within living memory, knowledge has always been passed on orally from parent to child. It's very interesting to learn that the word *taqbaylit* means "woman" as well as "Kabyle language." In spite of the fact that Arabic is the official language in Algeria, thanks to the mothers, Kabyle is still spoken in Algeria and outside the Kabylia. Our language is spoken in France, other parts of Europe, and Canada, where large Berber communities exist in Ottawa, Quebec City, Montréal, and Toronto. With the language, mothers teach us social communication—and beyond that, love, care, and compassion. We also learn from mothers to respect the earth, water, and all that is alive. Food and weaving are a gift of nature and we have to respect mothers' earth provenance as sacral.

PART II: THE SUCCESSION OF GENERATIONS IN ARTISTIC WORK

The honor, the privilege to be a woman, is so powerful that the Kabyle express motherhood in their artistic work. Tattoos, woven cloth, pottery, and murals constitute a secret language among women, which is exclusively passed on from mother to daughter. My initiation by old women-potters in the 1980s allowed me to decipher the secret code of these drawings that can only be appreciated by women, because they are directly connected to their femininity and maternity. I can share some of the most basic knowledge here, although much of it must stay within the community.

Figure 1: The Door Into The Woman's Womb

Tattoos appear on the face, on the neck and on the arms of the old women. All figures are based on the triangle and can also be found on pottery and murals. These four drawings (Figure 1) show the door into the woman's womb.

From this basic pattern—the triangle—other motifs are developed, such as the rhombus, which can be seen on all the old woven cloth. The succession of rhombuses represents the back of a snake. Like the earth, the snake metamorphoses once a year and puts on a new skin. Similar to the monthly changes of a woman's body in menstruation, the snake's moult is used in many rites and practices either to drive out or to enable the birth of a child (Makilam 2007/1, 238–239). These geometric patterns are also painted on the pottery (Figure 2).

Figure 3 of an oil lamp presents a human couple. This oil lamp is offered at weddings and we can observe that this pottery represents a human body with two heads.

The mystery of succession, the mystery of pregnancy and birth, are also painted as frescoes on the walls inside Kabyle houses. In Figure 4 we can see the oldest photo from a mural, both dating to 1942. All these paintings show the door into the woman's womb. We can observe that the legs are represented by the letter M—incorporating rhombus, the opening of the mother. These symbols of life, the succession of Ms, represent beams painted on the walls within the house. They illustrate the miracle of the conception of a human being in the motherly womb. They picture the eternal principle of life passing from mother to mother in endless generations. These trees of life can therefore be seen as totems in honor of the ancestral mothers.

Figure 2: Oil lamp showing a pregnant woman.

CONCLUSION

The philosophies, practices and artistic expressions I have described here show that the Kabyle society is one of the best examples of a mother-centered society. Yet, among the Kabyle, the woman-mothers have never reached the status of a goddess. The veneration of the mother does not refer to the woman alone but also to the earth: vegetation, ancient trees, springs, holy grottos and the moon. That why Kabyle say "If a mother dies, even the trees and the rocks weep."

Figure 3: Oil lamp presenting human couple.

The Kabyle women teach their daughters a magical script on the origin of human being with symbols of femininity and maternity. All these symbols mean *Women: you are the roots of the human culture.*

Figure 4: Mural inside Kabyle house, dating to 1942.

WORKS CITED

Abouda, Mohand. *Axxam, Maisons kabyles, espaces et fresques murales.* M. Abouda éditeur, Paris, 1985; Entretiens avec M. Virolle-Souibes, "Fresques kabyles", *Littérature orale arabo-berbère*, 1985–1986. Print.

Devulder, Marcel, "Rituel magique des femmes kabyles (tribu des Ouadhias, Grande Kabylie)." *Revue africaine*, t. 101, (1957), 229–361. Print.

—. "Peintures murales et pratiques magiques dans la tribu des Ouadhias," *Revue Africaine*, t. 95, 1e et 2e trim. 1951, 63–102. Print

Eliade, Mircea. *Le sacré et le profane.* Paris: Gallimard, 1972. Print.

Khellil, Mohand, *La Kabylie ou l'Ancêtre sacrifié.* Paris: L'Harmattan, 1985. Print.

Lacouste-Dujardin, C. *Le conte kabyle (1970).* Paris: F. Maspero. 1982. Print.

Laoust-Chantreaux, G., *Kabylie côté femmes: la vie féminine à Aït Hichem, 1937-1939.* Aix-en-Provence: Edisud, 1990. Print.

Makilam, M.G. *The Magical Life of Berber Women in Kabylia.* New York: Peter Lang, 2007. Print.

—. *Symbols and Magic in the Arts of Kabyle Women.* New York: Peter Lang, 2007. Print.

—. "The Central Position of Women among the Berber People of Northern Africa: the Four Seasons Life Cycle of a Kabyle Woman." *Societies of Peace (Matriarchies: Past, Present and Future).* Ed. Heide Goettner-Abendroth. Toronto, Canada: Innana Publications and Education Inc., 2008. 178–189. Print.

Rahmani, Slimane. "Coutumes kabyles du Cap Aokas." *Revue africaine*, 1e tr. 1939. Print.

Vaughan, Genevieve.*Women and the Gift Economy.* Toronto: Innana Publications, 2007. Print.

2.

"We Practically Lived Off The Land"

Generational Changes in Food Acquisition Patterns Among First Nation Mothers and Grandmothers

HANNAH TAIT NEUFELD

INTRODUCTION

Traditional foods, defined as plants and animals harvested from the local environment (Gagné 1), are central to health and culture for Indigenous peoples world-wide (Raschke and Cheema 662). Across the globe, how-ever, various processes of environmental dispossession have decreased access to traditional foods, leading to their gradual replacement with marketed or pre-manufactured products (Richmond and Ross 403). This shift from tra-ditional to market foods, has had dramatic consequences for dietary quality and cultural identity both on-reserve and off-reserve in Canada (Egeland et al. 1747; Johnson-Down and Egeland 1311). Under these circumstances, food insecurity, or the inability to acquire nutritionally adequate foods in culturally acceptable ways, (Anderson 1559) can lead to re-occurring hunger and lower caloric intake. It may also compromise the quality of the over-all family diet, as chronic food insecurity is often associated with a higher energy intake from foods containing more saturated fats and refined carbo-hydrates. Traditional foods tend to be more nutrient dense in protein and essential micronutrients (Gagné et al. 1748; Johnson-Down and Egeland

1314). Overall, this nutrition transition away from nutrient-rich locally-harvested foods has resulted in reduced dietary diversity associated with the increasing prevalence of obesity-related non-communicable diseases such as type 2 diabetes (Kuhnlein et al. 1447; Schuster et al. 287). Diabetes rates are 3 to 5 times higher in First Nations than in the general Canadian population (CDA S191). Gender differences also exist, with over 20% of First Nations women diagnosed with type 2 diabetes compared to 16% of men.

Dietary change is therefore leading to significant changes in the physical health status of Aboriginal[1] peoples in Canada, but so, too, have the effects of dietary change on cultural identity been significant (Lambden et al. 332). Food security is not necessarily narrowly defined as having enough to eat (Willows et al. 1150). Rather, its meaning encompasses the ability to acquire foods in socially acceptable ways, such as through traditional cultural practices (FAO 1) that may encompass access to traditional knowledge. For many Indigenous peoples, food is a physical, as well as a spiritual, medicine (Omura 150). Traditional, or perhaps more culturally-accepted foods are highly valued among Indigenous groups for maintaining health, preserving cultural identity, and promoting a sense of self-worth or autonomy (Kuhnlein et al. 112; Stroink and Nelson 268; Elliott et al. 6). Changes in these knowledge transmission patterns between mothers and their children, as a result of complex and continuing colonial policies in Canada, such as the residential school system, and elsewhere, have isolated children from their cultural roots and subsequently disrupted transmission of traditional knowledge to subsequent generations (Elias et al. 1561).

Although an emerging body of literature details the compromised nutritional circumstances resulting from a rapid transition in food practices, few studies have investigated the determinants of dietary change associated with loss of traditional knowledge and its potential effect on Indigenous mothering. In Canada, young single Aboriginal mothers have been identified as being most likely to be food insecure (Powers 96; Willows et al. 1150), yet few studies have described the dietary practices of First Nations women in Canada. First Nations groups living in southern regions have not been investigated as extensively, although lower incomes and high unemployment have been similarly found to contribute to food insecurity among southern communities (Neufeld 175; Willows et al. 1153). Furthermore, there has been little investigation on how traditional knowledge loss has impacted food security (Willows S35) or the importance of traditional food practices for Indigenous mothers. Those formal investigations that do exist employ almost exclusively self-reported dietary recall methodologies (Kuhnlein et al. 349; Ho et al. 335). Although these studies are helpful in quantifying dietary patterns, they are not able to address the complexities and meanings behind food choices and behaviours. Since very little has been documented on the changes in food knowledge for First Nations mothers, a qualitative study was undertaken with the purpose of exploring the determinants of food patterns and dietary practices during pregnancy with two generations of women living on a reserve located in southern Manitoba.

SETTING AND HISTORICAL CONTEXT

In examining cultural change and its impact on maternal food knowledge transmission across generations, it is important to briefly chronicle the unique history that has shaped the traditions of food procurement in the community where the study took place. The site of the present reserve is located in the Interlake region of Manitoba. Most community residents refer to themselves as Saulteaux, which is a branch of the Ojibway, or Anishinaabe. Their ancestors are thought to have migrated from the southeastern shores of Lake Superior, near the present site of Sault St. Marie, Ontario, towards the end of the eighteenth century (Van Der Goes Ladd 23). Once in Manitoba, the band settled along the banks of the Red River. Another group was also living in the area, having migrated there from Michigan. This band of Odawa peoples, also members of the Anishinaabe Nation, were extensively involved in agriculture, and taught the newcomers about planting potatoes and corn.

In 1817, tracts of land were set aside for the Saulteaux and Cree bands living along the Red River (Czuboka 16-7). During this period, these Indigenous peoples only depended on fur traders for goods such as firearms, ammunition, and iron implements, such as the axe. Economic autonomy was maintained, with most families satisfying their basic needs through hunting, fishing, wild rice gathering, and horticulture (Van Der Goes Ladd 63). By the 1830s, the British Colonial Office had already begun to put forward a policy of assimilation that encouraged First Nation communities to become settled in permanent villages and be educated in the English language, Christianity, as well as in agricultural methods (Cohen 40). The Anglican Church Missionary Society was very involved during this period in the area and set up a number of agricultural, pastoral communities along the Red River. The Saulteaux Chief became head of this "Indian Settlement" that included a school, mission houses, a church, grist mill, and farm. (Czuboka 90).

Treaty Number One was signed in 1871. It set aside this predominantly "Indian" settlement as the original reserve site for the Saulteaux community. European settlers continued, however, to take over land and, with amendments to the Indian Act in 1881, made it illegal for European settlers to purchase agricultural products from First Nation farmers (Waisberg and Holzkamm 186). Indian Agents also charged First Nation farmers for slaughtering their own cattle without permission. As a result, more and more First Nations groups began to shift away from agricultural practices towards hunting and fishing. The reserve was located on prime agricultural land. In 1907, pressure from various politicians and settlers, complaining that the land was not being cultivated, resulted in the illegal "surrender²" of these lands to the Canadian government (Tyler et al. 321). In 1909, Band members began their journey to the current reserve location set aside for them in the Interlake region of Manitoba. The new reserve was far more isolated and forested. It was, however, chosen by representatives from the community because of the abundance of fish in the local river and the potential for farming in the area. Many families eventually began to work at farming once again during the first half of the last century, on a much smaller scale (Thompson 58); however, cultivation traditions and their associated food practices have been diminishing gradually from one generation to the next.

THE PROCESS OF INTERVIEWING MOTHERS AND GRANDMOTHERS

Two generations of women who were long-term residents of the community were invited to participate in a study beginning in the spring of 2001, using theoretical sampling to interview women of differing ages, backgrounds, experiences, and beliefs (Corbin and Strauss 143). Half of the women were recognized in the community as grandmothers. The other half were of child-bearing age and, for the purposes of this paper, will be referred to as mothers. All had given birth to at least one child. Women selected to participate as grandmother and mother were not necessarily members of the same family. The fourteen grandmothers participating in the study ranged in age from fifty-nine to eighty-seven years. Almost 43% had never lived away from their reserve community, although close to 29% had spent some time working in mainly off-reserve urban locations when they were younger. The group of mothers was from eighteen years to thirty-six years of age. All fourteen had lived away from the community at some point for education or employment purposes. Over 64% had spent their childhoods in other locations; seven from non-First Nation communities and two from other reserves.

Both in-depth and semi-structured interviews were conducted with all of the women, followed by unstructured interviews with three grandmothers and four mothers, who were selected based on the results of their initial interviews. Women were asked for examples about their use of traditional or locally-harvested foods during pregnancy. The availability and accessibility of these foods, as well as marketed foods were also discussed. Concepts and themes that were raised during these semi-structured interviews then became the focus of later unstructured conversations, with the topics discussed varying according to age group. A more complete presentation of these methods and the overall results appear elsewhere (Neufeld; Neufeld and Marchessault). For the purposes of this paper, pseudonyms have been used for each participant. Names beginning with "G" and "M" refer to grandmothers and mothers, respectively. Additional participant description is included in Table 1.

CONTEMPORARY THEMES

Self-Sufficiency

When they were raising their children in the 1940s and 50s, grandmothers recalled having to purchase primarily staple items from the closest store or trading outpost. They also talked extensively about the knowledge that enabled them to live off the land, in addition to processes and technologies that were used to help them preserve the foods they procured for themselves. They spoke about a farming lifestyle that provided for their growing families during that period, even though not every grandmother raised her children on a working farm in the community. Each one talked at length about their vegetable gardens. Ginger stated: "of course we had a big garden! The only thing that we went to the store for was the flour, sugar and tea." Gail and her husband started planting a vegetable garden after their first child was born and "never bothered" buying food from the store. As Gail described it, "we practically lived off the land." Gladys also talked extensively about the days she spent in the garden while raising her large family, and the variety of vegetables she planted such as "potatoes, carrots, turnips, peas, beets, tomatoes, squash, pumpkins, and cucumbers."

Greta spoke frequently about "garden food." In addition to working

Name	Age	Description
Gladys	85	Retired mother of 13
Gertrude	80	Lived on the farm with 12 children
Gloria	77	Never left community, 7 children
Gail	67	Has 5 children at home
Georgia	68	From the north, 6 children
Geraldine	63	Works part-time, mother of 5
Gilda	70	Lives alone, raised 9 children
Glenda	59	Lived out-of-province with 6 children
Gennie	62	Always lived in community, has 10 children
Grace	79	Spent 20 years away from community, 3 children
Gillian	87	Lives by herself, had 8 pregnancies
Gina	66	Retired, raised 9 children
Greta	61	Raised 12 children
Ginger	75	Retired widow, 9 children
Miranda	31	Working full-time, expecting 5th child
Melanie	23	Single mother of 3
Mary	24	Student with 3 children
Matilda	23	Lives with extended family, new baby
Margaret	26	From nearby reserve, 5 children
Maud	30	Husband works seasonally, expecting 3rd child
Mabel	18	Recently moved to community, new baby
Marie	32	Pregnant with 8th child
Michelle	27	Works full-time, 4 children
Martha	34	Mother to 3 children and new baby
Marci	36	Has 3 children and new baby
Miriam	18	Lives with mom and 2 month old
Marissa	19	Newly married with 2 young children
Marlene	34	Raised outside community, 6 months pregnant

Table 1: Participant Descriptions

locally as an agricultural labourer while raising her children, she always grew a variety of her own vegetables in the summertime. Gardens were depended on as a vital source of food when her family was growing. She explained, "we couldn't afford to go out and go buy stuff like they do now, and [it is] very good to have a garden when you [have] children because they know fresh foods [are] coming from the garden, all the vegetables!" Both Greta and Gloria, as they increased in age, were also worried about the declining number of vegetable gardens on the reserve. Gloria blamed the lack of gardens for changes in the types of foods she observed pregnant women currently eating in the community, stating: "I think there's just too much junk! Not the right food and not too many people plant gardens, not too many people live on the farm."

Distant Awareness

More than half of the group of mothers discussed vegetable gardens in various contexts during their interviews; however, only one described her own. Maud told me about the small vegetable garden she had planted the previous summer, prior to her third pregnancy. She planted "carrots and beets and potatoes" for herself and her family. During the upcoming season, she planned to grow another garden to help keep food costs down. Only two other mothers spoke about having access to fresh locally grown vegetables while pregnant and raising their children. Martha said she really enjoyed fresh vegetables when she was pregnant, and was able to get them on occasion from her father's garden. Margaret also felt fortunate because she had access to her in-laws' garden, and knew a local farmer who regularly sold potatoes and onions. She appeared convinced of the superiority of fresh local food by exclaiming; "it tastes better, plus it's cheaper!"

Five other mothers were able to recall gardening in the past during their childhoods with older family members who grew vegetables on their land. As Melanie recounted, twenty years ago "there was quite a bit of people [who] had gardens. I remember going around and helping my aunties and that with their gardens." Miranda also talked about the vegetable garden her parents kept when she was young, where they grew "mostly potatoes." When I asked her if she still had access to fresh vegetables, she laughed as she replied; "I used to a long time ago, a few years ago, but not lately."

Resourcefulness

Close to half of the grandmothers spoke fondly about other methods of food production on the farm, such as raising livestock. When she was a young mother, Gloria remembered having "our own chickens, and pigs and turkeys and everything. We milked our cows. We had lots of milk and cream. It was wonderful!" Gladys vividly recalled "milking eight cows" every day by hand. Ginger spoke about a similar lifestyle, with access to a variety of fresh foods when she was pregnant and caring for her young children. Her family enjoyed a regular supply of milk from raising cattle, along with their own vegetables, chickens, and eggs. As she described; "we always had our own meat, but we used to kill animals too. It wasn't like now."

Nearly all of the grandmothers also spoke about methods of food preservation that allowed them to continue to enjoy their harvest of fresh meats, fruits and vegetables throughout the long winter that often lasted six months of the year. Gillian remembered that because there was no refrigeration on the reserve at the time, domestic and wild animals were often slaughtered in the fall, and meant to last as a source of meat until the spring. She explained that "a lot of people had their own cattle and they'd always butcher an animal or a pig or something in the fall, you know, after freeze-up." Gladys described how the fresh meat and milk were stored on her farm:

> I have a spring here. It comes right out of the ground. I'm used to having these big eight gallon cans [of milk]. My husband would stick them way in [the spring] and that's where we kept our milk [cold]. We even had outer cellars and then they had...in my Dad's day, I remember he'd put up an ice house. That's where we kept all the meat and stuff. We'd come in there and we'd have meat in white cotton bags so the sawdust wouldn't get on them, and [my mother] used to wrap up her butter in rhubarb leaves.

Gail similarly recalled learning from her own mother how to can a variety of foods such as meat and how preserved foods were stored:

> I remember watching mother doing wild meat in two quart jars, processing them in open canners. I remember that. [She] used to do chicken. The whole chicken into that two quart jar and preserving it like...dug a hole in the earth and put a box

in there. That was the deep freeze, or a cellar in the middle of the floor for all her preserves. And nothing spoiled. All stayed.

When I talked with Georgia about the short growing season in Manitoba and why canning was necessary to feed her young family, she explained, "I used to can everything, and unless I made enough…I got to know that I had to do more each year." Geraldine also remembered increasing the amounts of pickles and jams she canned when she was having her children. She said, "I always canned and jammed, always had dills and beet pickles, bread and butter pickles, yellow beans, mustard pickles. I remember my old cellar was just full."

Preserved Knowledge

In comparison, only three mothers spoke about storing or preserving foods, mainly in the context of freezing large quantities of wild meat for themselves and their families each year. Maud, for example, described how she would freeze moose meat and berries for the winter, explaining, "one moose will last just over the winter." She also advised me on where to pick the best berries in the community and how she extended her harvest by "either making jam with them or just freezing them." Another mother, Marci felt fortunate to have a fisherman in the family so they could "always stock up on fish in the fall." The frozen fish also helped to feed her and her family during the long winter months, and was especially helpful during her pregnancies, when only wild meat was palatable to her.

Three other mothers talked about preserving foods, but only in reference to extended family practices that had taken place in the past. Miranda remembered that her grandmother would regularly make and preserve jams made with wild berries. Margaret proudly told me about her grandmother's and mother-in-law's preserving skills and knowledge. Her grandmother had lived in northern Saskatchewan and knew how to "smoke moose meat". She also talked with great admiration while describing her mother-in-law's ability to can wild meat:

> I don't know exactly how she does it. She has one of those big canning pots and she cooks the meat in jars. And then she cooks it in the pot, and then once they're sealed then she lets them cool and puts them away. And then when we want to eat it, all we do is put it in a saucepan and add some flour and

water. Then we have our meat and gravy and it's really, really good!

Pride

All of the grandmothers spoke with a similar fondness about foods their mothers and grandmothers had taught them to prepare long ago when "everything was homemade." Several of their stories again focused in tandem on the economic as well as the health benefits of preparing foods at home. Those who had raised cattle talked about the dairy and meat products they procured themselves so they wouldn't have to depend on the store. Gladys churned butter using her own cow's milk, made her own cream, cheese, and lard when a pig was slaughtered on the farm. Her family also had its own source of flour. She remembered that, "when [my husband] would get through thrashing, he used to take barley and go, and in the mill there they'd thrash and he'd get flour from there. And there [were] other kinds of wheat granules and some other things that they got out of that flour and that's what we used."

Ten of the grandmothers talked about making homemade bread and bannock from grain they had ground or from flour purchased occasionally from the local store or trading post. Glenda described bread as an integral part of the meals she prepared for herself and her young children. At the time she would prepare "cereals in the morning, soups for lunch and have your meal at suppertime—potatoes and meats, some kind of meat. I always had home-made bread. I learned how to do that when I was young living at home watching my mom. It's still the same yet." Greta also told me that homemade bread and soup were an essential part of her diet when she was pregnant. Back then, she said, "we always had rabbit soup. We never had all this canned or store-bought stuff. And we made our own homemade bread, like you put in whole wheat. Brown bread we called it. We cooked our own."

Uncertainty

Few mothers spoke about food preparation methods when describing the foods they regularly consumed while pregnant. Those who brought up the topic of cooking, often did so to convey a perceived lack of knowledge or express a desire to change food patterns or routines. Four mothers described the foods they regularly prepared for themselves and their families to illustrate how their parents or partners cooked for them. Mabel, who was living with her parents when she was pregnant, explained that her father did all of the cooking. Marci told me her husband usually prepared the wild meat her family eats regularly, " 'cause I don't really like cooking, I don't cook it as good." Michelle learned how to cook from her mother who "always cooked just meat and potatoes," simultaneously conveying that she "never had vegetables" when she was pregnant and her children were small.

Two more mothers described their own difficulties cooking with produce purchased from the community's only grocery store. Miranda explained that she had a desire to eat fruits and vegetables more frequently, but was unsure about how to store them because, "if you don't eat it at that time, it just gets spoiled." Mary talked at length about her desire to learn how to cook, and had similar concerns: "when I do get that stuff, my carrots and celery usually lie in the fridge. Maybe I'll use it once and the rest of it goes to waste." She also confided, "I don't know how to cook either. I don't know how to cook fresh vegetables."

Mary and Marci talked about the reasons behind their preferences for prepared foods from the store. Marci was more inclined to choose foods that were fast to prepare to keep up with her family's activities. She purchased "meat and eggs, [items] that are easy to prepare, like something fast for the kids." Mary also talked about her busy lifestyle as a young mother and remarked, "since I've had [my baby], I don't have enough time to do what I usually do. A lot of times my husband can't do the same things I do, so a lot of times we're just eating cereal for supper, or sometimes we'll just have sandwiches and chips." Mary went on to describe shopping practices and how she would like to change established patterns: "when I go shopping, I always buy the same things. I can't think of anything else at the same time … I just pass right by the broccoli…don't even think about it."

DIVERGENT FOOD PRACTICES

Although a small group of mothers were aware of past practices, overall, a great divergence appears to exist with regard to the transference of food knowledge across generations. This apparent disconnection between women living in the same somewhat isolated community is surprising, yet reveals dramatic lifestyle changes have occurred over a relatively short time-span of less than four decades. Throughout their interviews, grandmothers conveyed pride in their skills, being able to provide and prepare food for themselves and their growing families. Comparatively, mothers conveyed a lack of confidence and sufficient knowledge base to independently acquire and prepare foods from the local environment. Earlier studies with women of child-bearing age in regions of northern Manitoba found that foods, particularly traditional foods, continue to be prepared and preserved by 61% of people in the communities surveyed (Campbell et al. 106). Traditional methods of food preservation, such as drying, salting, and smoking meats and fish, have gradually been replaced by freezing and canning. Older women tended to be more involved in preserving foods, with the most remote participating community reported the most extreme divergence between age groups (Campbell et al. 107). In British Columbia, research on dietary change among three generations of First Nations women also found a steady decline in the use of locally accessed plant and animal foods (Kuhnlein 273). In the Arctic, three other studies found a similar reduction in the use of locally-available foods by young people (Wein et al. 204; Kuhnlein et al. 149; Kuhnlein et al. 181).

Very few studies, however, have described plant propagation or food preparation methods in First Nation communities, or women's participation in these practices. Vegetable gardening was embraced along the west coast of British Columbia well before 1850, and the practice of gardening, as well as the growing availability of marketed foods, were thought to have displaced traditionally harvested foods from the diet, with 37% of families establishing home gardens in the early 1980s (Kuhnlein 264). More recent studies have been focused on the re-introduction of gardening practices, primarily in northern regions of Canada (Spiegelaar and Tsuji 10; Stroink and Nelson 264). One initiative included a series of workshops aimed at rebuilding a knowledge base in support of sustainable food systems in two First Nations communities located in northwestern Ontario (Stroink and Nelson 264). Male and female participants' self-rated knowledge of cultivated vegetable gardens and forest food systems was initially low to moderate with convenience and price primarily driving food choice towards the more dominant system of commercially available foods.

AGRICULTURAL TRADITIONS

Plant resources in northern Canada have historically played a less prominent role in terms of overall sustenance than wild meats and fish, in the diets of Indigenous groups in Canada (Waldram 43; Wien et al. 196). For many of the primarily northern communities previously studied, agricultural activities may have been directly tied to the operation of residential schools and/or church missions (Spiegelaar and Tsuji 9). This Saulteaux community, along with others in the same region, however, had a longer history of successful agricultural practices (Czuboka Van Der Goes Ladd; Waisberg and Holzkamm). In fact, it has been postulated that early ethnographies in this region were narrow in scope and did not include sufficient historical analysis to recognize earlier agricultural traditions first documented in the early 1800s (Waisberg and Holzkamm 177), or knowledge that has been passed down through oral tradition. Prior to the introduction of federal policy in Canada that discouraged agriculture by increasing the difficulties of commercial sales, many communities had their own Indigenous agricultural traditions, and engaged successfully in subsistence farming. The policy changes in favour of the surrender of reserves located on prime agricultural land were also justified, in part, by a presumption of a perceived unwillingness of First Nations to farm.

Foods that originated from the land were held in high esteem by both generations participating in this study, as being of superior quality compared to foods that were available to purchase from the store. The social and cultural significance of historical or more traditional food systems has been described by several authors (Kuhnlein et al. 121; Willows S33). Kuhnlein and Receveur contend that elements such as group identity and cultural expression may be closely tied to particular foods (421). Consuming locally accessible traditional foods is more than just about eating. It is the endpoint of culturally meaningful processes that require the continued enactment of culturally important ways of behaving which emphasize cooperation, sharing and generosity (Ohmagari and Berkes 199; Willows S33). Subsistence, as Ohmagari and Berkes have suggested, is not merely a way of obtaining food, but also a way of life, and mode of knowledge production that sustains social relationships and the distinctive cultural characteristics of families and communities (218). Grandmothers participating in this study did not tend to distinguish between wild or cultivated foods, such as fish or garden vegetables. They talked about the foods they harvested or stored for their families in a similar manner, reflecting the unique social and cultural identity, as well as the historical environment, of their community. Emotional and cultural health indicated by self-sufficiency and pride appeared to be tied to the variety of foods often started in the earth with their own hands, as well as the animals they helped to raise.

Many of the foods lovingly described by the group of grandmothers in the current study, however, were not always the traditional foods that First Nations groups in northern regions of Canada would have historically spent the vast proportion of their time hunting or gathering. For other communities, such as Sandy Lake First Nation in northwestern Ontario, a traditional diet may be considered more broadly to include foods available from local natural resources that are culturally accepted (deGonzague et al. 715; Ohmagari and Berkes 203; Robidoux et al. 17). Although both groups of mothers did talk about harvesting, preserving, and consuming wild meat and berries, the group of grandmothers mainly referred to the foods they planted, tended and preserved for their families, when they were young mothers, as those most associated with health benefits. It did not seem to make any difference to the grandmothers whether or not these foods were part of the diet prior to European contact. The practice of preparing and eating these foods, grown with their own hands, seemed to inform a sense of pride and tradition and identity as mother and caregiver.

MATERNAL INDIGENOUS KNOWLEDGE

There is considerable evidence that post-colonial traumas, resulting from the inter-generational impacts of children sent away from their communities to residential schools, place First Nations at greater risk of inequalities negatively impacting the transference of shared or lived experiences (De-Gagné S49). In Canada, these complex and continuing colonial policies have resulted in profound social and cultural disruption among all Aboriginal groups; however, there is a lack of research on the nature of the transmission of Indigenous knowledge and the magnitude of loss (Ohmagari and Berkes 198). The practice of learning by example from parents and grandparents was destroyed by the residential school system, including the transmission of food propagation and preparation skills. According to survey data collected from Cree communities in north-western Ontario, mothers were the principal teachers of these skills, accounting for two-thirds of transmission patterns (Ohmagari and Berkes 210).

A common experience of social insecurity resulting from continuous environmental and social changes may result in unhealthy lifestyles and eating patterns, as well as a potential reliance on the dominant food system as a result of the disappearance of community networks for sharing food (Stroink and Nelson 267). Individuals may feel disempowered, for example, by an inconsistent access to healthy foods (Spiegelaar and Tsuji 10), as well as a limited knowledge base of how to plant, procure, and prepare them. For the young mothers participating in this study, a shared experience of social and environmental disruptions, combined with a lack of food security, along with other insecurities in their lives, could translate into less perceived autonomy or self-determination as caregivers and providers. The lack of confidence and uncertainty mothers expressed illustrates an overall insecurity that was in stark contrast to the resourcefulness and pride exhibited by the generation of grandmothers.

During their interviews, mothers also expressed the desire to become more independent and self-reliant in their knowledge and ability to prepare healthy food for themselves and their families. As knowledgeable and resourceful providers whose experience and expertise is held in high esteem, grandmothers have a responsibility to share their wisdom and help to unravel patterns of insecurity that may be perpetuating unhealthy food patterns and eating behaviours. The complex history of food systems in First Nations communities also requires a more holistic approach towards security in many forms, such as the sustainability of the local food economy and the empowerment of mothers for future generations.

ACKNOWLEDGEMENTS

I would like to gratefully acknowledge the mothers and grandmothers who shared their experiences, Chief, Council and local Health Centre staff for their assistance, and members of my academic committee: Drs. T. Kue Young, John O'Neil, Gail Marchessault and Patricia Martens. This study was approved by the Faculty Committee on the Use of Human Subjects in Research, University of Manitoba, Winnipeg and the Chief and Council's delegate in the First Nation community. This research was made possible, in part, by the Canadian Institutes of Health Research (CIHR), through an Interdisciplinary Health Research Teams Studentship.

NOTES

[1] Aboriginal is a collective term used for the original peoples of North America and their descendants. The Canadian constitution recognizes three groups of Aboriginal people: First Nations, Métis and Inuit.

[2] According to the *Indian Act*, the surrender of reserve land must be approved by a majority of band members at a public meeting convened for that purpose, which was not achieved under these circumstances (Tyler et al. 321).

WORKS CITED

Anderson, Sue Ann. "Core Indicators of Nutritional Status for Difficult-to-Sample Populations." *The Journal of Nutrition* 120 (1990): 1559–1600. Print.

Campbell, Marion L., Ruth Diamant, Brian MacPherson, and Judy Halladay. "The Contemporary Food Supply of Three Northern Manitoba Cree Communities." *Canadian Journal of Public Health* 88 (1997): 105–108. Print.

Canadian Diabetes Association Clinical Practice Guidelines Expert Committee. "Canadian Diabetes Association 2013 Clinical Practice Guidelines for the Prevention and Management of Diabetes in Canada." *Canadian Journal of Diabetes* 37 supplement 1 (2013):S1–S212. Print.

Cohen, Bonita E. "The Development of Health Services in Peguis First Nation : A Descriptive Case Study." Unpublished dissertation. The University of Manitoba, 1994. Print.

Corbin, Juliet M., and Strauss Anselm. *Basics of Qualitative Research: Techniques and Procedures for Developing Grounded Theory*. Thousand Oaks: Sage Publications, 2008. Print.

Czuboka, Michael P. "St. Peter's: A Historical Study with Anthropological Observations on the Christian Aborigines of Red River (1811–1876)." Unpublished dissertation, University of Manitoba, 1960. Print.

DeGagné, Michael. "Toward an Aboriginal Paradigm of Healing: Addressing the Legacy of Residential Schools." *Australasian Psychiatry* 15 (2007):S49–S53.

deGonzague, Bernadette, Olivier Receveur, Don Wedll and Harriet Kuhnlein. "Dietary Intake and Body Mass Index of Adults in Two Ojibwe Communities." *Journal of the American Dietetic Association*, 99 (1999):710–716. Print.

Egeland, Grace M., Louise Johnson-Down, Zhirong R. Cao, Nelofar Sheikh and Hope Weiler. "Food Insecurity and Nutrition Transition Combine to Affect Nutrient Intakes in Canadian Arctic Communities." *The Journal of Nutrition* 141 (2011):1746–1753. Print.

Elias, Brenda, Javier Mignone, Madelyn Hall, Say P. Hong, Lyna Hart, and Jitender Sareen. "Trauma and Suicide Behaviour Histories Among a Canadian Indigenous Population: An Empirical Exploration of the Potential Role of Canada's Residential School System." *Social Science and*

Medicine 74 (2012):1560–1569. Print.

Elliott, Bethany, Deepthi Jayatilaka, Contessa Brown, Leslie Varley and Kitty K. Corbett. "We Are Not Being Heard: Aboriginal Perspectives on Traditional Foods Access and Food Security." *Journal of Environmental and Public Health* (2012). Print.

FAO. *World Food Summit Plan of Action*. Rome, Italy: United Nations, 1996. Print.

Gagné, Doris, Rosanne Blanchet, Julie Lauzière, Emilie Vaissière, Carole Vézina, Pierre Ayotte, Serge Déry and Huguette Turgeon O'Brien. "Traditional Food Consumption is Associated with Higher Nutrient Intakes in Inuit Children Attending Childcare Centres in Nunavik." *International Journal of Circumpolar Health* 71 (2012):18401. Print.

Ho, Lara S., Joel Gittlesohn, Sangita Sharma, Xia Cao, Margarita Treuth, Rajiv Rimal, Elizabeth Ford and Steward Harris. "Food-related Behavior, Physical Activity and Dietary Intake in First Nations—A Population at High Risk for Diabetes." Ethnicity and Health 13(2008):335–49. Print.

Johnson-Down, Louise and Grace Egeland "Adequate Nutrient Intakes are Associated with Traditional Food Consumption in Nunavut Inuit Children Aged 3-Years." *The Journal of Nutrition* 140 (2010):1311–1316. Print.

Kuhnlein, Harriet V. "Change in the Use of Traditional Foods by the Nuxalk Native People of British Columbia." *Ecology of Food and Nutrition* 27 (1992): 259–282. Print.

Kuhnlein, Harriet V., Donna Appavoo, Natalia Morrison, Rula Soueida and Patricia Pierrot. "Use and Nutrient Composition of Traditional Sahtu (Hareskin) Dene/Métis Foods." *Journal of Food Composition and Analysis* 7 (1994): 144–157. Print.

Kuhnlein, Harriet V., Rula Soueida and Olivier Receveur. "Baffin Inuit Food Use by Age and Gender." *Journal of the Canadian Dietetic Association* 56 (1995): 175–183. Print.

Kuhnlein, Harriet V., and Olivier Receveur. "Dietary Change and Traditional Food Systems of Indigenous Peoples." *Annual Review of Nutrition* 16 (1996): 417–442. Print.

Kuhnlein, Harriet V., Olivier Receveur, and Laurie H. M. Chan. "Traditional Food Systems Research with Canadian Indigenous Peoples." *International Journal of Circumpolar Health* 60 (2001): 112–122. Print.

Kuhnlein, Harriet V., Olivier Receveur, Rula Soueida and Grace M. Egelund. "Arctic Indigenous Peoples Experience the Nutrition Transition with Changing Dietary Patterns and Obesity." *The Journal of Nutrition* 134 (2004):1447–1453. Print.

Kuhnlein, Harriet V., Olivier Receveur, Rula Soueida and Peter Berti. "Unique Patterns of Dietary Adequacy in Three Cultures of Canadian Arctic Indigenous Peoples." *Public Health Nutrition* 11 (2008): 349–360. Print.

Lambden, Jill, Olivier Receveur, Joan Marshall and Harriet Kuhnlein. "Traditional and Market Food Access in Arctic Canada is Affected by Economic Factors." *International Journal of Circumpolar Health* 65 (2006): 331–340. Print

Neufeld, Hannah T. "Prenatal Dietary Reflections among Two Generations in a Southern First Nation Community." Unpublished thesis, The University of Manitoba, 2003. Print.

Neufeld, Hannah T. and Gail D.M. Marchessault. "Perceptions of Two Generations of Aboriginal Women on Causes of Diabetes during Pregnancy." *Canadian Journal of Diabetes* 30 (2006): 161–168. Print.

Ohmagari, Kayo and Fikret Berkes. "Transmission of Indigenous Knowledge and Bush Skills among the Western James Bay Cree Women of Subarctic Canada." *Human Ecology* 25 (1997): 197–222. Print.

Omura, Emily. "Mino-Miijim's 'Good Food for the Future: Beyond Culturally Appropriate Diabetes Programs.' " *Indigenous Peoples and Diabetes: Community Empowerment and Wellness.* Ed. M.L. Ferreira and G.C. Lang. Durham: Carolina Academic Press, 2006. 139–165. Print.

Powers, Elaine M. "Conceptualizing Food Security for Aboriginal People in Canada." *Canadian Journal of Public Health* 99 (2008): 95–97. Print.

Raschke, Verena and Bobby Cheema. "Colonisation, the New World Order, and the Eradication of Traditional Food Habits in East Africa: Historical Perspective on the Nutrition Transition." *Public Health Nutrition* 11 (2007): 662–674. Print.

Richmond, Chantelle A.M. and Nancy A. Ross. "The Determinants of First Nation and Inuit Health: A Critical Population Health Approach." *Health and Place* 15 (2009): 403–411. Print.

Robidoux, Michael A., Françoise Haman and Christabelle Sethna. "The Relationship of the Burbot (Lota lota L.) to the Reintroduction of Off-the-Land Foods in the Sandy Lake First Nation Community." *Biodemography and Social Biology* 55 (2009): 12–29. Print.

Schuster, Roseanne C., Eleanor E. Wein, Cindy Dickson and Chan Hing Man. "Importance of Traditional Foods for the Food Security of Two First Nations Communities in the Yukon, Canada." *International Journal of Circumpolar Health* 70 (2011): 286–300. Print.

Spiegelaar, Nicole F. and Leonard J.S. Tsuji. "Impact of Euro-Canadian Agrarian Practices: In Search of Sustainable Import-Substitution Strategies to Enhance Food Security in Subarctic Ontario, Canada." *Rural and Remote Health* 13 (2013): 2211. Print.

Stroink, Mirella L. and Connie H. Nelson. "Aboriginal Health Learning in the Forest and Cultivated Gardens: Building a Nutritious and Sustainable Food System." *Journal of Agromedicine* 14 (2009): 263–269. Print.

Thomas, Jeff. *Where are the Children? Healing the Legacy of the Residential Schools.* Ottawa: National Archives of Canada, 2003. Web.

Thompson, Albert E. *Chief Peguis and His Descendants.* Winnipeg: Peguis Publishers, 1973. Print.

Tyler, Wright and Daniel Limited. *The Illegal Surrender of St. Peter's Reserve.* Winnipeg: Treaty and Aboriginal Rights Research Centre of Manitoba, 1983. Print.

Van Der Goes Ladd, Georg. *Shall We Gather at the River?* Toronto: The United Church of Canada, 1986. Print.

Waisberg, Leo G. and Tim E. Holzkamm. "A Tendency to Discourage Them from Cultivating: Ojibwa Agriculture and Indian Affairs Administration in Northwestern Ontario." *Ethnohistory* 40 (1993): 175–211. Print.

Waldram, James B. "Hydroelectric Development and Dietary Delocalization in Northern Manitoba, Canada." *Human Organization* 44 (1985): 41–49. Print.

Wein, Eleanor E., Jean H. Sabry and Frederick T. Evers. "Food Consumption Patterns and Use of Country Foods by Native Canadians near Wood Buffalo National Park, Canada." *Arctic* 44 (1991): 196–205. Print.

Willows, Noreen D. "Determinants of Healthy Eating in Aboriginal Peoples in Canada: The Current State of Knowledge and Research Gaps." *Canadian Journal of Public Health* 96 (2005): S32–S36. Print.

Willows, Noreen D., Paul Veugelers, Kim Raine and Stefan Kuhle. "Prevalence and Sociodemographic Risk Factors Related to Household Food Security in Aboriginal Peoples in Canada." *Public Health Nutrition* 12 (2009): 1150–1156. Print.

3.

Risk and Resistance

Creating Maternal Risk Through Imposed Biomedical Safety in the Post-colonial Indigenous Philippines

PAUL KADETZ

INTRODUCTION: COLONIAL AND POST-COLONIAL HEALTH CAMPAIGNS FOR THE "UNHEALTHY NATIVE"

Over one hundred years ago, American colonists waged a war against cholera in the Philippines. It has been argued that there was little differentiation between the 1902 "war against cholera and the pacification of Filipinos" (Ileto 127). To combat Asiatic cholera, infected houses were burned, residents were strictly quarantined in detention camps, medicine needed to be administered with "the use of force", and bodies of the deceased were burned (Ileto 134). However, each of these measures threatened the integrity of indigenous Filipino identity and beliefs.

From the anthropologist Mary Douglas, we can identify that what is being threatened in this example are cultural systems of order that contain understanding and meaning. These systems of order essentially facilitate the ability for any given group to navigate through life. These ordered systems of understanding and meaning may be considered foundational to the integrity of social structure. Thus, Filipinos resisted these threats to their order, and inadvertently facilitated the further spread of cholera. Residents rebelled against colonial attempts to burn their homes and fires spread. Filipinos escaped quarantine and hid in outlying areas, thereby rapidly spreading cholera even further than if quarantine had never been instituted. Desecration of the dead via cremation was completely forbidden in indigenous Filipino ordered systems (Douglas). Therefore, Filipino families hid the bodies of their dead under homes and in swamps, which served as potent transmitters of cholera, ensuring an ongoing source for the spread of the disease.

Hence, in each instance that the Americans attempted to control cholera by following their own system of order and meaning (biomedicine and public health), they threatened the local ordered systems of understanding and meaning and were duly resisted. For even though the American colonists perceived their paternalism as not only justifiable but also beneficent, the dominance and acceptance of biomedicine in the West was irrelevant in a context wherein such biomedical measures were perceived as alien, threatening and the justification of a colonial form of control. Thus, the American insistence on imposing an alien order of safety for the good of the native Filipino ultimately resulted in chaos.

After more than a century, those in health and development may try to distance themselves from these behaviors by categorizing them as artifacts of colonialism. In the ensuing years, the fields of anthropology and development studies matured. We have supposedly learned from the egregious and naïve errors of our colonial pasts. We believe we no longer engage so blindly in ethnocentrism and dominance. We do, after all, include asset-based approaches and community participation in our development projects. We pride ourselves on embracing the inclusivity of *aspects of* local knowledge in modern development projects. Yet, the hegemonic dominance of biomedicine has been curiously shielded from most post-colonial critiques[1] as if it is somehow outside of culture and devoid of ethnocentrism.

But now, after more than a century of the attempted colonial control of cholera, a new biomedical war is being waged, this time for the purported good of Filipino women and their infants. This chapter reviews and problematizes the specific case of the attempted eradication and replacement of local and Indigenous non-biomedical means of delivery with skilled biomedical delivery in attempt to reduce risk and promote safety in maternal child health. This chapter will first review the global context of traditional birth attendant trainings of the World Health Organization (WHO) and UNICEF. The justification of the failure of these trainings to reduce maternal and infant mortality is then briefly assessed. The 2008 Department of Health of the Philippines Administrative Order requiring mandatory in-facility birthing with "skilled" birth attendants for all women in the Philippines is assessed through informant interviews and participant observation conducted in Indigenous communities of the rural Philippines and with State and multilateral stakeholders over a twenty-two month period. The myriad issues embedded in the ignorance and silencing of local and Indigenous systems of order, through the imposition of an alien system of order, are examined in this particular case study of a global maternal child health care campaign that is being implemented at local levels.

LOCATING INDIGENEITY IN THE PHILIPPINES

Before examining this research, it is important to briefly discuss the challenge of determining Indigeneity in the Philippines. Defining indigeneity in the Philippines can appear an ambiguous and relative distinction with no set boundaries. This is particularly evident when comparing Indigenous groups in the Philippines with other countries in which tribal distinctions are readily visually apparent, as in the distinctive *traje*, or traditional dress, amongst the different Maya communities of the highlands of Guatemala (Kadetz).

Indigeneity is often nuanced in the Philippines and can best be considered a function of differences in language, ritual, and most importantly, identification with a particular tribe and/or geographic area that may have formed a natural boundary from other tribes and colonial dominance. But what may be more important to distinguish for the purpose of this examination are the relationships between place and the heterogeneous influence of modernity and colonial systems of order on the landscape of Filipino identity.

One shortcoming of simple systems analyses and reductionist representations of modernity is that change can only be understood to occur in a hegemonic "all-or-nothing" manner within any population. However, colonization was not a uniform process amongst the 7,107 islands of the Philippine archipelago, nor within all of the areas of any given island, nor even uniformly throughout any town. The movement of modernity in the Philippines may be partly understood as an outcome of where colonists perceived they could safely travel. For example, the Spanish colonists of the Philippines tended to remain in the more accessible lowland areas and refrained from travel to the highlands, especially in Northern Luzon and Mindanao (Nelson). This may be partly due to the colonial fear and avoidance of the tribes of the Northern Luzon highlands who were associated with headhunting (Raedt; Rosaldo)

However, identifying the geography of colonial influence is even more nuanced within individual towns. The Spanish colonists remained near Manila and town centres (known as *poblacions*). The further a community (*barangay*) was located from the *poblacion*, the less likely it was to be under Spanish rule or even indirectly influenced by any colonisation. Those *barangays* far from the *poblacion* and difficult to navigate were very often relatively free from Spanish influences. Thereby, a gradual weakening of western influence can be detected the further one travels from the town centre.

The movement of western modernity can be traced via the temporality embedded in local practices. I had observed in Sunday church services near a rural *poblacion* that hymns and songs were sung. However, in churches further from the town centre, congregants would sing chants that appeared improvised and would, like the mesmerising atemporal music of the gamelan, continue for hours. One service I attended at 10 a.m. continued until 7 p.m. The Minister of Culture of the Philippines corroborated in interview that music can be used as a marker for the movement of modernity via the adoption of a western order of temporality. The further one travels from the *poblacion*, the less the music can be distinguished as a song. Songs and hymns sung nearer the town centre had a beginning, middle, and an end; whereas, in the improvised chants identified further from the centre of town, there were no such linear boundaries, and chanting simply continued until congregants were tired. Thereby, chanting can be understood to occur outside of a western conception of time, and illustrates that whatever influence colonialism or the modern world appears to exert on this *barangay*; it is ultimately eclipsed by local ordered systems of understanding and meaning.

This same phenomenon was observed in the sequence, or lack thereof, in serving a meal. The further one is from a *poblacion*, the less likely there will be any order in the serving or eating of a meal. Therefore, there are no first, second, or third courses, but only the placement of whatever is going to be served at the table and eaten in any order that a person chooses. Thus, we can conclude that the fully colonized Filipino did not merely mimic colonial order, but rather adopted the colonists order, particularly that of linearity and time. Hence, any representations of a uniform Filipino identity or sharp boundaries of Indigeneity are challenged in the field.

CONSTRUCTING COLONIAL ORDER: BIOMEDICAL HEGEMONY AND AUTHORITATIVE KNOWLEDGE

When western systems of order are present, they tend to dominate all others. Brigitte Jordan identifies that, even though "equally legitimate parallel knowledge systems exist", people may "move easily between...[often] one kind of knowledge gains ascendency and legitimacy" (56). She identifies this phenomenon as the domination of "authoritative knowledge" (Jones). A consequence of authoritative knowledge "is the devaluation, often dismissal, of all other kinds of knowing...as backward, ignorant, naive" (Jones). The power, then, of authoritative knowledge is not that it is "correct," per se, but that it is valued, reified and universalized as normative and "truth" (Jones 58).

The potential for expert or authoritative knowledge to control is also reflected in Antonio Gramsci's concept of hegemony, as the dominance and control "of a social group over the entire national society, exercised through private organizations, such as the Church, the unions, the schools" (67). However, as illustrated in the case example of cholera, authoritative knowledge can be resisted. History repeatedly demonstrates that to ignore local and Indigenous agency and resistance to a foreign imposition of order is, at best, naïve and, at worst, deleterious.

The advent of the biomedical expert

Prior to the twentieth century, biomedicine did not dominate healthcare in America, but was one of a plural system of health care practices that was not even considered the most popular (Starr). The hegemonic control of biomedicine in singularly determining the standards of safety for all health care can, at least in part, be traced to the 1910 "Flexner Report," which attempted to standardize and control biomedical education in North America. Backed by the Rockefeller Foundation, the recommendations of the Flexner Report were implemented, which led to the subsequent closure of over half (eighty-four) of North American medical schools from 1919 to 1928, as well as the majority of non-biomedical schools (Chapman 106). Of the seventy-six schools remaining, all offered the same curriculum, set the same academic standards, and followed the same entry requirements (Chapman). Thereby, they constituted a coherent ordered reflection of the biomedical Self.

In his 1910 report, Flexner posits that "modern medicine uses knowledge with no preconceptions," whereas "men possessed of vague preconceived ideas are strongly disposed to force facts to fit, defend, or explain them," thereby interfering with "the free search for truth" (156). He concludes that "modern medicine denies outright the relevancy or value of allopathy or homoeopathy" (156). Thereafter, "truth" in health care became the sole self-proclaimed domain of biomedicine and the biomedical expert. Thus, only by submitting one's ordered systems to the dominant biomedical system could the non-biomedical Self hope to survive. What is so powerful in Flexner's statement is the representation of the modernization and scientization of health care as a moral imperative.

Throughout the twentieth century, this moral imperative became embedded in international health policies and agencies. This episteme proved particularly central to the work of the first primary multilateral health agency, The League of Nations Health Organization (LNHO), forty percent of whose budget was funded by the Rockefeller Foundation (RF) (Loughlin and Berridge).

The RF's funds were specifically targeted to broaden the involvement of medical officers and medical researchers in the work of LNHO (Weindling 275). The LNHO emphasized "the development of a pool of international experts in public health" (Weindling 273). The RF used the LNHO as the means to improve health through the institutional resources of a scientific and medical "expert elite" (Weindling 269). A century later this moral imperative can be found in the WHO's discourse of safety, particularly concerning non-biomedical practices and practitioners, such as traditional birth attendants.

Re-ordering Indigenous Knowledge to make it "Safe:" The integration and eradication of traditional birth attendants.

Traditional birth attendants (TBAs) were the first (and often only) non-biomedical healthcare practitioners to be integrated into formal healthcare systems internationally, through training directed toward the reduction of maternal and infant mortality. Some of the first formal training of TBAs began in China as early as 1913 (Johnson). "As part of this process, midwives who had received some formal medical training were required [by the government] to be licensed, while simultaneously, those working without the prescribed training began to be forced out of the field and their once accepted skills and practices termed as deviant" (Johnson 283). In 1930, the Rockefeller Foundation instituted training for midwives through the

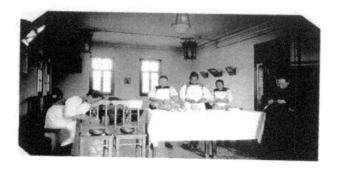

Figure 1: Training Exam of "Old-Type" midwives (from right to left) 1) cutting nails; 2) silver nitrate eye-drops for infant; 3) tie umbilical cord; 4) infant bath; 5) cleaning hands before delivery. *Source: Rockefeller Archive Center*

First National Midwifery School of the National Midwifery Board of China (Yang).

TBA training gradually became a global agenda. This training, sponsored by UNICEF and the WHO, beginning in the 1950s, predominantly focused on pre- and post-natal care, proper biomedical delivery and sterile techniques, and the recognition of obstetric emergencies for referral (Kruske and Barclay). According to the World Health Organization, initial assessments of TBA training programs demonstrated a reduction in maternal and infant mortality that purportedly "reached a plateau" in the 1990s (Kruske and Barclay 307). The identification of this "plateau" in the data triggered a dramatic shift in traditional birth attendant policy, which included the cessation of trainings and discouraged or prohibited use of TBAs worldwide (Kruske and Barclay 307).

This new policy toward TBA training and integration was formally announced in a 1992 joint WHO/UNFPA statement, declaring that the training and use of traditional birth attendants should only be used as an interim measure until all women have access to "acceptable, professional, modern health services" (WHO). "Four years later, WHO policy leaders insisted on 'skilled' rather than 'trained' birth attendants" (Kruske and Barclay 307). This was a significant policy change, as it is believed that (globally) "two-thirds of all births occur outside health facilities" (Bergström and Goodburn 79).

The literature suggests that these reported stagnant reductions in infant and maternal mortality rates may not reflect a TBA's innate ability to learn specific birthing techniques, as much as what and how TBAs were taught, and, particularly, how the training was evaluated. According to Bergström and Goodburn: "One of the reasons for continuing debate over TBA training is the haphazard way the programmes have been evaluated...there are surprisingly few methodologically sound evaluations, even of programme outputs" (2001: 84). The variety of training outcomes between countries corroborates this observation. For example, TBAs were considered to have been successfully integrated and demonstrated consistent marked reduction of maternal and infant mortality in both Malaysia and Samoa (Kruske and Barclay).

Furthermore, the determination of the success or failure of TBA training is based on infant and maternal mortality data of questionable rigor. There have been myriad issues identified with the unreliable data sets, and inappropriate data analysis employed in these findings of stagnant maternal and infant mortality rates. An independent analysis of neonatal and maternal mortality from the *Institute for Health Metrics and Evaluation* (IHME), at The University of Washington, used "three times as much data as the previous researchers" and demonstrated a marked reduction in both neonatal (Rajaratnam et al.) and maternal mortality (Hogan et al. 1609) during these reported periods of stagnation from WHO and UNICEF. Furthermore, any identified stagnation in maternal and infant mortality is demonstrated *after* WHO/UNICEF TBA training had ceased.

We can also question if maternal and neonatal mortality are accurate proxy measurements by which to access TBA training. Numerous factors can contribute to maternal and neonatal mortality including malnutrition, infectious environment and poor pre-natal/post-natal care. Although the IHME research did not specifically analyse TBA training as a factor in their research, both their findings and WHO's findings identify the most marked declines in maternal mortality rates from 1990–1995, which were the final years of WHO/UNICEF TBA training. Alternatively, the highest increase in maternal mortality rates were from 1995 to 2000, during the years after global WHO/UNICEF TBA training had ceased (Hogan et al 1612). IHME authors conclude "variation in the assessments of rates of decline indicates the availability and use of different data sets, different analytical methods, and different decisions about data quality by the analysts" (Rajaratnam et al. 1989).

At the time the IHME maternal mortality study was published online by *The Lancet* (Hogan et al.), a report published by a global alliance hosted by WHO, *The Partnership for Maternal, Newborn and Child Health*, claimed progress in maternal health as having "lagged" (Cheng).

> According to their detailed analysis, from 350,000 to 500,000 women still die in childbirth every year. The authors did not explain from where their data came or what kind of analysis was used to obtain this wide range of figures. However, in the same report, U.N. officials also claim needing $20 billion every year between 2011 and 2015 to save women and children in developing countries" (Cheng).

The editor of *The Lancet*, Dr. Richard Horton, reported to be "disappointed when maternal health advocates pressured him to delay publishing the IHME report until September, after several of their critical [maternal and child healthcare] fund raising meetings" (Cheng). Hence, it appears the data collection and analysis substantiating TBA policies may, in actuality, be more of a reflection of global and multilateral politics than of statistical neutrality.

Problematic Logic: "if we don't train them, they will just go away"

This change in health policy for TBAs at the global level may have influenced the change in the policy toward *hilots* (TBAs) in the Philippines. Since 1952, UNICEF and the Department of Health of the Philippines (DOHP) conducted training for *hilots* throughout the Philippines "as part of the country's midwifery programme" (Vuori 131). The training focused on sterile and hygienic techniques; pre-natal and post-natal education; and the warning signs of complications requiring referral to hospital (WHO). *Hilots* were especially discouraged from the practice of cutting the umbilical cord with bamboo and were given sterile birthing kits. *Hilots* interviewed found the trainings useful, reported to have practiced what they were taught, and were eager for more trainings. Some informants revealed they have kept their birthing kits since their initial trainings in the 1950s.

For example, one elderly *hilot* I interviewed in Guina-ang, Bontoc, brought her sterile birthing kit to the interview. It was a silver tackle box with "UNICEF" emblazoned across the top. She smiled broadly as she opened it with great care and revealed the contents with pride. One by one she removed from the tackle box: cotton, iodine, an old used razor blade, sutures, a packet of sterile gauze, surgical tape, surgical string, a lighter and a

Figure 2: In-Birthing Facility at Mainit, Bontoc with Sterile Birthing Kit from UNICEF (at far right)

scissors. She placed them before me almost ritualistically. She handled each object as if it was a priceless family heirloom. Then she looked and smiled and said "I've kept this for sixty years." If this was accurate, then she was one of the very first *hilots* to be trained in the Philippines in 1952. I asked, "Have you used this for sixty years?" She nodded, "Yes...and I'm waiting for another."

In 1958, *Republic Act 2644, An Act Regulating Midwifery Training and Practice*, authorized *hilots* to practice in areas not served by professional health workers. Training conducted for TBAs concerned sterile delivery technique and germ theory, in attempts to reduce infant and maternal morbidity and mortality.

In 1981, with the adoption of primary healthcare in the Philippines, trained *hilots* were recognized as qualified members of the Women's Health Team (Asian Development Bank). I observed that, in many communities, trained *hilots* were considered part of the health care team, even at the municipal rural health units (RHU). For example, in the RHU of the municipality of Murcia, a roster was kept on a wall of all the healthcare workers in the *barangays*. The category of trained *hilots* was included in this roster. Vuori identifies that "*Hilots* were encouraged to involve themselves in a wide variety of community health activities, such as notifying communicable diseases, organizing mothers' classes, registering births, helping to arrange mother and child referrals to health centres and hospitals, assisting in immunization and collaborating in family planning" (131).

Hilots were quietly integrated into most local health care systems. *Hilots* have been identified to be used by women even if physicians and midwives were readily available in their area (USAID). "Traditional Birth Attendants [in the Philippines] attend to 63% of deliveries by poor women versus only 23% for the non-poor" (USAID). However, there were regional differences in the use of *hilots*. In certain regions of the Philippines, half or more deliveries are identified to be attended by *hilots*. It appears from the table that the further from Manila, the higher is the reported use of *hilots*.

From 2004 to 2008, the World Bank, USAID, The European Commission, and The Asian Development Bank (ADB) issued reports concerning the funding of a project to reduce infant and maternal mortality in the Philippines via skilled deliveries within in-birthing facilities (USAID; ADB; European Commission). The ADB's independent evaluation was the only report to recommend *not* funding the project. The ADB identified the project as both infeasible and unsustainable, noting the seriously flawed data sets and statistical analyses provided by the DOHP (ADB). Unlike the other evaluations, ADB's suggested that the development of in-birthing facilities, especially in rural areas, was a project that, even if implementable, could only be implemented in small stages over time and that *hilots* continuing to attend to at-home births, were essential for this process to occur (ADB).

The director of this ADB evaluation stated, in interview, that their concern was that the cessation in training of, and the lack of a provision of a sterile birthing kit for, *hilots* would not dissuade women from seeking their help, nor would it encourage *hilots'* compliance with the policy, by virtue of their priorities to community women as dictated by their cultural role. For, although several *hilot* informants reported to be relieved to be able to give up their roles and gain more independence and control of their time, all stated that they would not be able to refuse a woman requesting their help.

Contrary to the other reports mentioned, the ADB evaluator identified numerous issues in the statistical correlation of infant and maternal mortality rate with *hilot* deliveries. She reported that when her team disaggregated the DOHP data, purportedly serving as the main data set for all of the above-mentioned reports, ADB found that, on the contrary, the training of *hilots* substantially *reduced* maternal and infant mortality in the Philippines and that the far lower number of in-facility deliveries actually resulted in a *higher* relative proportion of infant and maternal mortality.

Although these conclusions appear counter-intuitive, Penwell commonly identified poor hygiene, lack of medical equipment, lack of sterile technique and lack of appropriate care in labour, delivery and neonatal intensive care units of selected Philippine hospitals. Furthermore, it has been identified that "there is no conclusive evidence that trained TBAs can prevent maternal deaths unless they are closely linked with existing health services, and are supported to refer women to functioning hospitals providing essential obstetric care" (Bergström and Goodburn 79). However, it is also feasible that facility-based and biomedical deliveries may have been associated with higher maternal and infant mortality rates, because those mothers who went to hospital may have been at greater risk in delivery than those who remain at home, or with a *hilot*.

Yet, the same issues of scientific rigor that were identified in the global WHO/UNICEF maternal and infant mortality data were also found in the DOHP data. The independent evaluators at the ADB identified that essentially all at-home deliveries that resulted in maternal and infant mortality, including purposeful abortions by the mother, were statistically attributed to *hilots* (ADB). This is true, regardless of who assisted delivery, which, very often, was a family member or the mother by herself. Furthermore Bautista identifies: "All of the [DOHP] program implementation review reports begin with the caveat that data on infant and maternal mortality are unreliable" (Bautista 69). The ADB findings appear to be corroborated by the data of the Institute for Health Metrics and Evaluation, which illustrated that the periods with the largest decreases in the maternal mortality rate in the Philippines (from 1980–1990) were also identified as the periods with the highest number of *hilot* trainings.

Regardless of the numerous questions concerning the reliability of the data, the DOHP, with the help of substantial loans from the remaining project lenders, issued an Administrative Order in September 2008 that effectively instituted mandatory in-facility birthing across the Philippines (DOHP). This Order states that all women in the Philippines are to be considered at-risk during pregnancy and must only deliver in-facility by skilled professionals (i.e. physicians and biomedical midwives). *Hilots* are to be integrated into the maternal child health team only if they agree to not perform deliveries again. Hence, there is to be no more training of *hilots*, and they will no longer be provided with sterile birthing kits. It is simply assumed that all *hilots* and all women will comply with the Administrative Order. Furthermore, the definition of the new role for these re-integrated *hilots* and the specific activities they would be allowed to perform as part of the maternal child team, are quite vague, primarily identified as assistance to the biomedical midwife without further elaboration (DOHP). In interviewing the Director of the Maternal Child Health Unit of the DOHP who developed the policy, the role of the TBA was not further clarified. The Director stated:

> They [*hilots*] will assist the midwives, and they will do the other things they do…Like helping the mother, watching the children, washing her clothes. But they will no longer deliver. If they agree to this, then they will be integrated into the Maternal Child Health team. And if she is under forty and literate, we will pay for a scholarship for her to be trained as a midwife.

When I asked her how this would be feasible, especially in rural areas that were grossly under-served, she replied: "We are already building birthing facilities all over the Philippines. We have five years to get this going. Furthermore, we have incentives we can offer." She did not outline coherent plans beyond the fact that she perceived everyone would be eager to comply, including *hilots*. When I asked the reason for the urgency in executing the project, she replied: "The MDGs [Millennium Development Goals] …we *must* meet the MDGs!".

In listening to the Director speak for all women, I was interested to learn what Indigenous *barangay* women and *hilots* might have to say about the feasibility of this Administrative Order.

ASSESSING THE DOHP ADMINISTRATIVE ORDER THROUGH *BARANGAY* MEMBERS' PERCEPTIONS

Approximately 200 Indigenous *barangay* members (almost all females) were questioned in semi-structured interviews regarding who delivered their children; who they preferred to deliver their children; where they preferred to deliver their children; their reasoning for these preferences; the advantages and disadvantages to home and *hilot* delivery; any negative experiences they had or heard from others concerning *hilots*; if *hilots* should be allowed to continue to deliver; and if they perceived mandatory in-facility birthing with the prohibition of the practice of *hilots* appropriate for their *barangay*.

Results: Barangay *Members' Perceptions of Appropriateness of DOHP Policy*

In summary, nearly half of the total deliveries of all informants (46%) were handled by a physician or midwife and 36% of infants were delivered by a *hilot*. But it is important to note that few informants delivered their babies exclusively with *hilots* or biomedical practitioners; rather, a majority of informants delivered their babies with both *hilots* and midwives or physicians. Furthermore, although 66% of informants identified a preference for delivery by a physician or midwife, and 19% preferred delivery by a *hilot*, 63% of informants identified that they would prefer to deliver at home. Thus, even though the majority of women preferred to deliver their babies with physicians or midwives, they also strongly preferred to delivery at home, where only *hilots* were available at all hours for at-home delivery. Therefore, even if women did not necessarily prefer *hilots* to deliver their babies, *hilots* provided one of the few options for assistance in home delivery beyond the available midwife, family member or self-delivery.

Informants identified such reasons as cost (26%), comfort (24%), and lack of restrictions (16%) as the primary advantages of delivering at home, while 68% of informants identified emergencies during delivery as a potential disadvantage to delivering at home. Similarly, cost (58%), comfort (22%), and lack of restrictions (19%) were identified as the primary advantages for *hilot* delivery. Inability to handle emergencies (37%) and lack of medical equipment or medicines (25%) were identified as the primary disadvantages of delivery with *hilots*. Yet, only 2% of all informants reported having any complications with a *hilot* delivery and 8% reported ever hearing of anyone who had. Only 3% or less of informants reported any concern with the safety of *hilots*. Furthermore, 77% of informants believed that *hilots* should be allowed to practice in their *barangay* regardless of the DOHP Administrative Order. Informants identified skill (23%), access (29%), and affordability (29%) as the primary benefits of *hilots*.

Hence, the majority of informants believed *hilots* should be allowed to continue practicing and only 20% of all informants thought the DOHP policy for mandatory in-facility birthing was appropriate for their *barangay*. These findings are summarized in Table 1.

Indicator	% of informants
delivered by physician or midwife	46%
prefer physicisian or midwife delivery	66%
deliverd by *hilot*	36%
prefer *hilot* delivery	19%
prefer to deliver at home	63%
reporting any complications with *hilot* delivery	2%
hearing of others having complications with with *hilot* delivery	8%
perceive that *hilots* should be permitted to practice	77%
perceive this policy to be appropriate for their *barangay*	20%

Table 1: Results of *barangay* interviews assessing appropriateness of *hilot* reintegration

Factors Affecting the Perceived Appropriateness of this Policy

The appropriateness of this DOHP policy could be questioned through examining informant responses; as more than a third of informants identified they were delivered by *hilots*. Furthermore, informants generally perceived that *hilots* should not be prohibited from practice. *Hilots* were identified by informants to be highly skilled, always available, trusted members of the community, and always made women feel comfortable. Stauffer notes: "*Hilots* reportedly were willing to give highly personal service, beginning to call at the end of the 4th month of pregnancy and visiting the prospective mother frequently from then on. They will come day or night and stay long hours if necessary" (22). The primary reason that informants found the policy inappropriate was the shared perception that women would ultimately do what they wanted, regardless of the DOHP's policy.

Financial Access to In-Facility Birthing

A predominant perception identified from interviews with policy makers at municipal, state, and multilateral levels was that all women, given the financial opportunity, would naturally want to take advantage of delivery in hospital or facility. In adopting this perspective, the only factor that could be understood to be preventing women from delivering in-facility is financial access. Thus, in order to replace at-home delivery by *hilots*, it is planned that in-facility delivery costs for indigent women will be covered by the national health insurance, *Philhealth*, for up to US $130 per delivery for a maximum of four deliveries.

However, community informants identified that this amount does not fully cover the cost of in-hospital delivery, and women still must pay for medications (before reimbursement by *Philhealth*), transportation to the facility and any costs beyond the allocated coverage; all of which may be well beyond a family's budget. Furthermore, if there are complications resulting in costs beyond *Philhealth* coverage, families would be responsible for the difference. Yet, *barangay* informants did not generally identify financial access as the primary reason or even *a* reason they prefer to deliver at home. Furthermore, home delivery was identified in from half to three-quarters of all deliveries; with a national average of 61% in 2003 throughout the Philippines (ADB).

The perceived risk of leaving the home

One issue with making global policies from a Western paradigm, assuming universality in such social and cultural constructions as risk and safety, is that different perspectives will often not even be considered. Understandings of risk and safety are not universal. This relativity of understanding can be identified in pregnancy as well. In an interview, a representative of a non-governmental organization (NGO) described an Indigenous tribe in the Southern Philippine island of Mindanao. In this tribe's system of order, whereever a woman was located in her household when she realizes she is pregnant is where she is meant to deliver. From this particular group's order, risk was associated with not only delivering outside of the home, but also with delivering away from the exact spot in the home where the woman first realizes she is pregnant. Hence, for these families, safety was perceived to be preserved precisely by staying at home. Thereby, in-birthing facilities would be considered an extremely high risk that would be avoided at all costs. The NGO informant explained that no matter how much education was offered, these women would not deliver outside of their homes. Thus, in-facility birthing may be resisted regardless of intended beneficence, persuasive paternalism, or rationale.

Perceived Restrictions of In-Facility Birthing

Only 37% of all *barangay* informants identified a preference for in-hospital delivery and less than 1% identified a preference for a local birthing clinic or *barangay* health clinic. The locations of in-birthing facilities are chosen by a Municipal Health Officer with possible input from a provincial governor. However, facilities were not always planned for those communities furthest from hospitals, where women were least likely able to access emergent care.

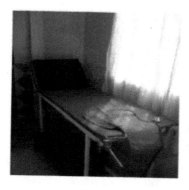

Figure 3: Birthing Table (left) and Birthing Facility (right) in Mainit, Bontoc

When queried how locations for birthing clinics were determined, one municipal health officer stated simply, "I just chose it." Another stated that the criteria were according to which community was most likely to sustain and utilize the clinic, which physicians could staff the clinic, and where greatest need was determined. From other interviews, the choice of which community receives an in-birthing facility appeared to be determined by a combination of political and feasibility criteria.

Regardless of the placement of the facility, several municipal health officers reported subsequent under-utilization of in-birthing facilities. For example, informants from one rural *barangay* that opened the only birthing facility in Bontoc in 2009 reported that, in that year, thirty-one women delivered at home and only one delivered in the in-birthing facility. When the women were queried why they did not use the new in-birthing facility, they stated that the table was too uncomfortable. The one woman who delivered in-facility agreed, stating that, in the future, she would not use the facility again. Female informants stated that when they delivered at home they could deliver in whatever position they found comfortable. The least comfortable position for most women interviewed was reclining. Few identified ever delivering on their back.[2]

Beyond the lack of comfort of the table, or the position they must maintain, many women complained about the restrictive environment of hospitals. A 68 year-old female from Caliban, Murcia delivered four children by herself and preferred this because "others hurry me...I like to take my time." A 29 year-old female from Sacasacan, Sadanga stated that "if you go to hospital, you will be forced to deliver immediately or you will be given a caesarean."

Several women stated that they preferred to stay home because they specifically did not want a Caesarean delivery, and they did not want to "get cut" referring to the obstetric procedure known as an episiotomy. Informants reported that Caesarean deliveries were commonly performed in Philippine hospitals, regardless of women's wishes. Food restrictions, lack of privacy, not being allowed to bathe, being treated poorly, the presence of male obstetricians and not being allowed to have children near or restricting the number of visiting family members could all be perceived as issues that would dissuade women from delivering in hospitals or birthing clinics. One 30 year-old female in Anabel, Sadanga stated that the policy would be feasible only if the "government forces women into the facility."

When questioned how communities would handle the situation of women who desired at-home deliveries with *hilots*, and did not comply with the DOHP policy, some informants reported tactics from persuasion and coercion to outright threats and apparent harassment. As of this writing, infants who are delivered by a *hilot* are not issued a birth certificate as only a skilled professional is authorized to sign the certificate. That a woman's choice of how, where, and by whom she would prefer delivery should be removed and dictated to her by a devolved department of health did not appear to be introduced into the consciousness of this discourse except by a very few of the *barangay* women interviewed (less than 8%).

Capacity and Human Resources

The feasibility of the capacity for increased hospital deliveries is also challenged by this policy. Several chiefs of hospitals who were interviewed reported that their number one admission of normal spontaneous deliveries was overtaxing an already overcrowded hospital system and that hospital obstetric staff have had to encourage women deemed not at-risk to deliver at home. Thus, women are more apprehensive to make what is, for some, a difficult and expensive journey to the hospital, only to risk possibly being turned away. For example, in one regional hospital, normal spontaneous deliveries increased from 1,858 deliveries in 2006 to 2,116 deliveries in 2009 (a 12% increase in 4 years), whilst the number of medical staff has remained constant or decreased (Figure 4)

Furthermore, though this policy has slashed the healthcare workforce by prohibiting *hilots* from delivering, it is of particular concern that no provisions have been offered for increasing the number of "skilled" birthing professionals. Nor does the policy address the issue of physicians who refuse to work in rural areas. This professional human resource imbalance may prove particularly difficult to overcome in a country with a well-documented mass migration of medical professionals (Choy).

A majority of biomedical midwife community health unit administrators interviewed (83%) believed the DOHP policy was neither appropriate, feasible, nor sustainable for their *barangays*. Although many midwives reported to be unaware of the policy (62%) the remainder identified that they ignore it. Considering that some midwife administrators can be responsible for as many as three to four different health stations, additionally having to be available around-the-clock for deliveries in several different *barangays* may stretch them beyond a functioning capacity.

Furthermore, many midwife administrators reported good collaborative working relationships with the *hilots* in their *barangays*, and reported few, if any, *hilot* delivery complications. Midwives identified that *hilots* made appropriate referrals either to them or to the hospital when complications did arise. However, several *hilot* informants on separate occasions relayed a similar story of taking their patient to hospital during an emergency and physicians refusing to admit the patient specifically because the patient was treated by a *hilot*. When I questioned physician informants about such practice, one 48 year-old male physician in Manila, shrugged his shoulders and said "Can you blame them? Obviously, they don't want to be sued." Yet, according to Bergström and Goodburn, even with appropriate TBA referrals: "a significant proportion of their patients do not comply with the referral advice. Reasons for non-compliance with referral by *hilots* include financial constraints, lack of transportation and fear of disrespectful or painful treatment from medical staff" (85).

Considering Potential Unintended Outcomes of this Policy

In general, appropriateness, feasibility, and sustainability for a given local context appear to have been neither assessed nor fully accounted for in this policy. A twenty-three year-old female in Demang, Sadanga stated: "The DOH policy will not work because most women currently seek a *hilot* and they will continue to do so." Hence, if the outcome of this policy is that Filipino women will continue to have at home births with *hilots* who are now no longer being trained nor supplied with a sterile birthing kit, then there is a justified concern for possible increases in maternal and infant morbidity and mortality and for the well-being of *barangay* women. This would especially be true for the most vulnerable women in remote, impoverished, and inaccessible areas. Therefore, the primary objective behind this policy and the cessation of TBA training; to improve maternal child health care access and outcomes, could potentially be severely compromised by this very policy.

CONCLUSION—MEDICINE OR POISON? COLONISING THE INDIGENOUS WOMAN'S BODY

The cessation of trainings of *hilots* appears to be neither justified as necessary, from a closer examination of the global and local data sets for maternal and child mortality rates, nor does it appear to be appropriate in this context, according to informants in communities studied. Equally important is the issue of health care access. In addition to substantially decreasing a trained health care workforce by not training TBAs, it is of particular concern if no provisions are offered for increasing the number of skilled birthing professionals, a goal which is often challenged in poor rural areas. But, more importantly in this instance, there appears to be a general disregard for what women and their families believe, prefer and practice. Can maternal child health policies formulated at international and global levels ever be truly appropriate or safe for Indigenous women by continuing to dictate rather than listen?

One noteworthy limitation of the western construction of safety is its reliance upon the idea of the liberal rational "individual" of the Enlightenment, which simply does not exist in many non-Western cultures and, even after 450 years of western colonization, does not commonly exist in the Philippines. Furthermore, what those who implemented both the colonial cholera policy in the Philippines and the policy for the eradication of *hilots* refuse to consider is that policies that defy local systems of order and understanding will ultimately be resisted. According to James C. Scott: "Everyday resistance is informal, often covert, and concerned largely with de facto gains...open insubordination in almost any context will provoke a more rapid and ferocious response than an insubordination that...never ventures to contest the formal definitions of hierarchy and power" (33). Thus, the failure to use of birthing clinics and the continued employment of *hilots* and home delivery are clear illustrations of resistance to a foreign imposition of safety.

Can biomedical constructions of "safe" motherhood that are embedded in our multilateral structures of global health governance ever truly be safe if their potential conflict with other systems of order, such as Indigenous systems, is perpetually ignored? The medicalization and commodification of birthing through the insistence on skilled attendants, whilst ignoring the beliefs and wishes of Indigenous women and their families, can potentially result in increased infant and maternal mortality.

Western modernity functions via a moralistic imperative to reorder the perceived disorder of the non-western Other for their own well-being and protection. But, arguably, imposing authoritative knowledge on other systems of order, regardless of the intended paternalistic beneficence, has never really wandered far from the swamp of colonialism. Colonizing Indigenous women's bodies and minds through the proven prescriptions of modernity has not shifted dramatically in the last hundred years. Is there really a marked difference between the American colonial obsession with toilet-training the Indigenous Filipino to sit on a commode in a particular way, and the current restriction toward birthing on one's back? The difference, mainly, appears to be in the packaging of the intent. Good medicine that is globally sanctioned by trustworthy experts could hardly be refuted as bad for the pregnant patient. However, it is important to consider what the expert may learn by witnessing the structure(s) already inherent in societies and perceiving the potential values that lie therein.

NOTES

[1] See, for example, Fanon 1967 and Comaroff and Comaroff 1992.

[2] Forcing the non-Westerner into an acceptable Western biomedical construction of appropriate positioning of the body through mimesis is also reflected in the American colonial obsession with forcing Filipino's to use toilets. But use of the toilet was not sufficient. The Filipino had to position their body on the toilet in the proper manner of colonial order. For one representative of the Rockefeller Foundation this was such an obsession that the toilet was specially designed "to make it impossible to sit on except in the desired position" (Anderson 2002: 687).

WORKS CITED

Anderson, Warwick. "Going Through the Motions: American Public Health and Colonial 'Mimicry'." *American Literary History* 14(4) (2002): 686–719. Print.

Asian Development Bank. *Philippines: Women's Health and Safe Motherhood Project. Performance Evaluation Report.* 2007. Web. 5 Jan. 2010.

Bautista, Victoria. *Area-Based Child Survival and Development Program: An Experiment in Devolution.* U.P. Assessments on the State of the Nation. Occasional Papers Series No. 94-004. (1994). Print.

Bergström, Steffan and Elizabeth Goodburn. "The Role of Traditional Birth Attendants in the Reduction of Maternal Mortality." *Studies in Health Services, Organization and Policy* 17 (2001): 77–96. Print.

Chapman, Carleton B. "The Flexner Report" by Abraham Flexner. *Daedalus* 103.1 (1974): 105–117. Print.

Cheng, Maria. *Lancet: Sharp Drop in Maternal Deaths Worldwide.* Associated Press. 2010. Web. 13 April 2010.

Choy, Catherine Ceniza. *Empire of Care. Nursing and Migration in Filipino American History.* Durham: Duke University Press, 2007. Print.

Comaroff, John L. and Jean Comaroff. *Ethnography and the Historical Imagination.* Chicago: University of Chicago Press, 1992. Print.

Department of Health of the Republic of the Philippines. Administrative Order 2008-0029. *Implementing Health Reforms for Rapid Reduction of Maternal and Neonatal Mortality.* 2008. Print.

Douglas, Mary. *Purity and Danger: An Analysis of Concepts of Pollution and Taboo.* Abingdon: Routledge, 1966. Print.

Fanon, Franz. *The Wretched of the Earth.* London: Penguin, 1967. Print.

Flexner, Abraham. *Medical Education in the United States and Canada: A Report to the Carnegie Foundation for the Advancement of Teaching.* New York: The Carnegie Foundation, 1910. Print.

Gramsci, Antonio. *Letters from Prison.* 2 vols. Ed. Frank Rosengarten. Trans. Ray Rosenthal. New York: Columbia University Press, 1994. Print.

Hogan, Margaret C., Kyle J. Foreman, Mohsen Naghavi, Stephanie Y. Ahn, Mengru Wang, Susanna M. Makela, Alan D. Lopez, Rafael Lozano and Christopher J. L. Murray. "Maternal Mortality for 181 Countries, 1980–2008: A Systematic Analysis of Progress Towards Millennium Development Goal 5." *Lancet* 375 (2010): 1609–23. Print.

Ileto, Raynaldo. "Cholera and the Origins of the American Sanitary Order in the Philippines". *Imperial Medicine and Indigenous Societies*. Ed. David Arnold. Manchester: Manchester University Press, 1988. Print.

Johnson, Tina Phillips. "Yang Chongrui and the First National Midwifery School: Childbirth Reform in Early Twentieth-Century China." *Asian Medicine* 4 (2008): 280–302. Print.

Jordan, Brigitte. "Authoritative Knowledge and its Construction." *Childbirth and Authoritative Knowledge*. Ed. R. Davis-Floyd and C. Sargent. Berkeley: University of California Press, 1997. Print.

Kadetz, Paul. *Government, NGO, and Community Factors Affecting Malnutrition in Twelve Indigenous Communities of Lake Atitlan, Guatemala: An Assessment for Sustainable Solutions*. Technical Report for the Royal Geographical Society. 2009. Print.

Kruske, Sue and Leslie Barclay. "Effect of Shifting Policies on Traditional Birth Attendant Training." *Journal of Midwifery and Women's Health* 49.4 (2004): 306–11. Print.

Loughlin, Kelly and Virginia Berridge, *Global Health Governance: Historical Dimensions of Global Governance*. London: Centre on Global Change and Health, London School of Hygiene and Tropical Medicine, 2002. Print.

Nelson, R. *The Philippines*. London: Thames and Hudson, 1968. Print.

Penwell, Vicki. "Mercy in Action. Bringing Mother- and Baby-Friendly Birth Centers to the Philippines." *Birth Models That Work*. Eds. Robbie Davis-Floyd, Lesley Barclay, Betty-Anne Daviss and Jan Tritten. Berkeley: University of California Press, 2009. Print.

Raedt, J. *Expansiveness and Restraint: A Relational Study of Myth, Ritual and Cosmology*. Unpublished PhD Dissertation. University of Chicago. 1969.

Rajaratnam, Julie Knoll, Jake R. Marcus, Abraham D. Flaxman, Haidong Wang, Alison Levin-Rector, Laura Dwyer, Megan Costa, Alan D. Lopez and Christopher J. L. Murray. "Neonatal, Post-neonatal, Childhood, and Under-5 Mortality for 187 Countries, 1970–2010: a Systematic Analysis of Progress Towards Millennium Development Goal 4." *Lancet* 375 (2010): 1988–2008. Print.

Republic of the Philippines. *Republic Act 2644: An Act Regulating Midwifery Training and Practice*. 1958. Print.

Rosaldo, Michelle Z. *Knowledge and Passion: Ilongot Notions of Self and Social Life*. Cambridge: Cambridge University Press, 1980. Print.

Scott, James C. *Weapons of the Weak: Everyday Forms of Peasant Resistance*. New Haven: Yale University Press, 1985. Print.

Stauffer, Robert B. *The Development of an Interest Group: the Philippine Medical Association*. Quezon City: University of the Philippines Press, 1966. Print.

Starr, Paul. *The Social Transformation of American Medicine*. New York: Basic Books, 1982. Print.

USAID. *Newborn Health in the Philippines: A Situation Analysis. Basics Support for Institutionalizing Child Survival Project (BASICS II)*. Arlington, Virginia: United States Agency for International Development, 2004. Print.

Vuori, Hannu. "The World Health Organization and Traditional Medicine." *Community Medicine* 4 (1982): 129–37. Print.

Walraven, Gijs and Andrew Weeks. "The Role of Traditional Birth Attendants with Midwifery Skills in the Reduction of Maternal Mortality." *Tropical Medicine and International Health* 4.8 (1999): 527–529. Print.

Weindling, Paul. "Philanthropy and World Health: The Rockefeller Foundation and the League of Nations Health Organization." *Minerva* 35 (1997): 269–81. Print.

World Health Organization. *The Traditional Birth Attendant in Maternal and Child Health and Family Planning. (WHO Offset Publication No. 18)* Geneva: WHO, 1975. Print.

World Health Organization. *Traditional Birth Attendants—A Joint WHO/UNFPA/MCH Statement*. Geneva: WHO, 1992. Print.

Yang, M. *Letter to John Grant by Marion Young*. Midwifery Education, Midwifery Training School, Beijing (report), folder 372, box 45, series 601, RG1, Rockefeller Foundation Archives, Rockefeller Archive Center. 1932. Print.

4.

Indigenous Midwifery as an Expression of Sovereignty

REBEKA TABOBONDUNG, SARA WOLFE, JANET SMYLIE,
LAURA SENESE, AND GENEVIEVE BLAIS

> A new cycle is starting—it will be a hard one, but in the end
> a powerful one...What will save us in the end is coming to-
> gether and putting our stories together...we will start a new
> kind of healing. (Maria Campbell)

INTRODUCTION

Indigenous midwifery is experiencing revitalization across Turtle Island.[1] There is a renewed understanding that birth is not only a deeply connecting community event, but also a political act that inspires the continued assertion of Indigenous identities and sovereignty. This chapter explores the positive and broad-reaching impacts of re-calling Indigenous midwifery, our traditional knowledges and our stories into our communities. We begin with central stories shared by community members Rebeka Tabobondung, Sara Wolfe, Janet Smylie, Genevieve Blais and Laura Senese, who describe their journeys and reflections in revitalizing the deeply rooted traditions of Aboriginal birth and midwifery knowledge at personal, professional, family and community levels as we worked together to establish an Indigenous grounded birth centre in Toronto.

Our stories as life-givers, knowledge workers, health care providers, allies and youth interested in re-calling and asserting Indigenous birth rights intersected in a powerful way in June of 2012, at the historic gathering *For Seven Generations: Visioning for a Toronto Aboriginal Birth Centre* which evolved out of a partnership between Seventh Generation Midwives Toronto [SGMT] and the Aboriginal Health research program, now known as the Well Living House (WLH)[2] at St. Michael's Hospital's Centre for Research on Inner City Health. The intent of this meeting was to create an opportunity for members of the Toronto Aboriginal community and relevant Aboriginal reproductive health stakeholders to inform the strategic development of an Aboriginal birth centre in the Greater Toronto Area (GTA). The following reflections, personal stories and insights highlight our diverse teachings and approaches to leadership and community engagement, as well as our efforts to resist and reverse colonial policies and practices.

Today, Aboriginal midwives are re-constructing the central role they have played in their communities since time immemorial. Their work demonstrates that Aboriginal frameworks of governance and approaches to research are effective when put into action. The result is increased access to quality care—with quality defined in our own terms. This, in turn, leads to more positive birth experiences and healing from the negative impacts of colonization in both Aboriginal and non-Aboriginal communities. Asserting their leadership in the creation of new standards for culturally inclusive care and education, Aboriginal midwives are challenging status quo policies. Together with their allies, they are unearthing, re-telling and sharing time-honoured Indigenous knowledge for the well-being of generations yet to be born.

COLONIAL ATTEMPTS TO SILENCE ABORIGINAL MIDWIFERY

From the earliest points of contact, processes of colonization attempted to destroy Aboriginal midwifery and birth knowledge. In the first half of the 20th century, the disruption of traditional birth practices escalated through the deliberate dispossession of land, the fragmentation of families and communities and the medicalization of birth, as part of the overall imposition of western beliefs, values and ideological frameworks upon our nations. According to Terry Carol and Calm Wind of the *Equay-Wuk* Women's Group, Sioux Lookout, the results have been:

...the separation of the midwife from the birthing process; the deterioration of the ties between a woman and her midwife, husband, children, family, community; the birth of children outside traditional areas; the breakdown of the rites of passages (for example: name giving ceremonies); the breakdown of kinship; the forced acceptance of the non-Aboriginal birthing values, norms and culture; further deterioration of Nishnawbe culture, tradition and language. (Do-Dis-Seem 77)

By the mid-20th century, the cumulative effects of colonization had devastated the highly developed birth cultures of Turtle Island. Aboriginal oral traditions, which had been used to ensure the passage of community birth knowledge from one generation to the next, were greatly diminished. Thankfully, many of our grandmothers and great-grandmothers worked to protect our birth knowledges and practices. These extraordinary acts of resistance and resilience have enabled a resurgence of Aboriginal midwifery traditions, largely driven by demand from a new generation of families seeking access to our traditional practices. Today Aboriginal midwives and researchers are actively producing, documenting and applying Aboriginal midwifery and birth knowledge in order to restore what was thought to have been silenced.

FIVE STORIES TO PIECE THE PUZZLE

We all carry a piece of the puzzle—if we come together, we can piece back the puzzle that was scattered by colonization. There is no such thing as no culture, story, language—it's not lost—it's out there and everyone has a piece of it. (Maria Campbell)

I, Creation—Poem by Rebeka Tabobondung

> Imagine O P E N
> body follows
> R I D E the crest
> Creation
> commands my body to slip
> deeper into water
> The wave grows
> seizes life
> throws me just beyond the spirit world
> I hover there
> A Spirit traveling water vessel
> Belly muscles rage me back
> hands cupping layers
> that tonight are opening
> Creation
> has flooded me
> a wet tangle of hair
> charges through pelvic bone
> First breadth about to form
> I, Creation
> bear down
> pull power
> from every woman and grandmother
> before me
> Will not rest
> Without you in my arms

Rebeka's Story

I had two experiences that I would describe as spiritual in the very early stages of my pregnancy. They occurred about a week after conception. It was winter, and I was about to leave the house. While I was putting on my hat, I noticed the faint sound of a drum, which seemed to be beating in my own ears! Of course, I knew there was a chance I was pregnant, and in that moment I wondered if I was hearing my baby's heart beating. That evening I had a vivid dream that I was bleeding from my belly button. When I awoke I interpreted that the blood in my dream represented the life force that flows through our bodies with the belly button being the essential opening to new life force, because this is where the umbilical cord attaches, and how a mother sustains life to her unborn child. Before I bought the pregnancy test, I knew at the level of my spiritual self that the results would be positive.

The mainstream knowledge that was offered to me while I was pregnant was devoid of the deep transformative journey that I intuitively knew I was on. This void resulted in personal feelings of isolation because I had no avenue to acknowledge, explore, or learn from my new experiences. Thus, I began to look to my own culture for an explanation of my experiences. In 2005, I sought out Aboriginal midwives in Toronto to attend the home-birth I had planned. I began to seek out traditional teachings about this life-changing journey. However, it soon became apparent that the midwives and I were on the same journey. We were urban Aboriginal women, dislocated from our traditional territories, seeking out traditional birth knowledges that had been silenced by the processes of colonization. I soon began to feel grateful for simply having access to the Aboriginal midwives that were providing my care.

My experience of pregnancy and birth initiated a journey of researching and disseminating traditional birth knowledges, first as a Masters student, then a magazine publisher, filmmaker, and research coordinator with Well Living House. Throughout that time I had continued to maintain close connections to the Aboriginal and non-Aboriginal midwives who were there to take care of me, eat the birthday cake my sister had made, and welcome my son Zeegwon on the night he was born. Since becoming a mother, this journey has brought me home to Wasauksing First Nation to spend time listening to the stories of our Aboriginal women, and to document our rich oral histories on traditional birth. I continue to work towards learning and sharing this knowledge in culturally appropriate ways within both my reserve and urban communities. At the Birth Centre visioning, my role was to produce a short documentary to be shared afterwards with the community and stakeholders.

My journey of pregnancy, birth and motherhood, as well as listening to stories, solidified what I had intuitively known all along: within Anishinawbe and Indigenous worldview, the states surrounding pregnancy are considered to be highly spiritual. Our traditional knowledge demonstrates the importance of paying close attention to our spiritual experiences, especially during pregnancy, because they have the capacity to hold vital teachings which can affect ourselves, our unborn children, and the community on individual, medicinal, political, and spiritual levels (Tabobondung 128).

Sara's Story

Choosing to (re)claim my identity as an Aboriginal person has forced me to think critically about my knowledge of history, and it has allowed me to learn how to locate myself in relation to colonial, political, family and community histories. I come from an Aboriginal family all too familiar with the legacy of colonization, the intergenerational impact of residential schools and the disruption of the cultural knowledge that is my birthright.

As I am an Anishnawbe midwife, many Indigenous women and families have come to me to guide them through their journey of pregnancy and birth, in what we know to be a good way. For many, this was the first time they had ever had a primary care provider who openly identified as Indigenous. They had many questions for which I did not know the answer.

On the advice of my mentors, I began to seek out Indigenous knowledge and teachings for pregnancy and birth. Thinking it was simply to enhance my knowledge and improve my credibility as an Aboriginal person, soon I also began to share their thirst for more knowledge. Learning about the traditions, knowledge and ways of my ancestors, I've become proud and confident in my identity as an Anishnawbe woman and midwife, and more deeply aware of my responsibilities in that role. Armed with the knowledge of our culture and teachings, I've found we become better at role modeling our individual and collective responsibilities. As fast as I was building my collected Indigenous knowledge around pregnancy and birth, others were coming to ask me to share my newly-acquired knowledge. In this journey, I am discovering what it means to be a midwife in my community, the obligations that come with claiming that prominent role and the power and beauty of awakening to the wisdom of our cultural knowledge.

What my teachers and mentors have taught me is that, as a gatekeeper of life, my role is to facilitate the sharing of our knowledge, beliefs, values and skills, and to help guide families to fulfill their own distinct roles. Midwives were traditionally seen as a community's nation builders. They were leaders as well as healers. The grandmothers who so bravely made sure to protect and pass down our knowledge and teachings on birth practices would be proud to know how Indigenous midwives once again are fulfilling their responsibilities, and in doing so, demonstrating the profound impact of balancing Indigenous and Western ideologies in healthcare delivery. The very act of salvaging this knowledge, and using the traditional practices of our culture in contemporary ways, is a continued demonstration of how Indigenous midwifery is an act of resistance.

In preparing for the For Seven Generations visioning meeting, I found the colonizers' tools to be very difficult to use, because they do not acknowledge or value many of our Indigenous ways of knowing and doing. Going through the various stages of getting approval, preparing a package for the ethics review board and writing a "report," were all things that challenged the intuitiveness of our vision, because the easiest way to move through the system was to use their formula. Their formulas don't work for our context, however, so we challenged that system by creating new tools, writing around policies, finding loopholes and, when all else failed, cried, only to re-group and try again. The interconnection of our stories demonstrates the powerful impact the restoration of Indigenous midwifery is having on personal, professional, family and community levels. Indigenous midwifery is empowering the next generations of Indigenous peoples and once again (re)building strong, sovereign Nations.

Genevieve's Story

For me, my path became very clear while working on the For Seven Generations visioning meeting. I was on my journey to finishing a degree in Biochemistry with plans to continue on to graduate work in molecular biology. However, I came into the gathering holding stories my mother and I had shared about her work as an Aboriginal midwife and high-risk prenatal and infant worker in the Aboriginal community. During my undergraduate years, I worked closely with her in a placement, where I witnessed firsthand the intergenerational effects of colonization on the health of my community. I sat and listened to the stories of the women, some of whom had lost their children to the child welfare system. They were pregnant and looking for ways to change their lifestyle through cultural support and guidance. I was left feeling lost and without a solution.

Their stories left me with a feeling of responsibility to learn more about the health inequities present in my community. With this in mind, I was led to take part in the birth centre meeting during my final year. My attendance at the gathering was a changing point in my life. Recognizing that midwifery and birthing connected women to the Indigenous knowledge that their bodies carry from previous to future generations seemed integral to the concept of health and identity. One simply could not be connected to their health without feeling connected to oneself. I realized that, as a youth, I have a responsibility to use my gifts in supporting individuals to reclaim their health for themselves, their families, and their community. I am now on a path to becoming a paediatrician and researcher to aid in the process of restoring Indigenous health by honouring and integrating our traditional knowledge into current health practices.

Janet's Story

On my mother's side, I come from a long line of strong and resilient Métis and First Nations women. I am a seventh generation half-breed. Like many Indigenous women, there are some broken threads in the fabric of my life. Growing up outside of our historic homeland, in a town north of Toronto, I always knew I was "part-Indian."

I believe that the embodiment of stressors catches up with us eventually—especially for those who are too busy trying to survive and support the survival of their families to attend to the wounds inflicted by day-to-day and historic traumas. I lost my strong, opinionated, organized and fiercely loving mother to breast cancer at the tender age of thirteen. It left a big hole that could only be partially filled by the generosity and love of my remaining family.

My interest in the science of living things and my confidence in things academic—notably nurtured by my mother, father and then my stepmother—survived the chaos. I found myself in medical school and then family practice residency in my early twenties. At the same time, I started to unravel who I was and how I was going to honour myself, my family, and my community, as an Indigenous woman.

The labour and delivery ward offered a lifeline amidst a medical curriculum that I was becoming increasingly disillusioned with. The complexity, beauty and balance of human physiology appealed to me tremendously—especially when further inter-linked with family and community systems. But it seemed that the large majority of medical "intervention" was about trying to break apart and control the inter-relationality and rhythms of life. The power of birth seemed to trump these attempts at imposing structure and control. Birthing clearly had an intrinsic timing, rhythm and power that the most skilled and experienced birth attendants knew was important to recognize and respect. Efforts to try to ignore this fundamental truth seemed to backfire. I hung on tightly to this proof of a different way of knowing and being within the health service contexts.

I arrived at Anishnawbe Health Toronto (AHT) as a newly graduated family physician in 1995. I was immediately overwhelmed by the significant health and social challenges facing many of the mothers and babies for whom I was providing care. I decided to take tobacco to Jan Kahehti:io Longboat, a Mohawk Elder and Traditional Counsellor who also worked at AHT, and ask for her assistance. She told me that if I wanted to help the infants, I needed to think about the grandparents.

As is often the case with the wisdom of our grandparents, at first it didn't seem entirely practical for the situation I was facing. I was already feeling stretched in my ability to respond to the complex needs of the mothers and babies, yet now I was being told that I also had to consider the grandparents. Fortunately, despite this initial resistance, these seeds of wisdom eventually took root in my mind and heart.

For years I continued to attend births, marveling at the power of this ceremony that seemed to retain a sense of sacredness, no matter what the medical intrusion. I could feel the energy in my hands for a long time after being the first one to touch the newborn as they crossed the eastern doorway into this realm of being.

I can still feel the energy on my hands even though it has been years now since I deferred my privilege of attending births to Indigenous midwives and took on a supportive clinical role as a family physician consultant. For the past ten years, I have spent most of my time as an Indigenous knowledge worker continuing to pursue an answer to the question that Jan framed for me so long ago—"Kokum (Grandmother), what makes a baby well?" I have had the opportunity of dialoguing with Indigenous community Elders and grandparents, and front-line health care providers in First Nations, Inuit and Métis communities in both urban and rural settings.

I try my best to work with these communities to respectfully document knowledge and support community wellbeing through its sharing and use. I also work to advocate for Indigenous knowledge and practice within mainstream health research and policy contexts. I was honoured to partner with Seventh Generation Midwives Toronto to acquire funding and co-facilitate the Toronto Indigenous Birth Visioning meeting.

Perhaps the most important knowledge work for me has been to work with Indigenous midwives through the pregnancy and birthing of my twin boys—and then to try and "walk the talk" on a day to day basis as I parent them.

Laura's Story

As a settler Canadian with largely Italian and Scottish roots, my path towards becoming an effective ally in supporting the revitalization of Indigenous midwifery has been neither straightforward nor clearly defined. My role has evolved out of relationships built through the community based, Indigenous-led health research that we do at the Well Living House (WLH).

My path began in a decidedly academic and somewhat abstract place. After I became aware of the egregious health inequities between Indigenous and non-Indigenous peoples in Canada, I completed a Master's degree in health geography in an effort to dig into the roots of these inequities. I approached this work from a critical, social justice perspective, focusing on gendered links between Indigenous rights and health. As I learned about these inequities, I was both shocked and angered. They are a part and a product of my existence, but had remained invisible because my position of privilege allowed me to remain ignorant of the legacy of colonialism as it continues to shape our contemporary Canadian existence. Persistent power differentials allow some people not to know about these injustices, while others live and breathe inequity every day. This realization was an important initial step on my ongoing path towards being an effective ally.

Working with the WLH on a number of community based health research projects focused on reclaiming and reintegrating Indigenous knowledge and traditions into health service work, I have had the chance to work with, and learn from, many brilliant and strong Indigenous women. I have learned so much and feel incredibly inspired by the diverse and powerful roles that these women play in their communities. Among the many teachings that I feel very privileged to have received through this work is the notion that you need to understand where you come from, where you are rooted, in order to truly understand who you are and to take up your role in a good way. This applies equally to Indigenous and non-Indigenous peoples, and has been the key to sorting out how to work effectively as an ally. It is only from an honest starting place that positive relationships can be built going forward.

Becoming more grounded in community and experience, I understand more clearly the important processes of reclamation that are occurring through the revitalization of Indigenous midwifery, and the ways in which I can help to nurture them. I understand more fully that birth is a deeply connecting, community event, as well as a political act—the continued assertion of Indigenous identities and sovereignty. We all have different roles to play in this process and I seek not to change where I am rooted, but to draw strength from this place in order to support this collective endeavour. In doing so, I am making an effort to share the power that I now know I am privileged to have and to contribute to the important work that I know needs to be done. By learning about and engaging with Indigenous ways of knowing and doing, we can all contribute to dismantling the power differentials that continue to structure our society, and to supporting more effective power sharing that centres fundamentally around respect.

FOR SEVEN GENERATIONS: VISIONING FOR A TORONTO ABORIGINAL BIRTH CENTRE

> Storytelling is the medicine we need now—What will help us through are the stories that we will say to each other. Even if you feel you have no story or culture, you do have a piece of it. Don't believe that your story is not important—it does not matter what kind of story it is. We need it—it's a little medicine that comes out. (Maria Campbell)

Indigenous midwifery has, and continues to have, life-long, multigenerational impacts across the family and community continuum. Community midwives carry the knowledge in the stories of how birth experiences influence the mother, infant-child, family over time—this is sacred, private knowledge. In our 2012 gathering, Métis Elder Maria Campbell explained "In our birth stories we carry the stories of our people." In this way, midwives are the carriers and caretakers of community knowledge.

Aboriginal women and midwives have been dreaming of securing a safe space for families to birth their babies with love and dignity since the sanctity of our homes was compromised by colonization. We planned a meeting to help balance the scholarly findings of the "official" research with input from community members and reproductive health care stakeholders. We were asking for broad community input about priorities, needs, aspirations and opportunities as we put forth a proposal to establish an Aboriginal Birth Centre in Toronto.

While our specific proposal was unique, over several decades there had been many failed attempts to establish a mainstream birth centre in Toronto. However, upon the cusp of our visioning meeting, the Ontario government announced a new plan to fund birth centres and the scope of our meeting took on broader significance. A birth centre in Toronto would be funded; the extent to which it would be grounded and led by Aboriginal midwives remained uncertain.

The three-day gathering brought together Elders, knowledge keepers, Aboriginal and non-Aboriginal midwives, Aboriginal health and knowledge researchers and community stakeholders, including previous SGMT clients, Aboriginal youth and artists, maternal-child and reproductive health front line workers, as well as a diverse mix of local, regional, provincial and national stakeholders (health workers, health managers and health policy makers). Our team was able to gather a great amount of information, rich in community experiences and understandings. Participants shared their clear directions and priorities for an Aboriginal grounded birth centre.

(RE)ENGAGING INDIGENOUS FRAMEWORKS

Regardless of all of the other things that happen at a birth, the transition of a baby coming through the door of the spirit world and into the physical world is considered a ceremony for the mother and child, and for her family and community. With this understanding that birth is a ceremony, it became clear that the meeting itself was to be a ceremony; we were birthing a birth centre. We offered tobacco to our Elders and knowledge keepers—Maria Campbell, Katsi Cook, and Jan Kahehti:io Longboat—who we also consider our grandmothers and aunties. Together, we implemented ceremonial protocols; the gathering was treated in accordance with the laws and customs for ceremony as we understand them.

We opened the meeting with a sunrise ceremony, and our Indigenous brothers took responsibility to light the sacred fire and tend to it the full three days of the meeting. With this act we were reminded that the sunrise ceremony is one of the first ceremonies that children are taught and everybody can learn it. We were told the story of Eagle travelling in all four directions to save humans who had forgotten the importance of acknowledging creation every day. In the end, Eagle finally spotted some grandparents teaching their grandchildren the sunrise ceremony.

The recognition of the spirituality and sacredness of birth poured into the framework and objectives of the meeting. It provided clarity and intent about its underlying purpose: to include, respect, and incorporate Indigenous values into midwifery practice. Throughout the three days, grandmothers, aunties and community participants shared many stories. The grandmothers reminded participants that teaching our communities and young people about the significance and power of birthing is firmly rooted in our cultural traditions. Traditional Knowledge keeper and midwife, Katsi Cook re-told aspects of the Haudenosaunee and Anishnawbe

Creation stories which demonstrate the central and sacred role that pregnancy, birth and mothering play in our cosmological vision.

> Sky woman falling from the sky to Turtle Island tells us about our relations with the universe and all things. There is a feeling of being part of something since this first birth story tells us about Indigenous ecosystems—foundations of social development and expanding cultural regeneration. This story belongs to Aboriginal midwifery and women's circle and ecosystems. Sky woman exemplifies compassion, courage, shaping of bodies by the cosmos. This is a life cycle teaching for women from puberty to Elderhood. A bird bringing Sky woman back to the turtle's back—egg leaving the ovary and travelling to the fallopian tube recapitulates Sky woman's fall, the ovary connection to Sky woman, the connection to our DNA. (retold by Katsi Cook).

ABORIGINAL MIDWIFERY AS A MOVEMENT OF RESISTANCE

In our birth stories, we carry the stories of our people. The links between the kinship relationships and positive birthing experiences in the stories shared by community members at the gathering also spoke to the ways that colonization disrupts cultural processes. The stories shared in our circles highlighted how these colonial abuses are manifested in the birth process and the care women receive. These impacts were not restricted to the women having the baby—the birth stories also expressed the powerful impact of the birth on their families and communities.

Community participants also shared the ways in which a positive birth experience has the potential to initiate significant, life-long change that is carried on into future generations. Their positive birth stories demonstrated the power of tradition, ceremony, and our ability to rediscover, re-engage and re-enter the sacred ceremonial practice of birth. Many times mothers recalled how during the birth of their children they themselves were reborn:

> I could hear and see everything my baby saw and I felt a great peace as I knew my baby was okay. And when he was born, I was born. In my birth I found a new meaning to life. I will not go one more day without speaking my language or let a history

book we did not write define myself or my people. It is we, the real people, who can deliver who we are within ourselves." (Birth story related by Katsi Cook.)

Many women at the meeting spoke about how important it was to receive midwifery care centered around Indigenous cultures and traditions, in order to foster the sense of acceptance and support needed to make their own decisions about their pregnancies and birth options. For example, one woman noted, "how healing it was not to explain my culture in order to receive care and not feel shame and embarrassment, but to feel supported for what I wanted in my pregnancy." The notion that participants drew strength from the culturally secure support they received from midwives came up often through the three days and some explained how this care had empowered them to demand this type of care in other care settings.

There were many reminders that midwives are often the heart and centre of a community, particularly when we are attempting to weave back together disrupted webs of Indigenous culture and ways of living. Katsi Cook told us how Indigenous midwifery knowledge encompasses the full environment of women's bodies and is not limited to just the physical but also includes dreams, relationships and ecology. Maria Campbell recalled how the midwives in her community, her aunties and grandmothers, were strong and gentle, wise and soft-spoken, laughing and singing. Maria described for us how midwives worked as advocates and provided security for our children and our communities—intervening in the community when this was required. Traditionally, they had medicines to treat sick children, counselled people who were fighting, taught about the culture through storytelling and attended to death as well as birth, transitioning the body from, and eventually back into, the spirit world.

Indigenous midwives today continue to hold many interconnected community roles and act as the glue that holds communities together. The knowledge of our birthing traditions is in the practice of Aboriginal midwifery. The resurgence of Aboriginal midwifery draws heavily on the knowledge of this power, and many have bound together to reclaim traditional roles as caretakers for the people. Maria Campbell noted, "Midwives work for the nation. They have authority as they birth everyone."

The visioning gathering was historic because it also accomplished bringing together many non-Aboriginal allied midwives and stakeholders to the meeting to support the strategic direction of an Aboriginal birth centre. Mohawk Elder Jan Longboat spoke about the wampum belts and teachings about cultures living in a good way together. Jan highlighted the Dish With One Spoon wampum, in which two nations came to an agreement that when people travelled into a territory, everyone from all nations would be fed and taken care of. Jan noted, "Women's council beads are laid out when women are meeting. They are made of wampum, from the ocean. There are links between water and woman; the birthing connection to water." Allies were asked to reflect on the power, privilege and authority they possess, including its source and consequences for others. They recognized a need for a shift in existing power dynamics and the confrontation of structural barriers. It was acknowledged that partnerships and collaborations between Aboriginal and non-Aboriginal groups have not historically worked out equitably, even when intentions were good and the aims were to divide resources fairly. Despite historical and ongoing colonial forces, the visioning gathering confirmed that Aboriginal peoples continue to maintain strong identities and that their contributions to midwifery care are a mark of strength that can contribute to healthy communities for everyone.

Indigenous midwives called on non-Indigenous midwives to support their proposal and an agreement was made to put their energies together to submit a single application for an Indigenous grounded birth centre in the city of Toronto. The application, philosophy of care and design of the physical space have been led by Aboriginal midwives and guided by an Indigenous framework that focuses on an holistic approach to health care—including emphasis on the physical, mental, emotional and spiritual aspects of birth. It is envisioned as a space where women, families and communities from all over Toronto can access care that is both medically and culturally safe. It was recently announced that the application was successful and the birth centre opened in Toronto in the winter of 2014.

CONCLUSION

Taking on a leadership role for the development of a visioning meeting is just one way Aboriginal midwives are interrupting the forces of colonization. Indigenous midwives across Turtle Island are actively demonstrating resiliency and resistance by reclaiming the knowledge, practices and traditions of birthing. Acknowledgement and gratitude is also owed to the groundwork that has been laid by many brave Indigenous men and women, warriors and midwives, who fought so long and hard to re-create a place where Aboriginal people could see themselves bridging gaps, leading innovation and, once again, healing our nations.

As we reflect on the five stories of how we all came together to support this gathering we discover many other quiet ways Indigenous people have been demonstrating this same resistance and how it dovetails with the stories shared at this meeting. Aboriginal midwifery offers us *Waakotawin*, a Cree understanding of what brings us all together. It reveals multiple pathways and roles in which we can do the work of coming together and engaging broader community and allies in culturally inclusive frameworks to build healthy communities. Everyone in our communities, at all stages of life, and regardless of genders and chosen paths, had individual and collective understandings of the central roles and responsibilities midwives played. Aboriginal midwives are reclaiming this responsibility and, in doing so, are role models for their clients and community to do the same. We will all know our rightful place again, and live the good life, because we are secure in our own knowledge and practice. Aboriginal midwives are facilitating community investment in culture, identity, self-determination, rights, values and putting birth as the central strategy to improve the health of our families, communities, nations and future generations.

NOTES

[1] Rooted within aspects of the Iroquois and Anishinawbe Creation stories, the term Turtle Island is an Indigenous understanding of the land included in North America.

[2] The Well Living House is an action research centre focused on Indigenous infant, child, and family health. It is housed within the Centre for Research on Inner City Health at St. Michael's Hospital, Toronto, ON. It was built from a foundation of collaborative work between Indigenous health researchers, frontline health practitioners and Indigenous community grandparents.

WORKS CITED

Carol, Terry, and Laura Calm Wind. "Do-Dis-Seem (Nishnawbe-Aski Nation Midwifery Practice)." *Canadian Woman Studies/Les Cahiers De La Femme* 14.3 (1994): 77–82. Print.

For Seven Generations: Visioning an Aboriginal Birth Centre in Toronto. Dir. Rebeka Tabobondung. Prod. Seventh Generation Midwives Toronto and Well Living House. Toronto. 2011. DVD.

Smylie, Janet, Wolfe, Sara, and Laura Senese. "For Seven Generations: Visioning for a Toronto Aboriginal Birth Centre Community Meeting Report." Toronto: *Seventh Generation Midwives Toronto* and *Well Living House*. Print.

Tabobondung, Rebeka. "Women Sharing Strength for All Generations: Aboriginal Birth Knowledge and New Media Creation." M.A. thesis, Ontario Institute for Studies in Education, University of Toronto, 2008. Print.

II: Voicing Resilience

5.

Stories of Mothers Living with HIV+ in Kibera, a Mega-slum in Sub-Saharan Africa

SAMAYA VAN TYLER

Biomedical and social science research relating to HIV/AIDS has accumulated at a dramatic rate over recent decades. The focus of these studies has been primarily on understanding the chronic disease as a medical, rather than a socio-economic and politico-cultural crisis. Research has leaned heavily on the side of prevention and clinical treatment without addressing the experienced reality of daily life for those living with HIV/AIDS outside of the United States of America (Doyal 173). This chapter is based on a study I conducted which focused on the day-to-day reality of nine mothers living with HIV/AIDS, all widows, and responsible for, in total, 36 children, who live in Kibera, an international mega-slum in Kenya, Africa.

This chapter has four main sections. In the first section, I provide a brief genealogy of Kibera, ending with italicized personal reflections of my first visit into the informal settlement. In section two, I discuss the methodology I used for my study, and provide an introduction of the participants. In the third section, I present four storylines that emerged from my findings: (i) If I die, who will take care of my children? (ii) They just come to you, (iii) If I sit there, that ten bob won't come and (iv) Being up, feeling down and stress-up. The fourth section presents an overall discussion and conclusion.

GENEALOGY OF KIBERA

To understand the present, we look to the past. Understanding the historical context of Kibera is important, as it is reflected in the lives of those who live there today. The informal settlement of Kibera first emerged due to the displacement of Africans by the arrival of British settlers and "owes its very existence to the forces of colonialism" (Ferraro 1). In the late 1880s, British colonists settled in an area once frequented by the pastoral Maasai people. This region became known as Nairobi, and was initially a colonial railroad camp on the Mombasa-to-Uganda railroad. Africans were not permitted to enter the city without a British government-issued permit. Africans, mostly men who were formally employed as menial workers, were also issued semi-permanent housing that met only the most basic of living requirements, were viewed as temporary residents, and forced to live in a separate enclave of the growing metropolis (Achola 2002; Macharia 1992).

In 1903, the British officially surveyed the area and publically designated it as a military reserve. Sudanese soldiers, all with Nubian lineage, were allowed to settle there, rent free, in recognition of services rendered to the British colonial cause, as a form of an unofficial pension (Parsons 90). This area became known as Kibera, which comes from the Nubi language word *kibra*, meaning "green forest", and "Kibera filled up very fast" (de Smedt 218).

In 1929, administration of Kibera was handed over to the Nairobi Municipal Council. The 1930s and 1940s witnessed a migratory flow into this informal settlement area, which quickly gained the reputation of being the cleanest and safest of Nairobi's slums in which to live (Bodewes 53). On December 12, 1963, Kenya became the Republic of Kenya, free from British rule, and, over the years, there have been many thwarted attempts to develop Kibera (Schwartz-Barcotte, 49). The Centre on Housing Rights and Evictions (COHRE) in 2006 reported that the Kenyan government had taken no steps to formally acknowledge the existence and rights of the residents of informal settlements, in relation to their rights to be protected from forced eviction, and access to basic infrastructure such as water and sanitation, electricity, garbage disposal, education, health services and paved roads (4).

Today, Kibera is a sprawling shanty town, an international "megaslum," and spreads over one hundred and ten hectares of land. Bodewes observed that "the normal measure for adequate space in refugee camps is about two or three times greater than the current density in most of Kibera"

(57). There is no accurate census data available; it is difficult to accurately estimate the number of those who make their home in Kibera, as the night population (the number sleeping there) is significantly higher than the day-time population. The numbers who sleep there may also vary considerably from night to night and add to the variables when thinking in terms of a re-liable count. "However, the majority of researchers estimate that between 600,000 and 700,000 people live in Kibera" (Bodewes 31). This approxi-mation of those who live in Kibera is over 10 years old, and is now likely to be closer to one million people.

Personal Reflections

> *It was another one of those stifling hot mid-afternoons in the summer of 2005, and I was walking with five African women on one of the earth-trodden paths in Kibera. As we walked I looked around, absorbing sights and smells that were strange and unusual for a privileged white woman. Live electrical wires hung loosely over and between the corrugated tin roofs of many of the wattle and mud buildings. Goats, dogs and the occasional pig were foraging in the mounds of garbage strewn around, while children played nearby, stopping now and again to stare at me or follow, shouting out repeatedly the friendly greeting in Kiswahili, "Habari gani? Habari gani?" which means, "How are you?" in English.*

> *I had been warned before we started to tread carefully, to watch out for black polythene bags that lay on the ground or flew through the air now and again. Because the numbers of pit latrines are not enough to meet the needs of Kibera's popula-tion, the menace of "flying toilets" continues. Those who have no money to pay to use a private latrine or who do not feel safe to venture out any distance at night to the latrines use a plas-tic bag to relieve themselves. Then they tie and throw them through the air or merely dump them outside their homes.*

> *We were walking to see the view from the railway line that cuts through the middle of the settlement; the railway track runs from Mombasa to Uganda, and is piled high on each side with smelling, rotting garbage. Four of the women walked ahead of me, one stayed close by my side, pointing to holes in the ground*

or pieces of cement, garbage, and animal and human waste
that may have caused me to stumble. They watched out for me
and included me at every turn as we meandered in and out
of the narrow throughways in the slum settlement. I observed
silently as I listened to the sounds. I heard the heaviness of our
solid tread as we moved together forward, and the vibrations
began to echo in my head resonating like a steady drum beat
with the rhythm of my heart.

METHODOLOGY

Fundamentally a narrative inquiry, my study was informed by feminist, Indigenous and neo-colonial perspectives. My de-colonizing agenda was complimented by the intersectionality of three research genres that enabled me to craft a methodological synthesis for the blending of the multiple perspectives of nine Indigenous mothers diagnosed with HIV/AIDS and living in poverty (Kincheloe 685). Given that I was able to locate little information regarding research specific to the diversity of Indigenous communities in Africa, I referred to the 2007 Canadian Institute of Health Research (CIHR) Guidelines for Health Research Involving Aboriginal People. It was crucial that my research was conducted in culturally competent ways that were ethical and in "keeping with Aboriginal [Indigenous] values and traditions" (CIHR 2). The use of a convergence of methodologies provided inclusive space to listen to stories that addressed the dynamism of mothers who are HIV+ and living in Kibera, while scratching the underbelly of the patriarchal beast. Issues such as gender inequality and colonization in relation to the experiences of mothers who are HIV+ were exposed in a world where, although change is escalating and dramatic, poverty remains a constant in their daily lives.

I developed relationships within Kibera over a five year period. Communication with a respected community leader, Winnie, was not only critical in the selection and recruitment of women for the study, it proved vitally important for every aspect of the research process, guiding it in ways that were culturally sensitive, relevant, respectful, responsive, equitable and reciprocal (CIHR 2007; Kovach 2009; Smith 1999).

The University of Victoria's Human Research Ethics Board reviewed and approved all aspects of the study. I received a research permit from the Kenya National Council of Science and Technology, a necessary requirement for official researchers in Kenya. I was concerned that participation in the study may expose women to the risks of identification as a woman with HIV/AIDS and any potential stigma that may ensure. This was not so; I was openly acknowledged whenever and wherever we met in Kibera. Issues of confidentiality and anonymity were explained during the initial meeting and again when asking for signatures on the "Participant Consent Form." Two women chose pseudonyms; the other seven and Winnie wished to use their own names.

The primary mode of collecting data was two, in-depth, semi-structured conversations which took place at a mutually agreeable time. These times were usually in the early morning before the local markets were open, and before the women began their daily activities in Kibera. At their request, I met with three women in their homes. However, home visits ended abruptly when Winnie became concerned for my safety. When I asked her for an explanation, she informed me that she had heard there were some in the community who thought I would be an easy target to rob. Kibera is an environment that can, at times, be dangerous. Further conversations took place in the secured compound in which Winnie taught tailoring skills to young women.

I drew upon dialogical/performance analysis to conduct the narrative analysis of my findings, and acknowledged that story and story-telling are expressive, and shaped by the relationship of the contextual, reciprocal interaction of teller and listener. As a non-Indigenous researcher, I became an active presence in the text, and engaged in an assortment of interdependent relationships with Indigenous women, research participants; together we created new stories (Riessman 105).

Meeting the nine mothers briefly

Amina A. tested positive for HIV infection in 2001, one month after the death of her husband from complications caused by the chronic illness. Identifying with the Nubian tribe, she was 33 and living with her three HIV negative children. Her mother and sister are very supportive of Amina B. who worked three days a week outside of Kibera cleaning and cooking for another family; she walks one hour each way to get to work in order to save money.

Amina's husband, a policeman, died of HIV/AIDS. Before he died, he apologized to her for infecting her with the HIV virus. She was 32, has three children, and identifies with the Nubian tribe. Amina B. is a community activist volunteering some of her time as a paralegal to deal with the many issues in Kibera regarding issues of family and child abuse.

Loise was a 34 year old mother of three children who identifies with the Buhuya people. She contracted the HIV virus from her husband who colluded with the doctor not to inform her because he didn't want Loise to leave him.

Lucy, a Kikuyu woman, learned of her HIV+ status when she was in hospital being treated for tuberculosis; she was 33, and a mother of five children. When she informed her husband, he immediately left her; he died soon after from HIV complications.

Mama May, a 43 year-old Kamba woman became a widow when her husband was killed in a work-related accident in the Congo. She has three female children of her own and is responsible for the care of one grandson, as his mother, Mama May's oldest daughter, disappeared.

Penninah lives with five children, and when she informed her husband of her positive status nine years ago, he left and went to live with another woman. She was 38 years old and identifies with the Kamba people.

Sara is a 41 year old Kalenjin woman who shares a two-roomed house with ten children and another HIV+ mother and her two children. She has five children of her own and cares for her sister's four children orphaned by HIV/AIDS and one grandson who is HIV+.

Zakia is a 43 year old Nubian woman, a devout Muslim woman. She was widowed when her husband was killed by robbers on the road, and was tested for the HIV virus because she began to notice marked changes in her health. She lives with her teenaged son and is very active in community education regarding the need to be "tested earlier than later."

Zuhura had three children and, pregnant with the fourth, she tested positively for the HIV virus. Her husband had died from HIV complications, and she became a widow in 2001. When she participated in my study she was 36 years old.

At the time of data gathering for my study, the nine mothers were responsible for the care of, in total, 36 children.

FINDINGS

Mothers living with the HIV virus are responsible for meeting their own physical, mental and social needs, as well as those of their children. Providing minimal physical needs such as clothing, shelter that is safe, nutritious food and a supply of safe drinking water is paramount to the overall well-being of any individual and requires a constant supply of money. These mothers receive neither government supplements nor financial support from the fathers of their children and must, therefore, work hard to generate enough money to keep themselves and their children alive.

When feeling well, these mothers get up early to prepare children for school and themselves for their daily business in Kibera.

If I die, who will take care of my children?

Mothers spoke of their greatest fear—dying and leaving their children. Amina B. expressed her wish to live until children are old enough to care for themselves:

> Oh, my God, if I die, who will take care of my children? Oh my God, just give me strength to take care of my kids because there is nobody else... Just give me life... I'm afraid of... dying and leaving my children when they're still very young. I'm praying so much ... so that I can stay until they become big and then ... what comes after, at least they know to support themselves outside there.

Sarah described some of her fears:

> What about these children ... when I pass away? They are going to stay where? I don't have house in my home. I don't have anybody in my home who says they are going to help me. What can I do? So... sometimes when I ... when I stay in my house ... my role is not feeling well. I'm feeling stress... When I am not, these children, they're going where? I don't have house in my place, in my name. I can't take... my children to my mum, my mum is somebody gone now... so, sometimes, I'm feeling stressed... When I am not here, what about these children small? They're going to where? They going to look like *chokora* [street children] in slums in Kibera.

Zuhura was able to take some comfort in thinking that her oldest children would take care of the baby. "Even if sometimes when I will be—you know, even when they [older children] get good education, even if I'm not around they can take care of the baby." Amina A. wanted to live to see grandchildren:

Let me pray to God, God will help me. Let me raise my sons, you see, my sons and grandsons, I want to see them. ...If I didn't take the drugs, I could died. I could passed away and left my son childrens. Yeah, and the children go to street to be a *chokora* [street kid.]

Loise did not want her children to suffer: "If I die now, my children will suffer and suffer because there is nobody to take care."

Whereas children may have traditionally been raised within the context of a multi-generational community, women recounted stories of presently having little or no relationship with immediate or extended family members. When Lucy was hospitalized, sick with HIV+ complications, she was shunned by her own mother:

Yeah, I have TB first. First, I finish my medicine for TB, and then I take ARV medicine. ...my family, they don't know what to say to me. They throw me out, ...they told my daughter, "If your mother die, I take these boys to the children's home and you go and find work for bar, ...I don't want to see your mother to buy your mother food.",...I tell my mother to give a little money to pay the rent. My mother told me, "ah, you know, I don't have money to waste....You are—have AIDS and you die tomorrow. Every day you—you sleep, every day you don't work, every day you—you don't have the power to go and find your food."

Lucy's story is similar to the stories of other women. When Zakia was very sick, she went with her son to stay with her mother; she remembered:

My Mama was the person who was telling me, "Oh now, you see, you bring ...us a lot of problems."...She reacted very badly..."I want you to move out of my house ...you can go and live with other people who are HIV. I don't want to see you in my house."

Loise's parents, in-laws and doctor were aware of her husband's death because of AIDS and suspected that she was infected with the HIV virus yet failed to inform her. Hospitalized for the first time, she described what happened: "Actually, they [in-laws] thought I was just going to die the very week. Even they had decided, taking my properties....Even the blankets, they were carrying—they saw me as I was just useless."

However, Amina B. and Amina A.'s experiences of family support contrast with the other women's stories. When Amina B. was desperately sick, she called her family in rural Kenya, and a sister came immediately to care for her and her children. Amina A. and her children have lived with her mother and sister since testing positively over ten years ago.

Mothers who are HIV+ meet the daily needs of children as best they can. Their children go to them with requests and demands because there is no one else to go to.

They just come to you

Each woman struggles to cope with mothering issues every day, as Zuhura expressed so well: "And the children come with their problems because they don't have anybody else to tell their problem. They just come to you...me who is responsible for them." There are days when mothers wake feeling ill and would like to stay on their beds sleeping, resting, restoring energy, yet they get up and face their single-parent responsibilities. In Loise's words, "Even at times you...wake up feeling very bad; a child asks you, 'Mum, how are you feeling?' You just say, 'I'm O.K.,' because you don't want to make them worried. They know when Mum is not here, they cannot eat. So that gives me a very big challenge."

Stories reflected the inner tumult on the part of mothers regarding, when, where, how and to which child to disclose their HIV+ status. Zuhura described her concerns:

> I'm waiting to tell the eldest, just the elder. I'm waiting to tell her because she's the elder—the others are young. I want them to become a little older. One day they understand, now they're young. Because, if I tell them now ...every time they are in class, they will start thinking, "My mother is HIV, my mother is HIV,"—a very hard fear. Now we will miss our mother, she will die....now I can't tell them...because they are still young and I want them to concentrate on their education. They are doing well in school and I don't want to stress them with anything. Right now, I'm thinking how to...tell her [her oldest daughter] but,—no I don't think she will take it badly because she's also in puberty.

I do not know why Zuhura equated her daughter's developmental stage of puberty with being a good time to disclose her HIV+ status. Perhaps it has to do with the fact that puberty is generally related to sexual awakening and sexual activity is one method of the HIV virus transference.

Older siblings often take on the parenting role and help out with home chores such as washing, cleaning, and cooking. Lucy drew attention to a mother's role, "I'm a good mother. I want to teach my children you know this…if you [I] don't wake up. If your children, they don't know how to work in the house, you get trouble….So you have children, you must do work to teach them how to clean the house and how cook, how to clean their clothes. Yeah!"

These mothers live every day with their children and a chronic illness. Chronic illness challenges a general western view that life is lived as a linear progression of events from birth to death in a predictable order. Life is no longer predictable when one has been infected with HIV (Scandlyn 132). The disappointment, frustration and depression that may occur during and after a period of crisis is not to be underestimated; "one consequence of chronic illness is that the responsibility for all aspects of management—physical, mental and social—increasingly falls on the shoulders of those who have the illness" (Scandlyn 133). That said, the reader is reminded that during the absence of crisis, individuals living with HIV+ must continue to care for themselves and children, and resume what could now constitute a normal life.

If I sit there, that ten bob won't come

These mothers are poor, like most adults in Kibera, yet they are not destitute. Four women sell consumables from individual makeshift, temporary constructions on the roadside. Penninah sells sweets. Zuhura makes and sells samosas [deep fried pastry filled with spiced vegetables and/or meat]. Lucy makes and sells *bajia* [spiced rounds of potatoes deep fried]. Sarah took out small loans from moneylenders in Kibera to start a chicken-selling business. Amina A. who has worked outside of Kibera for some time, commented, "Me now…I have another woman who is working at Kenyatta Hospital. I go there, I wash for her, her clothes, I clean her house. I go there Monday, Wednesday and Friday….She give me some little money."

Earning money honorably is important to Amina B. She will not just take any work: "Myself, I am educated. And I normally make sure I don't choose any…kind of job that comes across….if it is washing, I go for washing, washing for people's clothes, I get money. And I normally I do small ideas, like preparing ice—sometimes, I make ice." I was surprised to hear Amina B. talking about making ice which requires refrigeration. Having been inside her home, I knew she had no refrigerator. She told me she uses a neighbour's fridge at night to freeze the water. In the morning she crushes the ice, and then adds colour and sweet flavouring.

Since becoming physically weakened by their chronic illness, some mothers no longer earn money in ways they used to. Penninah reported, "I decided to live with selling sweets because I was not able to…carry heavy things. Business is…nothing big. I am selling sweets." Penninah used to go to a retail market in Nairobi very early in the morning and carry bundles of *sumawiki* [green vegetables] on her shoulders to sell in the slum markets in Kibera.

Zuhura was a professional cleaner for seven years in a well-known Nairobi hostel. She remembered, "Before I was working…I'm a professional cleaner…I got a very good job, a good pay…but when they wanted to grant test to me, now I decided to run away from there." It is illegal in Kenya for an employee to be fired because they are HIV+. However, many employers do fire workers who are HIV+. Employers know that few employees can afford court costs to challenge dismissal, and many employees are not informed of their legal rights. When Zuhura has no work washing or cleaning for neighbours, and is feeling strong, she makes samosas to sell from a makeshift kiosk she sets up at the road-side, close to home.

Since learning of her HIV+ status, Loise has had two hospital stays due to respiratory complications. Believing that cold water affects her breathing, she no longer washes clothes for other people. Instead, she buys reject soap from the industrial area of Nairobi, re-cycles it into another form of hardened soap and sells it. Loise also sells tomatoes and onions. She explained why she no longer sells from the roadside, "You can even stay there for even a day without even selling. Maybe you sell what is not even enough for you for the day. So I always, as you see me going up and down, at times when you just call me, you want some tomatoes, this if it is for ten shilling, I just go. I don't care whether—because, if I sit there, that ten bob won't come."

Before she tested positive, Zakia worked in a high end salon in Nairobi. She now makes and sells all-purpose liquid soap, braids hair, washes clothes and custom-makes crocheted table cloths and chair coverings. She spoke of the importance of networking when looking for work, "I make good relationship with women outside because if they hear about good things, they come and inform me."

Mama May used to work as a barmaid before she tested positive. Now she has no money and is dependent on the kindness of others for a place to stay and food to eat. She pays no rent and returns the hospitality by caring for the children in the home, and doing what she can to help out while there. She commented, "To make money, I educated my first child." Perhaps Mama May is eluding to the fact that she hoped her daughter would, in time, support her financially.

Being up, feeling down and stress-up

When mothers feel well, they described themselves as "being up." "Feeling down" or "stress up" were expressions used to describe negative physical and emotional responses to situations that personally affected them.

Loise noticed a correlation between her "down and up" state and her CD4 count. Twice hospitalized when "down," she reflected, "that is when I can be at least frightened." When Loise was hospitalized, she was unable to work and earn money to provide for her children; she could become depressed when thinking that her stay in hospital is a stark reminder that she is living with a chronic disease and the possibility of an early death is very real.

Amina B. talked of being "almost down" when she was too weak to work. She was still bleeding after giving birth and her husband had left her to marry another woman. Experiencing a high degree of stress during this time, she reflected, "I don' know if I am going to die, even, my baby is going to die. So I was so much stress-up." Amina B. did not die. She is well aware that stress is caused by the constant struggle of a single mother to earn money to keep her and her children alive. She explained, "You have AIDS, you have nothing to eat, you have—you have a lot of stress. You have no medication. Maybe the children are there. They are waiting for you, everyone's waiting for you, plus then you—you feel, you become so down, you feel stress up, you become sick, you have nothing to eat, that's when you can die very easily."

Mama May thought of suicide when she tested positive. She described herself as "going down" and "thinking that time of going in the coffin." She was very "up and down" before her body adjusted to the ARV treatment. Mama May talked of times she was hungry, had no money and so chewed her drugs. She was told by an AIDS specialist that chewing drugs in lieu of food was not considered taking the ARVs properly, "You are not using your tablets properly...unless maybe you are not eating well. What is happening for you? Listen, we are going to change this medicine because this one is not working. But if you don't use your...new medicines properly, Mama May, I'm telling you, there is no third life, if we put you on second life." Mama May was well aware that a nutritious diet is necessary for optimum results when taking ARVs; she said, "Now to eat properly is when you have money. I don't have money."

Lucy spoke of being "down" because of stress and not always feeling "up" enough to make her *bajia,* which means she has little money to buy food or pay the rent. She remembered when the landlord sought her out wanting back-rent money immediately and threatening eviction. Times like this she becomes stressed, "Stress, yeah, like that. You know...somebody come to ask for the money when you don't have money, that now—[I]...get stressed."

Penninah was very "down" when she tested positive. To "stay up," she was instructed by the doctor to learn self-care, to remove stress from her life and to eat a balanced diet. This medical advice given to Penninah and other mothers suffering with the HIV virus seems "out of touch" with the realities of their lives, and is indicative of gaps in service provider knowledge and infrastructure. No mother spoke of referrals to food distribution services, although some did refer to receiving counselling services. Penninah has come to understand that testing HIV+ is not a death sentence. With support from other HIV+ mothers in post-positive groups, she has become stronger, accepted her status and is not "tearing so much." She described herself now, " Me—I can say that, when I know my status, I can say that, I am well because I am going on well—because nowadays I'm not sleepy...I'm not sleeping at the bed that I am sick...Now I'm taking...that medication...I'm now encouraging. I'm coming up."

When Zuhura and I talked, she was feeling "down." She had tuberculosis and was taking medication for that as well as taking ARV drugs. She believes that stress is related to sickness and explained, "I stay alone a lot because I just stay home. You see...HIV is very painful. When you are sick, all your body is very painful. Now when children come from school...they need this and this, you start to stress, you become sick again....Stress, I think stress is the biggest thing that—that make people go down."

Sarah spoke of the time she was continually sick suffering with symptoms of her body's distress—coughing, vomiting and having diarrhea, before she finally consented to be tested, "Yes, [I] was sick. [I] was down. Every now and agains [sic], [I] wake up...I am not feeling well." She talked of the stress caused by wondering what would happen to her children in the future, "You are not staying two hundred years, no.... when I'm not here, when I am not, what about these children? [They're] staying... with who?... that give me the stress-up for these children."

Much has changed in Sarah's life since she accepted her positive status. She talked of seeing people in the community, and recognizing the looks on their faces as being similar to how her face looked when she was "down," had not been tested, and did not know she was HIV+. She is no longer so afraid, and will now sometimes approach such a person telling them, "I want to take you to doctor.... I want the doctor to help you. Even me, another time, [I] was down, like you." There are days or times in a day when Sarah is unable to sell her chickens in person because her HIV+ grandson is sick or she has to go to the clinic. However, her neighbors and friends sell for her and her business is slowly picking up. Most days she says she now feels well, not "stressed-up" because her chicken-selling business is showing a profit. She commented," I am blessed because I am profit... she's big to the business now, she's going up... I say, thank-you, because I know I reshape."

Amina A. has been living with HIV for over ten years. She observed, "The medication is free. But the problem is, how will you get the food?... The biggest stress is now the food, school fees, the house, the shelter, yeah... This is the biggest problem... About HIV, it's not the big issue for me because I have the drugs; I am taking the drugs, yeah."

Zakia knew little about HIV/AIDS before she was tested. She acknowledged that, "Living with HIV is a challenge." Her maternal grandmother, now dead, "taught her ways to... sit down and remove all stress you have in your—on your head." Zakia learnt how to care for herself and to stay "up." She now lives by the creed, "Forward ever, backward never," sees herself as an "up" person, and commented, "Yeah, I'm empowered. I'm walking like a lion because I'm proud, I know what I'm going through—I know how to life... Oh yeah."

After a full day of work, attending support groups, participating in community activities, exchanging news when talking with friends and going for medical check-ups, these mothers generally return to their homes to have an evening meal with their children, help with homework in some households, and then to sleep.

DISCUSSION AND CLOSING

Amina A., Amina B., Lucy, Mama May, Penninah, Sarah, Zakia and Zuhura continue to live as mothers with HIV/AIDS in Kibera, one of the biggest slums in the world. In February of 2013, Loise stopped taking her ARVs and bought a "cure" from a local traditional healer: she died. The lives of these mothers are far more complex than may be assumed by an apparent normalcy of waking each morning in their respective homes to begin their day.

The magnitude of poverty in Kibera cannot be overstated. Every waking day, these women confront social justice issues because they live in an environment of dire poverty. While bravely mothering their children, they struggle with the profound impacts of social determinants of health that impinge on their human right to live a flourishing life of well-being (WHO 1). They lack access to work, affordable health care, schools and education for their children. They lack the financial resources to live in adequate houses. As a result they must live in houses where the roof leaks during the rainy season, where the light is constantly dim because there is no electricity and the one window—if there is one—is only big enough to allow inside a small amount of daylight. The air is dusty and human and animal waste litter the ground outside; on hot days, the stench may become unbearable. Generating money to buy food and pay rent is the main preoccupation of daily life and there is little time for relaxation and leisure pursuits (Bodewes 2005; Davis 2006). These chronically ill mothers living with their children sometimes find themselves dependent on the goodwill of others for a meal and, at times, for somewhere to sleep.

These mothers share a vibrant economic activity, motivated by their quest for survival. They make saleable items to sell in markets or to private customers; they wash clothes, braid hair, and some clean and cook for others outside of Kibera. They are always alert to opportunities for generating income. Income earned by each woman is used to pay rent, buy food, water, household items and to educate children, and yet it is never enough. Their earned income is insufficient to purchase a quality of life that offers personal dignity, choice and freedom from stress and sickness.

Mothers spoke of their anguish when thinking what would happen if they were to die before their children were capable of fending for themselves. They fear children will gravitate to the streets and join the legions of orphans who have no alternative because nobody is left in their immediate family and no one in their extended family will have the means or the inclination to support them. They actively participate in post-positive and religious groups of choice, which affords them strength to face another day. Their lived experience speaks to a collective responsibility, and a willingness to help other women who are living with HIV/AIDS.

I admire Amina A., Amina B., Lucy, Mama May, Penninah, Sarah, Zakia and Zuhura, as I did Loise. Their generosity of spirit touched my heart and stimulated my intellect. As I listened to their stories of courage, strength and power, I was humbled by the human interconnectedness of their struggles to live, provide and care for their children. Their voices speak for millions of other mothers struggling to live with HIV/AIDS every day in similar circumstances around the globe.

WORKS CITED

Achola, Loice. "Colonial Policy and Urban Heath: The Case of Colonial Nairobi." *The Urban Experience in Eastern Africa, c. 1750–2000*. Ed. A. Burton. Nairobi: The British Institute in Eastern Africa. 2002. 110–137. Print.

Bodewes, Christine. *Parish Transformation in Urban Slums: Voices of Kibera, Kenya*. Nairobi, Kenya: Paulines Publications, 2005. Print.

Canadian Institutes of Health Research. *CIHR Guidelines for Health Research Involving Aboriginal People*. Ottawa: CIHR, 2007. Print.

Centre on Housing Rights and Evictions. *Listening to the Poor: Housing Rights in Nairobi*. Kenya. COHRE Fact-Finding Mission to Nairobi, Kenya. Final Report, June 2006. Web. 10 July 2013.

de Smedt, Johan. " 'Kill me quick': A history of Nubian Gin in Kibera." *International Journal of African Historical Studies* 42.2 (2009a): 201–220. Print.

Doyal, Lesley. "Challenges in Researching Life with HIV/AIDS: An Intersectional Analysis of Black African Migrants in London." *Culture, Health and Sexuality* 11.2 (2009): 173–188. Print.

Ferro, G. P. "Nairobi: Overview of an East African City." *African Urban Studies* 3 (Winter) (1978/9): 1–14. Print.

Kincheloe, Joe Lyons. "Describing the Bricolage: Conceptualizing a New Rigor in Qualitative Research." *Qualitative Inquiry* 7 (2001): 679–692. Print.

Kovach, Margaret. *Indigenous Methodologies: Characteristics, Conversations, and Contexts*. Toronto: University of Toronto Press. 2009. Print.

Macharia, Kamau. "Slum Clearance and the Informal Economy in Nairobi." *The Journal of Modern African Studies* 30.2 (1992): 221–236. Print.

Parsons, Timothy. "Kibera is Our Blood: The Sudanese Military Legacy in Nairobi's Kibera Location, 1902–1968." *International Journal of African Historical Studies* 30, 1 (1997): 87–122. Print.

Riessman, Catherine, Kohler. *Narrative Methods for the Human Sciences.* London: Sage, 2008. Print.

Scandlyn, Jean. "When AIDS Became a Chronic Disease." *Western Journal of Medicine* 17, 2 (2000): 103–133. Print.

Schwartz-Barcotte, Rye. "Youth, Culture, NGO Involvement and Collective Violence in Kibera, Nairobi—East Africa's Largest Slum." Diss. University of North Carolina, 2001. Print.

Smith, Linda T. (1999). *Decolonizing Methodologies: Research and Indigenous Peoples.* New York: Palgrave, 1999. Print.

World Health Organization. *Closing the Gap in a Generation: Health Equality through Action on the Social Determinants of Health.* Geneva: WHO, 2008. Print.

6.

Towards the Wellbeing of Aboriginal Mothers and Their Families

You Can't Mandate Time

CYNDY BASKIN AND BELA MCPHERSON

In memory of, and with deep gratitude to, Joann Kakekavash.

INTRODUCTION

This chapter explores findings from a research project entitled "Developing Collaborative Relationships Between Aboriginal[1] Mothers, Substance Misuse Treatment Counsellors and Child Welfare Workers," conducted in the city of Toronto by a team of academics, community partners and an Anishnaabe Elder. The academics in the project were a Mi'kmaq Associate Professor in the School of Social Work at Ryerson University (Cyndy Baskin) and a Scientist at the Centre for Addictions and Mental Health (CAMH) who was also teaching in the Dalla Lana School of Public Health at the University of Toronto (Carol Strike). Community partners included both Aboriginal and non-Aboriginal women who worked at the Jean Tweed Centre, CAMH, Native Child and Family Services of Toronto (NCFST) and Metro Children's Aid Society (CAS) and a Mohawk community researcher (Bela McPherson). Our Anishnaabe Elder was Joann Kakekayash, who lived in Toronto at the time of this research project, but has since moved on to the spirit world.

Nine social services agencies and community centres assisted in the recruitment of Aboriginal mothers, and four agencies assisted in the recruitment of substance misuse counsellors and child welfare workers for our research project. We conducted four focus groups with service providers: one with substance misuse treatment counsellors; one with child welfare workers; another with both of these groups together; and finally, a sharing circle was done with members of the research team, who also work with Aboriginal women with CAS involvement and substance misuse challenges. A total of thirty-eight mothers who self-identified as Aboriginal (i.e., First Nations, Inuit or Métis) and who, in the last five years, had involvement with a child protection agency and a substance misuse treatment facility in Toronto participated in this project through three sharing circles. Eleven substance misuse treatment counsellors and twelve child welfare workers who had worked with a pregnant or parenting Aboriginal woman in Toronto in the last five years participated. All of the sharing circles and focus groups took place at community centres, treatment centres and workplaces of the participants. The project began in 2007 and the final report was completed in 2010.

The aim of the research project was to explore how to increase the well-being of Aboriginal families experiencing substance misuse challenges and child welfare involvement by improving collaboration amongst three key stakeholders: Aboriginal women, substance misuse treatment counsellors and child welfare workers. The researchers implemented Aboriginal research methodologies, including storytelling and the Medicine Wheel. Within many Aboriginal Nations in Canada, the Medicine Wheel is a symbol of holistic health which includes the four aspects of a person: spiritual—how one connects with the self, all of creation and the spirit world; physical—all that affects the body in terms of both wellness and illness/injury; emotional—feelings about the self, others and events that have happened to us and around us; and psychological—one's thinking and understanding of the self and what happens to us.

Our chapter will focus on one emerging theme from the study: time. Analysis of the findings reveals how system-imposed deadlines create an environment where the interests of mothers and children are socially constructed as being in competition. Mothers in the project lamented that they are rarely given the needed time to meet child welfare requirements and thus find themselves constantly working against the clock. Treatment counsellors spoke of long waiting lists hindering mothers' access to necessary services, while child welfare workers cited legislatively-imposed time constraints, such as court processes, as unrealistic. All participants shared stories of how the time needed for healing is not specific or universal. One remarked, "Pain, grief and loss takes its own time to heal. You can't mandate time. You can't force that time."

LITERATURE REVIEW: OVERVIEW OF WOMEN WHO USE SUBSTANCES WHILE PREGNANT AND/OR PARENTING

Women of childbearing age account for approximately one third of all who misuse substances in Canada, highlighting the need to examine how this population of women are being (under) served by our current systems of care (Niccols, Dell & Clarke 324). Women's experiences with substance misuse are impacted by their gender, class, age, race, culture and sexuality which are described as the intersection of colonialism for Aboriginal women (Boyd 17; Crowe-Salazar 5). According to Niccols, Dell and Clarke, compared to men, women who misuse substances typically present with more complex precursors to use, including more negative life experiences such as trauma, more difficulty in accessing treatment and co-occurring mental health challenges (324). Aboriginal women are also more likely to have involvement with the child welfare and criminal justice systems and to experience socioeconomic hardships (Elizabeth Fry; Niccols, Dell & Clarke 311).

The literature speaks in great detail about the discourse that underlies stigma which labels certain women as "bad mothers," "unfit" and "undeserving" of having children (British Columbia Centre of Excellence for Women's Health 3; Boyd 11; Carter 170; Crowe-Salazar 5; Gustafson 27; Rutman et al. 241). According to Weaver, this stigmatizing discourse is reflective of our contemporary "shaming culture" in which women who use substances while pregnant are condemned for what is viewed as "selfish" and "unloving" behaviour towards their children (76). Gustafson discusses the binary that is created in this discourse of "good mothers," who are most representative of White, middle-class women of Judeo-Christian values, epitomizing selfless qualities of putting their children's needs ahead of their own at all times (27). On the flip side of this polarization are the "bad mothers" who typically are represented by poor, Aboriginal, immigrant, racialized and/or queer women who are viewed as "self absorbed," "self indulgent" and "selfish" by not performing "motherly duties" to protect, nurture, care and love their children (Gustafson 28). These women face being labeled as "pregnant addicts," thereby de-humanizing their sense of self to the behaviour of substance misuse alone (Rutman et al. 229). The contributions of the child welfare system and some of the workers within it in maintaining this troubling discourse are also noted in the literature (Carter 169; Niccols, Dell & Clarke 322; Rutman et al. 237; Weaver 81).

Pregnant and/or parenting Aboriginal women who use substances are at high risk for child apprehension which is compounded by the history of the child welfare system with Aboriginal peoples. Hence, Aboriginal women often fear and distrust those working in the system, which is a barrier to improving their health and wellbeing (Boyd 12; Crowe-Salazar 7; Horejsi, Heavy Runner Craig & Pablo 331; Niccols, Dell & Clarke 323; Ordolis 31; Rutman et al. 227). In a study by Rutman et al. (2007), Aboriginal women remarked on how workers' attitudes were often insidiously racist; they discussed how they were very much aware of the negative and prejudicial attitudes held by many professionals because of their substance misuse while pregnant (246).

FINDINGS FROM OUR RESEARCH

While nine major concerns regarding the need for time emerged from this project we chose to highlight those that focused on direct services and the relationships among the three groups that participated in the research. These areas include the following:

- Time for healing
- Building relationships, partnerships and trust
- Time for holistic approaches
- Time to learn

TIME FOR HEALING

What we heard most often from Aboriginal mothers in this project was the need for enough time to heal from the enduring colonial legacy that is widely understood to be a major contributor to the contemporary social ills that plague Aboriginal peoples. For Aboriginal women particularly, these ills include countless experiences of discrimination, violence, involvement with the child welfare system, mental health challenges and substance misuse (Bombay, Matheson & Anisman 8; Chansonneuve 3; de Leeuw, Greenwood, & Cameron 287; Ordolis 33; Shepard, O'Neill & Guenette 229). As noted by Christine,[2] one of the mothers in our research project:

Because we have a family history, as soon as I had my child, they're [CAS] at the hospital trying to take my kid, or they want to know what I'm doing. My kids never got taken away from me, but it's just like they're constantly there. They never leave you alone. Just because something happens in a family, it doesn't mean the next generation is going to continue on in the same pattern.

This woman's point is well taken, as there are many people who were neglected, abused or had child welfare involvement as children who grow up to be capable, confident parents. This is a case of a mother being targeted for child welfare involvement not for any behaviours on her part, but simply because she is an Aboriginal mother with a family history of such involvement. It is true that intergenerational/historical trauma, understood as traumatic experiences caused by colonialism, can carry over from one generation to the next (Bombay, Matheson & Anisman 15). It is important for anyone who works with Aboriginal families to have an understanding of this collective history and intergenerational trauma in order to help foster helpful ways to support these families. However, such trauma can also be used by child welfare authorities to maintain essentially racist and colonist prejudices that foster beliefs that Aboriginal mothers are destined to be inadequate because their parents and grandparents experienced abuse.

Two intergenerational experiences that have greatly impacted Aboriginal women and families in particular are residential schools and involvement with the child welfare system. Breakdown of traditional Aboriginal kinship and family structures are attributed to these experiences and they impact parenting across generations, disrupting traditional systems of social support (Horejsi, Heavy Runner Craig & Pablo 334; Niccols, Dell & Clarke 326; Rutman et al. 230; Shepard, O'Neill & Guenette 229; Thibodeau & Peigan 55).

Four separate qualitative research projects by Rutman et al., conducted in 2005 and 2007, reveal that both child welfare and substance misuse treatment systems are unrealistic in their expectations of Aboriginal mothers carrying so many traumas (241). They highlight concerns associated with risk assessments that demand a fast, linear process of recovery, critiquing the predominance of "traditional" abstinence based models which do not recognize that "recovery and healing take considerable time and tremendous effort and are fraught with backslides" (242). Bastien, Carrière, and Strega further explain:

> Because child welfare is concerned with immediate safety of the child as well as development and attachment issues, it wants to see significant change on the part of parents within a fairly short time. Substance abuse services accept that process of recovery and relapse prevention take time and acknowledge that when clients are Indigenous or otherwise marginalized, a long-term healing approach will be more effective than short-term treatment. Child welfare is concerned with children's developmental timelines, whereas alcohol and drug workers see recovery as a process that might involve relapse and that often must take place in conjunction with other types of healing. This is especially true for Indigenous parents, who often need to reconnect with cultural and spiritual influences that they may have been deprived of (230).

The mothers who shared their stories with us stressed how long it takes for them to begin a healing process and then complete it.

One mother, named Angela, shared that she has been involved with both mainstream Children's Aid Society (CAS) and Native Child and Family Services of Toronto (NCFST), which provides culturally-based prevention, protection and healing services specifically for Aboriginal families, for five years and that she has been involved in many treatment programs. She described this journey as being "a long gruelling process" and that she is still working on herself in order to "turn that cycle back to where I was" before her struggles with substances and child welfare involvement. Family support staff at NCFST concurred by stating "in terms of success, sometimes you can't really see it until maybe years later" and "if someone has stayed clean from crack cocaine for two years, there's a good chance they will remain clean."

The substance misuse treatment counsellors we interviewed added a great deal to this conversation, stating that the timelines for mothers are unrealistic and that typical twenty-one day programs are "ridiculously short." They called attention to the misconceptions that a woman will be "mysteriously healed after a few weeks or a few months." This perception that "one size fits all" is embedded in most treatment programs when it comes to time. Treatment counsellors explained to us that the general public, policy makers and child welfare workers do not understand the individualistic nature of the healing process. They suggested that mothers have the opportunity to try a variety of programs until they find the right fit for them and take these programs more than once if they wish. One counsellor explicitly explained this position by comparing it to her own learning process: "Each time I've attended the very same training, I've gotten something different out of it. I don't think the number of times matters at all." Another agreed, stating that the necessary time it takes to connect a woman to appropriate services is not given, so "we try to make her fit into a program and if it doesn't work out, we say she's not ready [for help]. But really she's just not ready for our idea of what we're rushing her into."

On a structural level, Aboriginal mothers are often not only struggling with substance misuse, but are also struggling with poverty, inadequate housing and violence (de Leeuw, Greenwood & Cameron 285). Their lives are incredibly complex, their needs are great and safe, affordable housing in a city like Toronto is rare even without the additional barriers created by racism and sexism on the part of landlords. Those involved in the helping process do not have the time to gather a holistic understanding of their clients' lives or the necessary resources to address all of their challenges. Thus, one worker's time is put into ensuring children are safe, another is dealing with the addiction concerns and someone else is trying to help with housing, all of which take their own time. As one counsellor empathetically put it, "I'm overwhelmed thinking of all that needs to be done in a very short time, never mind how she [the mother] feels."

All of the participants agreed that the time allotted to mothers to get their children returned to them after apprehension in accord with child welfare legislation is insufficient. The Child and Family Services Act (CFSA) of Ontario legislates that children under the age of six years, taken into care, who are not returned to their parent(s) within one year become wards of the state, putting enormous pressure on everyone involved, including child welfare workers. Often mothers respond to the apprehension of children by becoming depressed, fearful and hopeless which can last weeks, months or years. Already struggling with substance misuse, chances are a woman's way to deal with such strong emotions is to use even more. As Raven said:

> You just took my only child from me. You took the only thing that I have in life from me and you think that I'm going to go and get help. I'm going to my dealer. I'm getting a rock and I'm going to smoke my face silly until I puke.

Raven noted how the experience of losing her child made her situation worse: "From that day, it didn't end; it got really bad."

Raven's experience is congruent with what many Aboriginal mothers face in terms of timing around addressing substance misuse: if a mother disappears into serious substance misuse for three months and then resurfaces seeking custody of her children, the court system is already pressuring the child protection worker to provide proof that the mother is on a healing journey. With nine months remaining, she is placed on a two to three month wait-list for treatment and must detoxify before entering, leaving only six to seven months remaining. She spends twenty-one days in residential treatment, moves into a shelter, continues with aftercare, and works on getting housing. Only a few months left, and the clock is ticking faster and faster. Even if she achieves all the requirements of CAS, she has only touched the tip of the iceberg. One worker, Charlene, commented on this dilemma:

> It is going to take her years and years to look at all her trauma. Drug abuse isn't the problem. It's a solution to the problem. There's something underneath that, and if we're not looking at that, we're wasting our time because there's going to be an underlying issue that's always there. Meanwhile, there is no time to look at underlying issues.

This position was emphasized during a focus group, when CAS workers were asked "If everyone was working towards helping the mother to be a stronger, healthier parent, what would you, drug treatment counsellors and the court system need to make that a reality?" Every person in that circle responded "time!"

BUILDING RELATIONSHIPS, PARTNERSHIPS & TRUST

Another area much discussed by everyone involved in this project was the importance of time to develop trust by building relationships and partnerships. Aboriginal scholars write about the necessity of developing relationships between those who are in the helping profession and the people they attempt to serve, as this is critical to Aboriginal worldviews (Baskin 96). Several CAS workers and treatment counsellors spoke about the need of mothers to develop trust before accepting support which, of course, takes time. They suggested "spending time together," "getting to know each other" and "going with them to their appointments" to facilitate safe relationship building. These supportive behaviours were appreciated by the mothers in our research project. As one mother named Sam noted "I was really scared to go to a doctor's appointment, it was bad news, but at least I had somebody there. I didn't have to leave there alone. I had someone to talk to right then and there."

Staff at NCFST noted the importance of developing relationships with mothers on a cultural level to build rapport, communication and engagement. Fostering mothers' trust is an extremely difficult process as, collectively, Aboriginal peoples' trust has been repeatedly betrayed for decades. One worker, who described herself as "wearing the face of child welfare," as that is how she is seen by Aboriginal mothers, shared a moving story about trust:

> One of the most honouring things that a client can do is ask me to be at her birth, which is a ceremony in itself. This mom invited me to be her labour coach. Her plan was to put this baby up for crown wardship because she didn't feel her lifestyle was healthy for raising a child. In the end though, she was so moved by the support of me and the agency that she chose to try to get clean and work towards getting her baby back. She's been clean for three or four months now, but whether or not she stays clean or whether or not she gets her child back, something inside of her has shifted and changed.

Another worker provided a similar story about an experience where she had been able to offer many supports to a mother, supports which she believes led to a trusting relationship:

> Recently, this mom told me, "I'm so honest now. I can sit and talk to you and I'm not afraid because you know everything." She felt free to tell me she smoked a joint. I just asked her, "What supports do you need to not do that again?" I felt very good about my work and this individual who said "I don't lie about anything to you. This is neat!"

Clearly, it is possible for child welfare workers to build trust with those they provide services to through the development of supportive, rather than judgmental, relationships.

Nevertheless, however, most of the CAS workers talked about how they "don't trust the women and the women don't trust us." One worker reflected:

If we were able to say to clients "You know, it's okay if you have a relapse" because the reality is they are going to have relapses...We can work with that and I think if we can be honest with our clients, the outcomes might be a bit different. Besides, the better you know a client and the better you know their family and other supports, the better plans you can make for the children. So much of this work is based on relationships and when we have a strong one, we have a better place to go from.

If workers have enough time with mothers, they are able to build relationships, learn their history, and know how they cope. Should a mother run into difficulties that may lead to using again, the relationship is strong enough that a safety plan they have created can work. Furthermore, when CAS workers have more time with mothers, they see their positive parenting and the good work that is happening. Janine shared:

I wasn't allowed to leave the hospital until Native Child and Family Services came and that was fine. I spoke with the woman. She's a very nice woman about my age and I told her "You know, I've been clean and sober and I'm ready. I'm ready to take care of my daughter. This is what I want and you know I have major family support." She just said, "Okay I believe you." I am really grateful that she believed me because I have been doing good ever since.

A treatment counsellor working in outreach with Aboriginal women who are pregnant and homeless explained how the development of relationships is critical so that women will feel able to speak freely, explore possible options and make decisions. This enables her to ask difficult questions, including how the woman is feeling about the pregnancy and parenting. She elaborated, "Usually women will say 'I know we need to call child welfare.' So we talk about that, what the process is and I kind of map out the system for them." In this way, women feel supported and valued enough to participate in discussions that will impact their entire lives.

Development of positive relationships between child welfare workers and mothers, and substance misuse treatment counsellors and mothers, is not all that is needed. The conflicting paradigms and approaches of child welfare workers and treatment counsellors is a barrier to forming meaningful working relationships (Boyd 18; Centre for Addiction & Mental Health

6; Rutman, Callahan & Swift 272; Rutman et al. 231; Weaver 82). As one of the counsellors stated, these conflicting approaches can "set up separation between agencies, between the helpers, silos between traditional and non-traditional medical, harm-reduction versus abstinence, parenting that's different than what we're used to dealing with, and I think that things are broken up." She added "...people end up feeling that they have to get protective over the expertise that they carry, and then they don't learn to see the connectiveness, and how that can happen. I think it's about communication on this kind of level."

Some of the CAS workers agreed with this counsellor. One offered, "I can see why maybe drug treatment people don't trust us. Plus, we have two totally different sorts of timelines." Another agreed, adding "We don't have those conversations, those partnership conversations with treatment people. Like 'Are you seeing what I'm seeing?' and 'How can we get her [the mother] back on track again?'"

Both the treatment counsellors and child welfare workers we interviewed discussed how communication and collaboration can greatly strengthen the work they do with families as a whole. A CAS worker suggested how helpful it would be if there could be a dialogue with treatment counsellors identifying a mother's triggers that cause her to misuse drugs. In such cases, partnerships could be formed, the work with a mother and her family could be shared and the results might be more effective. One treatment counsellor shared how she works hard to build strong relationships with child welfare workers, so that if a mother relapses, she can talk to that worker to help her understand what happened, what needs to be done now, and what the mother learned from the experience.

TIME FOR HOLISTIC APPROACHES

Another major component of Aboriginal worldviews is a holistic approach when addressing healing, which includes connections to family and community. A thorough approach needs whatever time it takes and is particularly significant to services at NCFST and Aboriginal counsellors in other agencies. Simply focusing on a presenting problem can mean missing co-occurring problems. Workers at NCFST discussed how the period of time given to complete holistic assessments is insufficient to cover family struggles, substance misuse, relationship stressors, concerns with children and mental health challenges. After assessment, workers have very little time to determine what direction to take with the family.

Holistic approaches must also contend with mainstream child welfare mandates as the former tends to conflict with the rigid, linear legislation, policies and court processes of the latter. However, some CAS workers acknowledge that failing to take a holistic approach with Aboriginal mothers is problematic. One worker asked thoughtfully:

> How is it [that] we send them [mothers] off to treatment and say, "Come back clean, but I don't want to know how you got there and I don't want to know what led you there? I just want to know that you're clean."

Another worker suggested a better approach:

> We should have more options instead of looking down on women, pointing our fingers at them and telling them what they have to do. It would likely be helpful to be able to work with the entire family, such as involving them in the consideration of treatment options. We should be able to look at the whole woman, not just the drugs, but that takes a long time.

Counsellors from one treatment centre shared how their assessment package was recently re-designed to better fit the needs of Aboriginal mothers. It now includes information on a mother's biological family and adopted family if she has one. The question areas are not as intrusive and triggering for mothers, and there is more conversation within the assessment process.

Involving family as supports to women is an important aspect of a holistic approach, and this was taken up by all the groups who participated in this research project. One supportive worker remarked that in the case of Aboriginal mothers, "We can't have a discussion without the family's presence." In some cases, Aboriginal mothers do not think they have any family members who can help, but staff at NCFST can locate someone, such as an auntie, who may or may not be biologically related to the family, such as a close friend, older woman in the community or someone who generally cares for children, who can care for the children until the mother is ready to do so again. In addition, several counsellors stressed the importance of talking to mothers about where they would prefer their children to be. As one stated, "We need to really look at whose needs are we addressing. Are we asking women about where they want their children to be if they are not going to be with them?" All of the participants in the project acknowledged that locating family members, connecting with them and getting them involved is a time consuming process which connects with our overall theme about time in this chapter.

Reaching out to communities is also seen as a part of a holistic approach. Some participants pointed out how the CFSA incorporates legislation intended to ensure the involvement of First Nations communities. Legislation in the province of Ontario, where our research took place, contains provisions whereby child welfare workers must consult with First Nations communities if apprehended children are registered members of these communities according to the Indian Act. The *Indian Act* is federal legislation that provides the basic legal status and rights of Aboriginal peoples in Canada, such as the legal definition of who may claim Indian status, the rights and duties which accompany that status, the structure of First Nations communities and the nature of Aboriginal self-government (Makarenko). Such legislation means that child welfare workers can ask for placement of the child in his/her own First Nations community or, if the child is placed in a non-Aboriginal family, they can ask that culture-based services be implemented in order to support the child. Such services could include access to celebrations and ceremonies, participation in programming at Aboriginal community centres and lessons in the child's Aboriginal language. In reality, these forms of collaboration are difficult as many communities do not have the resources to participate in supporting off-reserve families and are already overworked with the cases they carry in their communities. Self-determination and self-governance for Aboriginal peoples, although in negotiations, will take many years to come to fruition in most First Nations communities. This will involve dismantling legislation that continues to be oppressive towards Aboriginal people, such as the CFSA, and creating policies and practices based on the values of Aboriginal worldviews in the raising of children—such as involving all community members since everyone is affected. It will take a great deal of time to build the trust necessary to do this work. The challenge is to learn how to communicate with one another non-judgmentally in order to create truly Aboriginal foundations for practice, rather than simply embedding culturally-appropriate services within dominant structures.

Another concern raised by participants focused on having time for community development and capacity building. This is critical for everyone involved in supporting Aboriginal families, especially within urban centres. As one of the Aboriginal counsellors pondered:

I wonder why so many of us in the Aboriginal community [of Toronto] who are doing well, have never been asked to be a customary care home or respite care or something like that. We get referred to as the middle class "Indians"...Is there not somewhere for us to help? Everyone has something to offer...If a child needs to be protected, then that's the sacred duty of the community to do that.

This counsellor spoke to the need for child welfare services to be more assertive and cohesive when it comes to the care of children in the Aboriginal community of Toronto such as in the recruitment of customary care homes, respite care and other ways to assist in the raising of children. Perhaps this would result in a community of Aboriginal caregivers within the larger Toronto community, thereby both strengthening what already exists and building more capacity to care for our own.

TIME TO LEARN

Having time for genuine learning about Aboriginal mothers and their circumstances, along with the types of services they need is another significant theme that emerged from this research project. As stated, Aboriginal mothers face unique circumstances of marginalization, must deal with the impacts of colonization, and have distinct worldviews, all of which is important to understand when offering services to them.

Some CAS workers discussed educating themselves about Aboriginal mothers and their environment so they can work collaboratively. They noted that, at present, only the mothers have to learn, as they must know about CAS and their mandate. One admitted, "I think maybe we see it as a one-sided thing—like everyone has to work with us for our agenda." Others agreed, stating there is not much of a difference in their approach with Aboriginal mothers as compared to anyone else. They referred to CAS as "predominately a white agency," and deliberated on how they could better engage with Aboriginal mothers. One hopeful initiative within CAS is the newly adopted anti-racist, anti-oppressive framework, which is a method of attempting to bring systemic change into the field of child welfare. Workers in Ontario are struggling to understand and implement how to bring about progressive changes in their practice while taking into account the many challenges of doing so. At the very least, such a framework could be a catalyst for critical review of CAS practices and processes (Yee, Hackbusch & Wong 5).

Treatment counsellors emphasize implementing anti-oppressive practice to learn a holistic approach and to learn how to consult with Aboriginal families. They believe this will lead to decision-making that is beneficial rather than detrimental to mothers. However, counsellors did not suggest that involving family is necessary. In fact, it was noted such involvement can backfire if the family relationship is not healthy. Time is needed to learn about the full circumstances a mother is facing. As one worker noted:

> So Children's Aid right now is big on finding family members or friends that clear security checks and stuff to keep the kids in the community. [T]he backfire to that is…having women being returned back to their parents and the women themselves were abused by mom or dad and so she's [mother] constantly being triggered but she's willing to because it gives her greater access to raise her child.

This is a frightening situation for a mother to be in as she must sacrifice her own wellbeing so that she can have access to her children. She may also be concerned that her children could also face abuse if her family continues to be unhealthy. It is imperative that CAS and NCFST workers have the time to fully learn about a mother's family and her relationships with them.

Counsellors also discussed the continuum of substance misuse and aspects of treatment. One reasoned that a mother may never get past her addiction, but could manage her life in a fairly healthy way and keep the family together with the help of relatives and friends. They also suggested that child welfare examine eligibility criteria for those who want to care for children. One counsellor offered a poignant reason for this:

> A woman says she wants her children to go to her brother, but he has a criminal record. When we look at the Native population and the racist criminal justice system, we see another barrier because he can't take the children. Therefore, the children are removed from their family. Instead why aren't we learning about what does the brother need to provide a successful family environment for the children?

Such a position does not provide the opportunity to look at people individually in terms of the crime they committed, the reasons and circumstances around it and how they live their lives in the present.

Workers at NCFST discussed how Aboriginal women need time to learn about history and the continuing legacy of that history since, for many, there have not been opportunities to do so. It is important that Aboriginal mothers understand how the history of colonization has influenced their lives. Having this insight into the struggles they face may help mothers see that they are not "bad people," which will allow them to move forward without shame.

CAS workers shared their own lack of knowledge surrounding the experiences of mothers who are misusing substances. As one noted:

> It was just not my experience of [people who use] drugs, that some mothers can manage drugs. This speaks to the need for everything to be an individualized plan as some people [who use drugs] can function and some can't.

Another worker supported this stance, adding that she had involvement with a mother who was using a serious drug and her training directed her to apprehend the children based on this. However, this worker was willing to look at the whole picture, rather than only this one aspect of the mother's life:

> I looked into it. The kids were not displaying any problematic behaviours in the community. She had a very supportive ex-husband [who was the children's father] who lived close by. She tested off the map for crack and cocaine, but she was still functioning. This was an eye-opener for me. I learned that I was out in left field when it comes to drug use and parenting.

Such knowledge can make a difference as to whether or not children will be apprehended by child welfare workers.

Treatment counsellors talked about the importance of learning what services are appropriate for a particular woman who is mothering. One critiqued CAS workers who think that any treatment program is fine for all women, rather than understanding, for example, that not all programs take into consideration gender issues. This concern is compounded when the specific needs of Aboriginal mothers must be taken into consideration. Another counsellor added that "Child welfare just sees the kid. When we talk about the mother's needs and how she might best heal, CAS says 'She can go to this continuing care group because the real issue is the child.' To me, this means " 'You're [the mother] not important to me.' " Such a position that views the needs of the child as separate from those of the mother is unfathomable, particularly when looking at this through the lens of Aboriginal worldviews. One of the primary needs of a child is a healthy mother. If we do not provide necessary resources to the mother and assist her in her healing process, she cannot thrive. If she cannot thrive, neither will her child. She cannot give to her child what she does not have. Mother and child are inescapably connected which must be reflected in the services provided to them, such as family treatment programs that include both of them.

Another counsellor talked about the importance of bringing an understanding of the history of Aboriginal families into programming:

> A lot of people don't understand the incredible amount of forced family separation and the effects of residential schools, how that's affected parenting over the generations. [It is] programming that particularly addresses this that is of value for healing and helping moms find their place.

The above examples also support the literature referring to the need for CAS workers to develop a better understanding of the historical relationship between Aboriginal peoples and child welfare and the ongoing impacts of colonization on their lives (Chansonneuve 4; de Leeuw, Greenwood & Cameron 290; Horejsi, Heavy Runner Craig & Pablo 335; Ordolis 35; Shepard, O'Neill & Guenette 232; Thibodeau & Peigan 55).

Child welfare workers also need to be better informed about Aboriginal services for substance misuse treatment which is another reason for the need to have time to learn. As one said, "This isn't even on our radar." Workers revealed they typically do not understand treatment models other than abstinence (such as harm reduction). One worker shared "Methadone is a new treatment for us and I don't have a good understanding of how it works, which means I can't okay it since I don't know how it might impact on her [mother's] parenting." Another added:

> We're good at telling them what the treatment goals are going to be which are "You need to be abstinent." I can't remember any of us asking mothers "What are your goals for treatment?" We seem to always want them to go to residential treatment,

but if they don't want that, we say they are resistant. We do not have the education about what else is available.

Workers agreed that they may indeed be setting mothers up to fail when it comes to treatment because they are neither knowledgeable about available options, nor taught enough about the complexities of substance misuse for Aboriginal mothers. One worker expressed:

> You really need to set up realistic goals and objectives and be a part of it and I think being a part of it is us having that understanding of what exactly the treatment is and how it relates to parenting. I think we need to do a better job of helping [mothers], which means learning a lot more.

CONCLUSION

This chapter includes important information and experiences from Aboriginal mothers, substance misuse treatment counsellors and child welfare workers. The concerns that each of these groups raised were all connected to time: having enough time to heal, to build partnerships, to implement holistic approaches and learn from one another. There is a need for all service providers working with Aboriginal mothers for professional development where both groups can come together to educate each other about what they do, about who they service, and about the barriers that they face in their everyday work, but this requires a commitment to the time to do so. Having time to come up with protocols that work for everyone involved could create much needed collaborations amongst these helpers. Through some of their examples, they have shown that such collaborations benefit Aboriginal mothers and their children. One final thought from a member of the research team clearly sums up the collaborative process:

> [If] we were having that open dialogue, we could help [the mother]. She's not alone. But it's going to take time to build the trust and learn how to communicate with one another as workers, to lift [these mothers] up...So it's a really delicate balance, and it's really grandiose ideas of what we need to change, and I'm told a lot that this stuff has been in place over 100 years and it's not changing. It's the way it is, suck it up. But if that had always been our ancestors' attitudes, we wouldn't be sitting here today, doing this project!

NOTES

[1] Aboriginal Peoples of Canada include First Nations, Inuit, and Métis people (Constitution Act, 1982). First Nations People are "Status" Indian if they are registered under the Indian Act or "non-Status" if they are not registered (Isaac, 1995) and a "treaty Indian" if one's ancestors signed treaties in Canada (Smylie, 2000). The Métis are people whose ancestry comprises First Nations women who intermarried with European men in the 17th century (Métis Nation of Ontario, 2010; Smylie, 2000). Inuit historically lived above the tree line in Canada and there are four Inuit specific regions in Canada, which include Nunavut (east of the Northwest Territories), Inuvialuit (western Arctic), Nunavik (northern Quebec), and Nunatsiavut (northern Labrador) (Smylie, 2000).

[2] All of the research participants' names have been changed to protect their privacy.

WORKS CITED

Baskin, Cyndy. *Strong Helpers' Teachings: The Value of Indigenous Knowledges in the Helping Professions.* Toronto: Canadian Scholars' Press, 2011. Print.

Bastien, Betty, Jeannine Carrière and Susan Strega. "Healing Versus Treatment: Substance Misuse, Child Welfare and Indigenous Families." *Walking This Path Together: Anti-racist and Anti-oppressive Child Welfare Practice.* Eds. Susan Strega and Jeannine Carrière. Halifax: Fernwood Publishing, 2009. 221–37. Print.

Bombay, Amy, Kim Matheson and Hymie Anisman. "Intergenerational Trauma: Convergence of Multiple Processes Among First Nations Peoples in Canada." *Journal of Aboriginal Health* 5.3 (2009): 6–47. Print.

Boyd, Susan. "The Journey to Compassionate Care." *With Child: Substance Use During Pregnancy: A Woman-Centered Approach.* Eds. Susan Boyd and Lenora Marcellus. Halifax: Fernwood Publishing, 2007. 10–19. Print.

British Columbia Centre of Excellence for Women's Health. "Gendering the National Framework. Mothering and Substance Use: Approaches to Prevention, Harm Reduction, and Treatment." *Coalescing on Women and Substance Use.* Vancouver: BCCEWH, 2010. Web. 2 July 2013.

Carter, Carolyn S. "Perinatal Care for Women Who Are Addicted: Implications for Empowerment." *Health and Social Work* 27.3 (2002): 166–74. Print.

Centre for Addiction and Mental Health. "Practice Guidelines Between Toronto Substance Abuse Treatment Agencies and Children's Aid Societies." Toronto: CAMH, 2005. 1–19. Print.

Chansonneuve, Deborah. "A Residential Addictions Treatment Facility for Aboriginal Women and Their Children in the City of Ottawa: A Feasibility Study—Final Report." Ottawa: Minwaashin Lodge, 2008. Web. 2 July 2013.

Crowe-Salazar, Noela. "Substance Use During Pregnancy and a Women-Centered Harm Reduction Approach: Challenging the Mother and Baby Divide to Support Family Well-being and the Prevention of Child Maltreatment." White Bear First Nation, Saskatchewan: White Bear First Nation, 2009. Web. 2 July 2013.

De Leeuw, Sarah, Margo Greenwood and Emile Cameron. "Deviant Constructions: How Governments Preserve Colonial Narratives of Addictions and Poor Mental Health to Intervene Into the Lives of Indigenous Children and Families in Canada." *International Journal of Mental Health and Addiction* 8.2 (2010): 282–295. Print.

Elizabeth Fry Society. "Aboriginal Women: National Elizabeth Fry Week 2010". *Fact Sheets.* Ottawa: Elizabeth Fry, 2010. Web. 2 July 2013.

—. "Violence Against Women and Children: National Elizabeth Fry Week 2010". *Fact Sheets.* Ottawa: Elizabeth Fry, 2010. Web. 2 July 2013.

Gustafson, Diana L. "The Social Construction of Maternal Absence". *Unbecoming Mothers—The Social Production of Maternal Absence.* Ed. Diana L. Gustafson. New York: Haworth Clinical Practice Press, 2005. 23–50. Print.

Horejsi, Charles, Bonnie Heavy Runner Craig and Joe Pablo. "Reactions by Native American Parents to Child Protection Agencies: Cultural and Community Factors." *Child Welfare* 71.4 (1992): 329–40. Print.

Makarenko, Jay. "The Indian Act: A Historical Overview". *Judicial System and Legal Issues.* Web. 2 June 2008.

Niccols, Alison, Colleen Anne Dell and Sharon Clarke. "Treatment Issues for Aboriginal Mothers with Substance Use Problems and Their Children." *International Journal of Mental Health and Addiction* 8.2 (2010): 320–35. Print.

Niccols, Alison, Maureen Dobbins, Wendy Sword, Ainsley Smith, Joanna Henderson and Karen Milligan. "A National Survey of Services for Women with Substance Use Issues and Their Children in Canada: Challenges for Knowledge Translation." *International Journal of Mental Health and Addiction* 8.2 (2010): 310–19. Print.

Ordolis, Emilia. "A Story of Their Own: Adolescent Pregnancy and Child Welfare in Aboriginal Communities." *First Peoples Child and Family Review* 3.4 (2007): 30–41. Print.

Rutman, Deborah, Marilyn Callahan and Karen Swift. "Risk Assessment and Mothers Who Use Substances: Contradictions in Child Welfare Practice and Policy." *Highs and Lows: Canadian Perspectives on Women and Substance Use.* Eds. Nancy Poole and Lorraine Greaves. Toronto: Centre for Addiction and Mental Health, 2007. 269–82. Print.

Rutman, Deborah, Barbara Field, Suzanne Jackson, Audrey Lundquist and Marilyn Callahan. (2005). "Perspectives of Substance-using Women and Human Service Practitioners: Reflections From the Margins." *Unbecoming Mothers—The Social Production of Maternal Absence.* Ed. Diana L. Gustafson. New York: Haworth Clinical Practice Press, 2005. 227–49. Print.

Shepard, Blythe, Linda O'Neill and Francis Guenette. "Counselling with First Nations Women: Considerations of Oppression and Renewal." *International Journal for the Advancement of Counselling* 28.3 (2006): 227–40. Print.

Thibodeau, Steven and Faye North Peigan. "Loss of Trust Among First Nation People: Implications when Implementing Child Protection Treatment Initiatives." *First Peoples Child and Family Review* 3.4 (2007): 50–58. Web. 3 July 2013.

Weaver, Sydney. "Make it More Welcome: Best-Practice Child Welfare Work With Substance-using Mothers—Diminishing Risks by Promoting Strengths." *With Child: Substance Use During Pregnancy: A Woman-Centered Approach.* Eds. Susan Boyd and Lenora Marcellus. Halifax: Fernwood Publishing, 2007. 76–90. Print.

Yee, June Ying, Christian Hackbausch and Helen Wong. "An Anti-Oppression (AO) Framework for Child Welfare in Ontario, Canada: Possibilities for Systemic Change." *British Journal of Social Work* (2013). Web. 7 September 2013.

7.

The Impact of Sexual Violence on Indigenous Motherhood in Guatemala

INTRODUCTION

Wars have destroyed local infrastructure, displaced masses, and left people within the iron fist of poverty. In every war, alongside cataclysmic tolls of civilian deaths, a major hurdle is the large-scale perpetration of violence against women, making them arguably the worst victims of conflict. The occurrence of sexual violence has been a stark reality in every conflict setting. Whether in Haiti or Yugoslavia, in Afghanistan and DR Congo, or in Syria and Guatemala, conflict has always proved to be a hotbed of violence and flagrant disregard for the sanctity of the human body. Sexual violence in conflict is, oftentimes, a manifestation of the already prevailing undercurrent of gender-based antagonism in peacetime. Armed conflict paves the way for its manifestation in horrendous ways. As the men of the household take to armed forefronts, women find themselves being made vulnerable to political and criminal violence, while holding fort as the sole breadwinner of their families. While the freedom of opportunity is the first factor that sets the ball rolling on conflict-related sexual violence, the crime continues to remain afloat because of the impact it has on the social fabric.

x

131

The reason underlying the use of gender violence as a war tactic is oftentimes because of how "effective" it is. In sum, sexual violence in conflict
is a means of attacking men by proxy—as it aims at humiliating or degrad-
ing the men for their failure in protecting the women in their families. This
stems from a largely prevalent notion that women are "property" and become "damaged goods" post-violence. Gender violence effectively breaks,
humiliates and destroys both the mental and physical health of the person it
is inflicted upon. When this impact is further extended by the sheer volume
and magnitude of occurrences in a conflict zone, the whole social fabric of
a community is destroyed. When women are subjected to sexual violence,
in many instances, the family is broken, and social functioning comes to a
grinding halt.

The impact of sexual violence on men and women differ, and is arguably worse on a woman from an Indigenous community—and there are
several reasons for this. A community that is built on certain values of sanctity attached to womanhood, a community that is often marginalized and
disenfranchised, a community that is worn out by poverty and a myriad of
economic and social difficulties is easily more vulnerable to the disparaging
effects of conflict-related sexual violence. The impact of conflict-related sexual violence is most tangibly felt on the life and livelihood of an Indigenous
mother. Everything from her ability to physically bear and mother a child
to being able to bring up her child, while having to deal with the stigma of
a child conceived in rape, are encumbered by the effects of sexual violence.

This paper will seek to make an in-road into understanding the impact
of sexual violence on Indigenous motherhood, with specific reference to,
and close analysis of, the lives of Mayan Ixil women in Guatemala. In this
environment, women "were raped not only as the 'spoils of war,' but as part
of the systematic and intentional plan to destroy the Ixil ethnic group by
exercising violence on women's bodies as a way to destroy the social fabric
and thereby ensure the destruction of the Ixil population" (Open Society
Justice Initiative). The lack of sufficient administrative and executive machinery to enforce the inherent rights of women during this conflict proves
that a culture of impunity thrives due to the culture of silence, consequent
to a lack of legal attention to the issues.

In Guatemala, the occurrence of the protracted civil war has provided
the proverbial hotbed for crimes such as genocide and sexual violence to
thrive, and among the many victims are a massive number of Mayan Ixil
women. The Maya Ixil are a people indigenous to Guatemala, specifically.
Geographically, they inhabit three municipalities in the Cuchumatanes

Mountains in North El Quiché, forming what is famously known as the Ixil Triangle. Part I of this paper will examine the heady mix of sexual violence in conflict by drawing out references to the Guatemalan conflict. The second part will proceed to examine the specific impacts that the conflict-related sexual violence has had on Indigenous mothers in the Mayan Ixil community. The final part will draw conclusions from the study to prove the contention of the author that Indigenous mothers as victims of sexual violence suffer immensely among the victims of sexual violence in a conflict setting.

SEXUAL VIOLENCE IN WAR: EVERY WOMAN'S REALITY

Wars do not have clearly defined "end" points, and one cannot necessarily find comfortable distinctions between relief and development (International Federation of Red Cross and Red Crescent Societies). Wars create complex humanitarian emergency situations, characterized by massive needs for food, water, health-care, and medical aid. In every war, alongside cataclysmic statistical tolls of civilian deaths, a major issue is the large-scale perpetration of sexual violence against women (Jayakumar). War turns a woman's body into a battleground. When women are subjected to sexual violence, the family is the first social institution to be adversely affected (Jayakumar).

The reason for the use of sexual violence as a war weapon or war strategy is that it is an effective tool in "breaking the enemy" (US Senate). Armed groups, combatants, and non-combatants use rape as a means to terrorize and control women and by extension entire communities. In addition to physical and psychological harm, subjecting women to sexual violence stigmatizes the woman. Families turn these women out of their homes. Men refuse to marry victims of sexual violence, regarding such women as "damaged goods," unworthy of marriage and family life because of the violence they suffered. Even married women who have survived sexual violence are often kicked out of the house by their husbands. Women in the Maya Ixil community suffer a stigma as a consequence of rape, and literature shows that many survivors of sexual violence and aggression have even run away "to other communities to avoid living with the shame of being marked as a raped woman" (Rothenberg 54). A report by the Open Society Foundation on the Guatemalan Civil War noted:

At the collective psycho-social level, the social fabric was torn; it has been established within this framework that, among other consequences for the group, there was a breakdown of relationships of trust; the creation of communication voids in the Ixil group, for which oral transmission is of paramount importance; the silence and mistrust have in turn caused the social isolation of families and communities that returned from their displacement, due to stigmatization. (Open Society Foundation)

When women are spurned the family, community, and ultimately the backbone of the entire societal structure is broken. It is therefore no surprise that the use of sexual violence is calculated and brutal (US Senate). Using sexual violence as a modus operandi in warfare is intricately woven with the hegemonic desire for power. A close reading of the civil war in Guatemala reveals how sexual violence was used as a campaign, as a war tactic, and a war weapon.

THE GUATEMALAN STORY

Stretching over thirty years, the Guatemalan Civil War started in 1960 (Schirmer). It was largely fought between the government of Guatemala and several leftist rebel groups that were supported by many ethnic Mayan Indigenous people and economically disadvantaged Ladino peasants. The government of Guatemala has been oft condemned for having committed the crime of genocide and of having committed widespread human rights violations against the Mayan people. Statistics reveal that as many as 200,000 people died or went missing during the war, including 40,000 to 50,000 people who were subjected to enforced disappearances.[1]

The Mayan Ixil people are Indigenous to Guatemala, living in primarily three municipalities in the Cuchumatanes Mountains in the northern part of the department El Quiché. Known as the Ixil triangle (comprising Santa Maria Nebaj, San Gaspar Chajul and San Juan Cotzal), these municipalities became a centre of violence during the peak of the war. The Ixil community became the principal target of what appears to be a genocide operation that involved systematic rape, displacement and imposed hunger during the conflict (Briggs).

A skewed land tenure (2 per cent of the population owns 60 per cent of the country's arable land), as well as grinding poverty, dire working conditions for Indigenous campesinos in the large coffee, sugar and cotton export plantations and the appalling lack of state services for health or education, gave rise to mass Indigenous incorporation into the rebel forces (Eade and Macleod). As in every war, the army deliberately incited terror in the hope of suppressing rebellions, including sexual violence in their repertoire of war crimes.

In the aftermath of the war, instead of a trade-off between peace and justice as it often happens, a *Tribunal of Conscience against Sexual Violence towards Women during the Armed Conflict* was established in Guatemala in March 2010 (Crosby, Alison and Lykes, M. Brinton). Through the Tribunal, it came to light that the rape of Indigenous women continues to be commonplace as a reprisal against social organizing, especially in the forced evictions of Indigenous campesinos in land conflicts (Eade and Macleod, 2011). The most under-reported human rights violations were the incidents of rape of Indigenous women, and 88.7% of the 1465 cases of rape that were documented by the Truth Commission were those of Mayan women (Eade and Macleod). Women were "routinely raped in front of their children, often gang-raped, and others were forced into slave labour—cooking, washing clothes and providing sexual favours under duress—for the army or the civil patrol leaders" (Eade and Macleod 56). In the Guatemalan Civil War most of the sexual violence took the form of femicide. Over 5,000 women and girls in Guatemala have been murdered in the past ten years, many of them raped and mutilated, their bodies discarded in public places (Madre et al.). From the many testimonies that were narrated in the Tribunal, it came to light that the brutal sexual violence inflicted upon the women included forced nudity, rape, gang rape, penetration with objects, rape as a form of torture during interrogation, rape before, during, and after massacres, rape in front of family members or neighbours, rape and mutilation, forced pregnancy, forced common-law marriage to soldiers, military commissioners or members of the civil self-defense patrols, forced sterilizations, miscarriages due to rape and/or other sorts of violence and sexual and domestic slavery obligating the women to always be ready to "service the needs" of the troop, garrison or other military group (Latin American and Caribbean Women's Health Network).

SEXUAL VIOLENCE AND MOTHERHOOD IN THE MAYAN IXIL COMMUNITY

Predominantly residents of the northern highlands in Guatemala, the Mayan Ixil community are entrenched in their traditional life. Women in the community spend their time tending to the household and raising their children, while their husbands are agrarian, working on the fields of corn and beans that help sustain their families. The essence of the Mayan Ixil life is the continued importance of the principle of communality, rather than individuality (Roberts). The Indigenous communities of Guatemala have their own traditions, community values and mores that deal with issues of gender equality, violence and the role of women in public spaces and cultures (Roberts, 2013). Gender equality in the Mayan Ixil Community hinges on the recognition of equal rights for the community at large (Roberts). However, the notion of gender equality has been eroded, in that the colonial influence of patriarchy appears to have taken root in the fabric of the Mayan Ixil society.

The everyday life of the Maya Ixil Community is deeply entwined with the profound respect for nature and for the dead, the performance of spiritual ceremonies for specific events, their own linguistic traditions and the accordance of a special status and place for animals (Roberts). Women play a significant role in the community as they transmit culture within the family. As the backbone of a familial set up, Mayan Ixil mothers maintain the interconnected ways of the people, nature and the universe at large (Roberts). Considering the fact that there is so much importance attached to communal values and the cohesiveness of the community, sexual violence can have disparaging and damaging effects on the fabric of the community itself.

Undoubtedly, whole communities do suffer the consequences of armed conflict, but it is the women and girls that are particularly affected because of their gender and status in society. While it is definitely not for anyone to lay claim that the impact is worse on one community in comparison with another, this argument holds water in the Maya Ixil context:

> The war has left the people of Guatemala years behind in development, especially the Maya. Maya women may feel the effects of their people's history even more acutely than the men. Many men died or disappeared during the war. Women were killed as well, but more often their husband and sons were killed, while mothers and daughters were raped and tortured,

then left for dead. Many of these female survivors bear physical and mental scars. Maya women are also considered to be the most marginalized individuals in Guatemala. They have two strikes against them. Despite the fact that the civil war is over, there are still major problems with racism in Guatemala. Many of the ladinos (people of mixed European descent) view themselves as far superior to the indigenous Maya. There is also a problem with machismo in the country. Men view themselves as superior to women. Therefore Maya women suffer not only because they are indigenous but also because they are women in a male dominated society and, under these circumstances, the women have begun to view themselves as inferior (Sundberg).

In the Maya Ixil Community childbirth is a rite of passage of sorts, one that completes the transition of a girl into womanhood (Walsh; Tedlock). Deliveries of children in the community are often done with the assistance of midwives in the Mayan society, who are ordained into the order of midwifery through divinity. Legend has it that these midwives gain their training and their calling to the profession entirely from God through their dreams. Midwives are considered significant and sacred in society, sometimes being ordained to abstain from sex. For the Mayan Ixil Community, these midwives are the liaison—sometimes, the only ones at that—to any form of healthcare, and, in some instances, the only health care provider for women. Midwives are summoned anytime around the third to fifth months of pregnancy, from which point they pay monthly visits that become weekly visits in the final month of pregnancy. Mothers receive prenatal care in the form of massages, examinations and physical assistance from midwives. During delivery, and after, midwives provide assistance to the mother and the newborn. Post-delivery, the mother is made to rest. Following this, the midwife performs ritual cleansings that signify that her work here is over. The baby is bathed and dressed, and the hammock that the baby uses is prayed over and the mother receives a hair-washing ceremony in a semi-public setting (Paul and Paul).

As a community, clearly, the Mayan Ixil of Guatemala are rooted in their own traditional practices when it comes to motherhood. Keeping to themselves, these communities are already disenfranchised and marginalized. Their access to healthcare systems outside their communities is limited, and, oftentimes, non-existent. Once their children are born, they all share a common experience: they grow up stigmatized by marginalization and exclusion as Indigenous peoples in multi-cultural societies (Madrid and Fuentes). The level of chronic malnutrition in the country is the highest in Latin America and out of every 1000 children born, 39 die before reaching their first birthday (Guatemala National Survey on Maternal and Child Health). Not surprisingly, the rural areas that are inhabited by the Indigenous communities are the ones that have "the lowest levels of public investment and have the worst social indications" (Guatemala National Survey on Maternal and Child Health 44).

Keeping these factors in mind, it is important to understand that sexual violence and rape in the Guatemalan Civil War had immense ramifications not only for the individual woman, but for the community as a whole. Sexual violence was chillingly premeditated, widespread, systematic and an overall uniform practice in the conflict. The idea was, clearly, to erode the sanctity of the social set up, to severely harm or destroy the women of the Maya Ixil community as a specific target group. None of the incidents of rape and sexual violence were isolated acts of individuals but rather acts committed under the sanction of the superiors in charge of each of the troops. These acts were legitimized, authorized and carried out with a grotesque aspiration of erasing the Maya Ixil population. One of the Maya Ixil women who survived the ordeal heard a clear and strong voice of a soldier saying: "Rios Montt told us to finish off all of this Ixil trash since they collaborate with the guerrilla" (AJR et al.). The analysis that follows will attempt to put in words the impact of sexual violence on the Mayan Ixil mothers.

Physical injuries and obliteration of reproductive capacity

Sexual violence and rape have been determined to be acts of genocide by international tribunals, (Prosecutor v. Akayesu, ICTR) and with good reason. Testimonies of women at the Tribunal of Conscience recount the most horrific incidents of sexual violence that harmed women so terribly that reproduction capacities were damaged or completely obliterated. This also impacts the survival of the community at large as many individual incidents come together to erode the community's ability to exist. A 46-year old woman witness stated: "I have an infection in my belly; my uterus always hurts..." (AJR et al.). Another recounted, "They grabbed us and took us to a room in the parish hall and there they raped us group of women; there were several soldiers that used [raped] me and I was left hemorrhaging for almost a year..." (AJR et al.).

Women were used as sexual slaves in the conflict. A horrific testimony explains, "They took us to the base and there many soldiers raped us; I was there ten days and I was raped many times, and other women as well" (AJR et al.). Another testimony describes how "They raped me the entire night; there were about 20 soldiers. But by the end, I had lost consciousness" (AJR et al.). Soldiers would take women, keep them in their custody and would rape them over several days. They were forced to cook, to "keep house" for the soldier under threats of death and continued perpetration of unabashed sexual violence. One of the women who was used as a slave at the mercy of soldiers narrated to the Tribunal of Conscience, "They stabbed me and I have scars; I could no longer walk when they raped me and they threw me around like a ball...I had to cook for them so they wouldn't kill me." (AJR et al.)

Unwanted pregnancies and forced abortions

The purpose of the counter-insurgency was to instill a sense of fear and terror in the people—especially among the women. This was accomplished through sexual violence, nearly all of which left the women with permanent injuries that affected them both physically and mentally. Testimony from a survivor describes how "They wanted me to become their wife [to rape me], but I resisted; but they stabbed me in the head and then I could no longer resist...I was 6 months pregnant and 15 days later I gave birth to my dead baby..."(AJR et al.). A state of abject terror prevailed as the brutal, monstrous treatment of women and their bodies continued without restraint.

An oft occurring consequence of wartime rape is unwanted pregnancy. Unlike other instances where the woman is left to bear the child that was conceived out of rape, in Guatemala the women were brutally forced to abort their children since the rape was integral to the pursuit of genocide. In a bid to prevent newborns among the Indigenous groups they would take pregnant women and beat their wombs until they would involuntarily wind up aborting (Genocide Watch, 2012). In some other instances, women were knifed—where their stomachs were stabbed and cut open in acts of violence by Rios Montt's troops. Invariably, and unsurprisingly, the mothers died after being cut open. In the few instances where mothers remained pregnant and did not face abortion, there was a general proclivity towards accepting the child born out of war rape: "Well what that man did to me was against my will. But my son was born and grew up, and now he's 19. He's my consolation. He always leaves me a bit of money when he comes, and tells me not to worry. If it weren't for my son I would hang myself" (Eade and Macleod 56).

Displacement and stigmatization

Irrespective of when or where the rape takes place, whether in peace or in war, women face stigmatization. In many Indigenous communities, the stigmatization is inevitable as the defilement of a woman is often seen as a defilement of the community. This is especially so in the context of the Maya Ixil community—where the emphasis is largely on the community and not on the individual. The Maya live in ways similar to how they have for hundreds of years, living and working together in small supportive agrarian communities. There are clearly defined roles as to what women do and what men do. Women perform many of the traditionally female responsibilities including cleaning, cooking, taking care of the children and weaving. Men are responsible for the planting of the crops, work in the fields (this includes the traditional practice of slash and burn agriculture) and most of the family income (normally generated by means of agriculture, either selling one's own excess crops or working at large plantations). Mayan women suffer not only because they are Indigenous, but also because they are women in a male-dominated society and, under these circumstances, the women have begun to view themselves as inferior (Sundberg). Maya Ixil women were primarily seen as housewives and their work at home was viewed as not significantly helping their families or communities in regards to development, and had to only function as breeders.[2] Therefore, women who have survived rape or sexual violence are seen as an aberration in the community as much as it is in the individual. Consequently, many young and unmarried women are considered "damaged goods" or "used goods," and are deemed unsuitable for marriage. Women who were already married before the incident, who have suffered sexual violence in conflict, are considered adulterous, characterless, and loose. These women are often either thrown out of their homes, or are subjected to more violence. For many of the women who were thrown out of the house and spurned by their families, the only option available was to leave their community, rather than spending the rest of their lives in an ostracized state. In Guatemala, most women were rejected by their families—and those of them who were pregnant accepted the children they had conceived through violence (AJR et al.).

For the women who remained, the destruction of the mode of liveli-hood of the Mayan Ixil population forced them to move out of their com-munities and living spaces. The army was systematic in erasing and exter-minating the Indigenous ways of life entirely. One Mayan woman testify-ing before the Tribunal stated: "The soldiers burned all our houses, right in front of our eyes. They burned our millstones, our maize, our sacred life-giving maize...they told us that by whatever means, they were going to make all Indians disappear" (Eade and Macleod 6).

Physical and psychological trauma

As with any form of violence, the sexual violence inflicted on the women and girls left immense physical and psychological injuries. Already marginalized and disenfranchised these women were not in a position to ac-cess medical care outside their communities. Psychologically, the impact of sexual violence on women is tremendous. As one testimony notes, "I'm ex-tremely sad; I'm always sick and I don't leave my house...My heart hurts." (AJR et al.) Those suffering from the trauma of sexual violence or wartime rape need a lot of counseling and psycho-social assistance in order to help them heal. For the Maya Ixil women, mainstream counseling may not be as easily accessible, and many turn instead to Mayan spirituality. Certain rituals under the Mayan spiritual faith have assisted in providing solace and comfort and have contributed to reparation. For one of the Maya Ixil women, the "cleansing powers of burning pom (resin) and lighting candles means: *Now I don't feel dirty any more, I feel that my body is innocent, my body is all right because it is clean and I am clean.*" (Eade and Macleod 57)

Impact on raising children

Given that the sexual violence thrived and continued in a bid to assert a sense of dominance over a population that was to be destroyed, the cam-paign of violence was undertaken in way that ensured the effects would spill over into the community. There was, as anticipated and expected, a ripple effect. In addition to breaking families' networks as the women were driven out of the community, there was also a direct impact on the lives of the children in the community. Seeing their mothers being raped has left a dis-astrous mark in the minds of children (AJR et al.). Without psycho-social rehabilitation to help these children understand what happened, and begin the necessary healing, these children are likely to have difficulties coping with the resulting trauma. A painful testimony by a young girl is proof of this. "They grabbed my mother and they dragged her like a dog...As if we were animals so they could do anything to us" (AJR et al.).

It is also possible that the mothers themselves might find it difficult to relate to their children's needs in the aftermath of violence. With its impact on the physical and psychological levels on the women, sexual violence disrupted traditional mothering practices. While having to cope with recuperation from their own trauma, many mothers were unable to deal with the psycho-social needs of their children.

CONCLUSION

Clearly, the sexual violence against the women and girls of the Mayan Ixil community in Guatemala was part of a much larger campaign to assert power and domination over the Indigenous community. This violence was a demonstration of power and hatred, which was manifested on their bodies, leading to degradation, humiliation and terrible physical trauma. In a patriarchal system where women's bodies are already not valued, the conflict led these bodies to become battlegrounds.

Throughout the course of the Civil War, the impact of sexual violence on the lives of the Mayan women was terrible. In fact, these women were the most affected. And yet, it is disheartening to note that there was absolutely no inclusion of the Mayan Ixil women in the peace negotiations between the government-army and rebel forces mediated by the United Nations. Nevertheless, without any consultation with them for their needs, the 1996 Peace Accords did include an agreement on Indigenous peoples' identity and rights. They contained specific provisions addressing women's needs, and also spoke of the creation of an Indigenous Women's Defense Commission (or the Defensoría). Nevertheless, the implementation of the accords has been minimal because of the extent of dependence on international aid. Indigenous women in Guatemala continue to face underrepresentation, although it is true that, in a first in Guatemalan history, a few Mayan women have been included in the Cabinet as ministers.

An ex-rebel explained in painful words what the impact of the armed conflict has been on Mayan community life: "Our village never recovered. It was as if our communal heart had been cut out." Yet, as much as they suffered, Guatemala's Maya Ixil women have been resilient and strong in their fight to survive. One clear-cut example of counter-hegemonic behavior and the resilience of the Maya Ixil women is their acceptance of the children born out of rape. This stems from the resilience inherent in their culture. The Maya Ixil community has a complementary dynamic between women and men—and the connection between our human species and the ecosystem to which we belong. This interdependence is central to Ixil philosophical thought, and has been a source of resilience during war, genocide, repression (UMAL IQ').

NOTES

[1]Forced disappearances, or enforced disappearances are instances where a person is abducted or imprisoned clandestinely, augmented by a refusal to acknowledge the fact that the abductor/imprisoning authorities are aware of the person's whereabouts. This is usually done to take the person outside the scope of legal protection. (See Jean-Marie Henckaerts; Louise Doswald-Beck; International Committee of the Red Cross (2005). Customary International Humanitarian Law: Rules. Cambridge University Press. p. 342.) Forced disappearances are a crime against humanity under the ambit of the Rome Statute of the International Criminal Court. Forced disappearances were carried out for the first time among other states, in Guatemala during the 30-year-long civil war. Estimates say that as many as 40,000–50,000 people were forcibly disappeared by the military and security forces in Guatemala during the civil war.

[2]http://cas.umw.edu/geography/files/2011/09/Huffman-Thesis-1.pdf

WORKS CITED

Asociación para la Justicia y Reconciliación AJR [Association for Justice and Reconciliation], Centro para la Acción Legal en Derechos Humanos CALDH [Center for Legal Action in Human Rights], Colectivo Nosotras las Mujeres [We Women Collective], Centro Medios Independientes [Independent Media Center], Alai, America Latina en Movimiento. *Guatemala—Testimonies of the Trial against Rioss Montt: Sexual Violence is Genocide: Their Truth is Our Truth.* 12 April 2013. Web. 10 June 2013.

Briggs, Billy. *Billy Briggs on the Atrocities of Guatemala's Civil War.* The Guardian (London). 2 Feb. 2007. Web. 10 June 2013.

Crosby, Alison and Brinton M. Lykes. *Mayan Women Survivors Speak: The Gendered Relations of Truth Telling in Postwar Guatemala IJTJ.* Oxford Journals. 15 Sept. 2011. Web. 10 June 2013.

Eade, Deborah and Morna Macleod. "Women and armed conflict: from victims to activists." *State of the World's Minorities and Indigenous Peoples 2011.* 2011. Web. 10 June 2013.

Guatemala National Survey of Maternal and Child Health. *Encuesta Nacional de Salud Materno Infantil.* ENSMI (2008-2009). Web. 10 June 2013.

Huffman, Amber. "The Gendered Aspect of Maya Development in Guatemala." Thesis, University of Mary Washington, 2011. Print.

International Federation of Red Cross and Red Crescent Societies. *World Disasters Report.* Oxford: Oxford University Press, 1996. Print.

Jayakumar, Kirthi, "The Rule of Law in Conflict Zones: A Means to Handle Gender-Based Violence." *Addressing Inequalities: The Heart of the Post-2015 Development Agenda and the Future We Want for All.* Global Thematic Consultation. 2012. Print.

Latin American and Caribbean Women's Health Network. Tribunal of Conscience against Sexual Violence in Guatemala. March 2010. Web.

MADRE: the International Women's Human Rights Clinic at the City University of New York School of Law, Muixil, Barcenas Women Workers Committee, Colectivo Artesana, Women's Link Worldwide and the Guatemala Human Rights Commission. *Demanding Rights, Resources and Results for Women Worldwide.* 2012. Web. 10 June 2013.

Madrid, Kathia, ávila Loyzaga, and Patricia Figueroa Fuentes. "A Shared Challenge Indigenous Childhood and Education." *Bernard van Leer Foundation Early Childhood Matters.* June 2007. Print.

Open Society Justice Initiative. "Judging a Dictator: The Trial of Guatemala's Efrain Rios Montt." 2013. Web.

Paul, Lois, and Benjamin D. Paul. "The Maya Midwife as Sacred Specialist: A Guatemalan Case." *American Ethnologist* 2.4 (1975). Print.

Pike, John, "Guatemalan Civil War—1960–1996." *Global Security.* Web. 10 June 2013.

Prosecutor v. Akayesu, (ICTR). *Case No. ICTR-96-4 (Trial Chamber).* 2 Sept. 1998. Web. 10 June 2013.

Roberts, Tobias. *Gender Equity and Mayan Spirituality.* Huffington Post. Web. 8 May 2013.

Rothenberg, Daniel. *Memory of Silence: The Guatemalan Truth Commission Report*. Basingstoke: Palgrave Macmillan, 2012. Print.

Schirmer, Jennifer. *The Guatemalan Military Project: A Violence Called Democracy*. Penn Press, 1998. Print.

Sundberg, Juanita. "Identities in the Making: Conservation, Gender, and Race in the Maya Biosphere Reserve, Guatemala." *Gender, Place and Culture* 11.1(2004): 43–66. Print.

Tedlock, Barbara. "The Role of Dreams and Visionary Narratives in Mayan Cultural Survival." *Ethos* 20. 4 (1992): 453–476. Print.

UMAL IQ'. "Monument to the Resilience of the Ixil-Maya." 2013. Web.

US Senate. *Rape as a Weapon of War: Accountability for Sexual Violence in Conflict*. Hearing before the Subcommittee on Human Rights and the Law of the Committee on the Judiciary. 1 April 2008. Web. 10 June 2013.

Walsh, Linda. "Beliefs and Rituals in Traditional Birth Attendant Practice in Guatemala." *Journal of Transcultural Nursing* 17.2 (2006): 148–154. Print.

8.

Camera, a Collective, and a Critical Concern

Feminist Research Aimed at Capturing New Images of Aboriginal Motherhood

MARY ANDERSON

The ideas and representations surrounding Aboriginal mothers in Canada have long been stereotypical and unjust. Colonial narratives have helped shape notions of the "un-fit," Aboriginal mother and the negative stereotypes have served to trap many women in a certain framework that sustains their marginalization (Cull 141). This chapter visually portrays research conducted by a group of individuals dedicated to revamping the negative representations of Aboriginal mothers in a current Canadian context. A collaborative art project, created by a feminist researcher and five Aboriginal mothers in Saskatoon, Saskatchewan, aimed to address and alter the oppressive and stereotypical image of the "unfit" Aboriginal mother. Feminist research, scholarly literature, and photographic theory shaped the nature and direction of the project.

Photography functions best when it engages with something that is visual, or at least easily envisioned, and since much of the discourse surrounding Aboriginal motherhood can be essentially "pictured," photography becomes an ideal medium for such exploration. It becomes a matter of strategy and creativity when constructing new imagery, especially when the motive is to reveal previously ignored perspectives and generate new meanings. Photographs were taken of the participating mothers and text was applied to give a personal perspective on their Aboriginal mothering experiences. These images were then placed publicly in the streets of Saskatoon as tools that aimed to educate and transform negative notions about Aboriginal motherhood. Following in the tradition of Collins who suggested we shift the focus from the dominant, patriarchal notion of what constitutes appropriate motherhood to a community of mothers who practice in alternative ways, this collaborative research project deliberately set out to make a political statement against the dominant ideology of motherhood and the systemic oppression that many Aboriginal mothers experience. As Collins argued, "we must distinguish between what has been said about subordinated groups in the dominant discourse, and what such groups might say about themselves if given the opportunity" (314).

Motherhood is significant for many Aboriginal women and communities, as it continues to stand as a site for empowerment and cultural relevance—ideas and practices that provide a sense of freedom from the confines of patriarchal, western motherhood (Anderson 768). Mothering from the outside in this case, allows for opportunity and resistance, which again, provides resistance and independence. O'Reilly finds this positionality quite promising and refers to this kind of mothering practice as "feminist mothering." As she explains, "Feminist mothering may refer to any practice of mothering that seeks to challenge and change various aspects of patriarchal motherhood that cause mothering to be limiting or oppressive to women" (796). Although the mothering experiences differ amongst Aboriginal communities, even amongst the five women who participated in the project, these kinds of practices are highly political. It may keep mothers on the outskirts, and in turn excluded from mainstream motherhood discourse, but it may also provide alternative theories and practices that could potentially revolutionize mothering experiences. One cannot help but find that potential promising.

Thank you to the five women who created this project alongside me. Your insights and experiences are what shaped the work and I am forever grateful. Thank you for teaching me what it looks like to be incredible mothers.

WORKS CITED

Anderson, Kim. "Giving Life to the People: An Indigenous Ideology of Motherhood." *Maternal Theory: Essential Readings.* Ed. Andrea

O'Reilly. Toronto: Demeter Press, 2007. 761–781. Print.

O'Reilly, Andrea. "Feminist Mothering." *Maternal Theory: Essential Readings*. Ed. Andrea O'Reilly. Toronto: Demeter Press, 2007. 792–821. Print.

Collins, Patricia Hill. "Shifting the Center: Race, Class, and Feminist Theorizing About Motherhood." *Maternal Theory: Essential Readings*. Ed. Andrea O'Reilly. Toronto: Demeter Press, 2007. 311–330. Print.

As I raise my two children, I use my mom and dad's methods. They taught me to respect one's self, other people, to love, and to not be arrogant. —Aboriginal Mother, Two Children

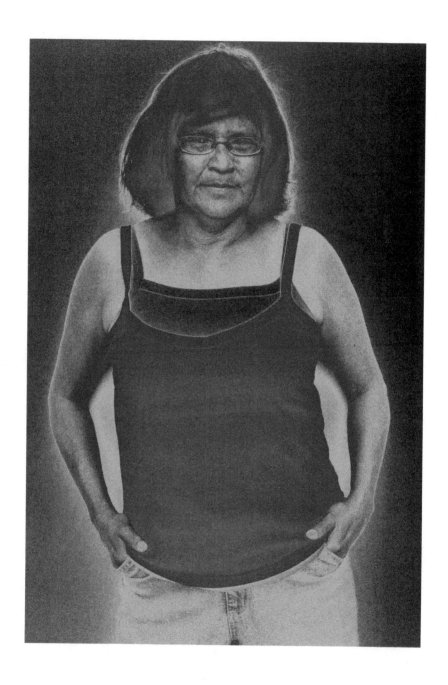

Can't keep a good woman down.—Aboriginal Mother, Nine Children

You have a divine animal right to protect your own life and the life of your child. —Aboriginal Mother, One Child

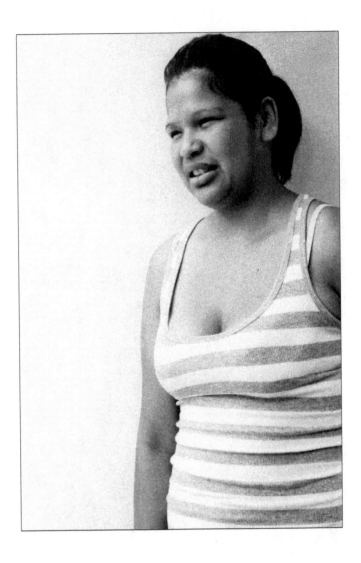

While in one area of your life you are moving ahead in leaps and bounds, in another you are standing still, much to your frustration. Don't worry, it simply means you are not quite ready for a particular challenge.—Aboriginal Mother, 4 Children

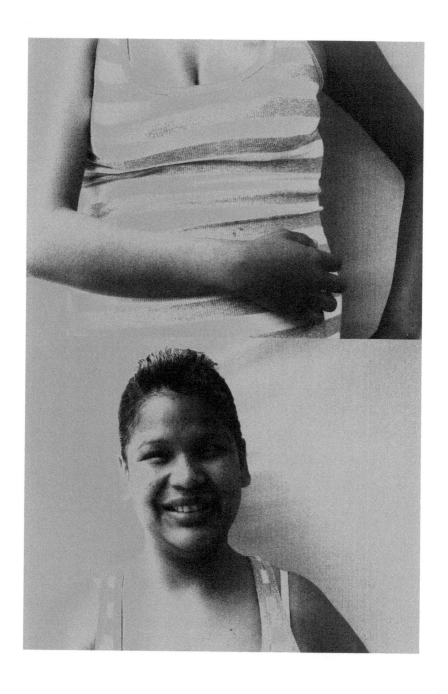

I feel good as an Aboriginal Mom. —Aboriginal Mother, 2 Children

III: Othermothering Spaces and Multiple Moms

9.

Storying the Untold

Indigenous Motherhood and Street Sex Work

SINÉAD CHARBONNEAU, ROBINA THOMAS, CAITLIN
JANZEN, JEANNINE CARRIÈRE, SUSAN STREGA AND
LESLIE BROWN

> We get busted for standing out there and fuckin' trying to feed
> our kids or feed the neighbours or take care of our girlfriend
> who's sick or…somebody has a cold…people don't realize we
> take care of each other, of our own out there. They forget,
> they forget, they forget. That human side is completely gone.
> (Edmonton Participant)

Here we share the often-untold stories of Indigenous mothers in street sex
work who lead within their families and communities. Focusing on experiences of mothering is a way to breathe form into the ghostly contours
of the sex worker mother, to challenge the dehumanization of Indigenous
sex worker mothers, and to hold up the many mothers we spoke to who,
through their mothering practices and identities, were, and are, leaders. Using the idea of leadership in this way recognizes that everyone—even those
living in dire situations—possesses a full and complex life, knowledge, and
sense of identity and self (Dean 24).

We focus on mothering as a form of leadership among Indigenous street
sex workers[1] and mothers of street sex workers. These stories include the
voices of Métis, Inuit, and First Nations women. When we talk about leadership in this context, we refer to the often unacknowledged, informal and

formal ways that women involved in street sex work and their families strive toward bettering their lives, their children and their families' lives, the lives of sex workers, and society as a whole. Our writing draws on 99 interviews conducted with street sex workers and family members of street sex workers in Winnipeg, Regina, Edmonton, and Calgary by a group of Indigenous and White social work researchers who have personal, familial, and other close experiences with the sex industry. While we interviewed both Indigenous and non-Indigenous sex workers and family members in our research, this chapter only draws from interviews with Indigenous women. In our research, we intentionally defined "family" very broadly, so as to include various family forms including adoptive, foster, extended, queer, chosen, and street families. Our project, entitled *Someone's Mother, Sister, or Daughter*, explored the lives of street sex workers, their families, and transitioning out of street sex work (see Janzen et al.; Strega et al. for more publications from this project).

Most of the people we spoke with were mothers; some were mothers working in sex work, some were mothers whose daughters were in sex work, some were aunties and grandmas raising their families' children, and others were non-biological mothers who fulfilled a mothering role on and off the street. Our research thus confirms a fact that is publicly disavowed: most street sex workers are mothers. Though little data has been collected on this subject, three researchers based in the U.S. found that 69% to 91% of street sex workers are mothers (Sloss, Harper, and Budd 102). Despite these findings, there is little research, writing, or programming aimed at understanding and supporting women at the intersection of mothering and sex work. Exceptions include the work of: Basu and Dutta; Bletzer; Castañeda et al.; Dalla; Deischer et al.; Hardman; McClelland and Newall; Peled and Levin-Rotberg; Rivers-Moore; Sloss et al.

The stories that we share illuminate how Indigenous mothers and grandmothers carry out sacred motherhood duties in many places and spaces, in creative and strategic ways, that strengthen both family and the broader community. Mothering in these stories is characterized through one's actions, and is and not a predetermined role reserved for those who physically bear children. This conception of mothering is guided by the definition provided by the National Collaborating Centre for Aboriginal Health: "Mothering, as a relationship and practice, is a social and cultural act that occurs between multiple configurations of people of many generations—individually and communally. Mothering, understood in this way as a complex web of relational practices, was and is fundamental to life" (National Collaborating Centre for Aboriginal Health 3).

Colonization as Sexual Violence

Colonization is a gendered process that sets Indigenous mothering in the crosshairs of racist invasions legitimated through government policy. The *Gradual Disenfranchisement Act* (1869) and the *Indian Act* (1876) removed some of the recognition, authority, and responsibilities from women that had been long established in Indigenous communities. A long history of legislation aimed at colonizing the family has deteriorated traditional governance systems, with resultant displacement of Indigenous women's central political, economic, and social roles in traditional (and contemporary) Indigenous societies (Emberley; Native Women's Association of Canada). Indigenous mothering has long been a particular target of the colonial state. Mothers (and communities) lost their children when they were taken en masse and placed, for decades, in residential schools; when children were taken during the "Sixties scoop" for out-of-community and frequently out-of-country adoption; and, for the last several decades, when Indigenous children continue to be disproportionately subjected to apprehension by child welfare authorities. Indigenous women were also sterilized without their knowledge or consent and were thereby prevented from ever becoming pregnant (Grekul et al.).

The capacity of Indigenous women to birth the next generation; Indigenous women's role as keepers of knowledge and transmitters of culture, language, and tradition; as well as the often community-centered and non-biological practice of Indigenous mothering (carried out by aunties, grandmas, and the community at large), pose a direct threat to the eugenicist policies of colonial governments and the cultural mythologies of the "vanishing Indian." The cumulative effects of colonization, specifically on motherhood, are not readily ascertainable, though they are deeply felt in many areas of Indigenous individual and collective life. Yet, attempts to control and re-define Indigenous motherhood have not succeeded.

Indigenous mothers in street sex work face the ongoing colonial violence perpetuated through child welfare, the criminal justice system, and other structures they may interact with. Street sex work in Canada is inextricably bound up with colonization, and, specifically, the dispossession of Indigenous land, and the violent sexualization of Indigenous women. These streets are not natural, and the violence enacted upon them is not neutral or momentary, but historical, systematic, and strategic. Indigenous sex workers are more likely to be negotiating personal histories of violence and trauma, intergenerational poverty, and to have substance abuse problems, as well as to experience increased morbidity and mortality, in comparison to non- Indigenous sex workers living and working in the same area (Benoit et al.; Hanger; PACE). Moreover, Indigenous women in street sex work are more likely than other street sex workers to experience violence when in the sex industry and tend to access health supports less (Culhane; Phillips et al.). Although street sex work is the smallest sector of the sex industry in Canada, accounting for less than 20% of the overall industry in Canada (Lowman et al.), street sex workers are disproportionately targeted by policing efforts, and disproportionately covered by media (Benoit and Millar; Janzen et al.), where negative portrayals dominate.

Throughout the stories we heard, many Indigenous and non-Indigenous people shared that they witnessed differences in the way Indigenous women are treated on the street, by police and by customers. As one woman from Winnipeg said: "Aboriginal women are still being triggered, you know, still being, like blamed on. Like 'oh she didn't work,' or 'she deserved it,' know what I mean?" Although our relationships to sexuality are diverse and sovereign, tied to individual identity and collective cultural stories, by framing the sex industry as a part of colonization as sexual violence, we point to the structural factors that define street level sex work, and that disproportionately impact Indigenous women.

LEADING WITHIN THE FAMILY

Many people who shared their stories with us practiced mothering across generations, both individually and communally. Raising children within this inclusive definition of family had many different meanings: taking care of siblings as a child, raising nieces and nephews, grandmothers raising their grandchildren, and mothering the whole community. Family is not only about the people to whom one is directly related, or only about the children that mothers give birth to; family includes the people that truly understand because they have shared experiences and complex empathy.

Many stories were shared with us about people finding strength in their families, about building family on the street and in the social service agencies that supported them, and about leading within the family. What was common across the interviews was the desire for belonging, hope, and a sense of self that can come with family—however family is defined. Sex working mothers' roles as leaders within their families showed in their commitment to keep their families together. Contrary to the notion that sex work is exclusively a divisive factor for families, for some women, keeping their families together meant doing sex work in order to provide.

Keeping the Family Together

We heard many stories of people working hard to keep their families together with creative and strategic actions, and by putting their family's needs first. The struggle to keep the family together is often an economic one; it is hard to support everyone's basic needs when living in poverty and facing discrimination. Sex work was their only option when it came to putting food on the table, as illustrated by a mother from Edmonton:

> There's a lot of women out there too that do, that work because they need food for the house or you know, they need to feed their kids or you know what I mean? Like pay their rent or whatever...

This participant's words are echoed in the literature, as Marie Ashe notes, "while caring for children is never easy, being poor makes it harder; experiencing racism makes it harder; experiencing homophobia makes it harder; and experiencing the fear of violence within one's own household makes it harder still" (149).

Others spoke to making their families within their street sex work community and working hard to nurture, teach, and share equally with all the people in this family. Taking up a mothering role in sex work communities is important, not only to the people in that "street family," but also to the families who cannot or will not support their family members entrenched in sex work. Many people worked in their communities to fill the void created by damaging family experiences, as illustrated by a transwoman who spoke with us in Winnipeg:

> *Participant*: I've seen a lot of things. I've defended a lot of girls. Even though we're mad at each other at some point, if we're a leader we'll still help.
>
> *Interviewer*: So it sounds like you've got quite a mothering role.
>
> *Participant*: Oh yeah. I had those instincts already 'cause I was raising my siblings. Like they always called me momma, which is now I'm momma.

This woman depicts the intimate connectedness between mothering and leadership precisely: a leader takes care of those around her through mothering. This maternal role is learned through a lifetime of caregiving. This "momma" lives through a "complex web of relational practices" including inclusive definitions of mothering in a colonial context (NCCAH 3). This way of being flies in the face of colonial models of family and motherhood that privilege the biologically succinct family and the exercise of mothering to specific bodies and spaces. This woman's story shows us that mothering is a process and an action, a role learned and earned, not a codified identity that can be given and taken by colonial powers.

The women we spoke with sketched their communities in vibrant images that show how "relational practices" are fundamental ways of being, and how their obligation to family is taken up as an obligation to the whole community (NCCAH). As one woman in Calgary expressed:

> A lot of the women I know are out there, are there to provide for their children because they cannot get welfare, and they cannot do all this other stuff. So it really kind of pisses me off that the media takes and like makes everybody's views of us, like we're the ones damaging the community and whatever else, and its not like that, we are our own community trying to survive in your community.

This mother's story clearly urges us to recognize how these communities, connected by time, place, culture, identity, and by sex work, generate their own leadership. Often street sex work communities are portrayed as merely surviving. Left out of these characterizations is the understanding that surviving requires spiritual, mental, and intellectual work; it is culture and tradition.

DECOLONIZING THROUGH MOTHERHOOD

Despite incessant colonialist attacks on Indigenous mothers and families, some Indigenous communities practice traditions of mothering that are rooted in more egalitarian and communal worldviews, and mothering continues to be an empowering role for many Indigenous women (Lavell-Harvard and Corbiere Lavell). Because the family—often led by mothers—is at the centre of much Indigenous community and social organization, the breakdown of families has repercussions across many generations, with disastrous effects on the lives of women in particular. In the quote below, the connections between colonialism, the denigration of families, and the over-representation of Indigenous women in the sex industry are tied together:

> So right now I have a fifteen-year-old cousin who lives in [youth detention centre] who's experiencing a lot of the same things as me. Uhm…she wasn't fortunate to be adopted, she's been through numerous foster homes…I've been asked to be a part of her life to try to find the natural family…so she had some connection to family. And so I've been doing my best to do that…What…what…what could've somebody said to me at fifteen? (Edmonton Participant)

This woman is fighting intergenerational colonialism by building connections with her cousin. Seeing where the state regulated child welfare system has failed her family, she is beginning the brave work of finding the tools to support her family through their shared experiences. Although colonization has wrought profound loss of language, of land, of children, this cousin is focusing not only on what has been lost, but on what remains. She does this by recognizing that there is a child she can reach, and by seeing that her own experiences of loss have equipped her with the potential to nurture her cousin.

Mothers we spoke with also challenged colonialism in their day-to-day acts of raising their children, as demonstrated by one woman from Calgary:

> And I don't want them to be men like the kind of men I know so the only way I'm learning to break that cycle is to go and pray…like in our culture, you know? Like take them to pow-wows and you know, and I'm trying to show them the pride I guess, you know in their people rather than you know like look pitiful on them…I don't know how I'm going do it you know, like, but I just try every day. (Calgary Participant)

For this mother, being a leader in the family means resistance to the constant onslaught of discrimination and negative images of Indigenous peoples. She teaches her children to have pride in themselves through love and day-to-day actions of decolonization. Her mothering work demonstrates that patriarchy is not an Indigenous tradition, and that unlearning colonial modes of thinking can occur through cultural teachings and community rootedness. Child welfare and residential school systems treated children as objects, existing at the whim of the state. This mother uses culture to disrupt the objectifying process and reject the pitiable images projected by the dominant culture. Building up identity through prayer and culture disempowers the objectification of Indigenous children. There is no road map for decolonization—this mother is working it out on her own—but there are guiding lights: culture is one of them.

In recognizing that dominant ideals of motherhood were inaccessible and undesirable, many of the women we spoke with engaged in strategic mothering acts that defied the dominant role of mothers and challenged the perceived incompatibility between motherhood and sex work. One of the women we spoke with clearly rejects the idea that sex work and motherhood are incompatible, "I don't think because I'm in a sexual way, it's not my…my compassion and my love for them hasn't changed, if anything it's probably grown stronger" (Calgary Participant). In this woman's life, compassion and love are what are important in motherhood and being in sex work does not diminish these traits. Rather, experiences in sex work can engender a set of skills and knowledge that are important to motherhood. Her words poke holes in the colonial veneer of "good motherhood."

Breaking Colonial Cycles

Women we spoke with also worked at making life better for the next generation by breaking cycles of abuse, honouring the skills and strengths of family members, and teaching empowering and self-sustaining ways of being. Breaking cycles within the family can mean re-connecting with teachings, traditions, and community, and using these teachings to reclaim sustaining ideas of Indigenous personhood. One woman we interviewed in Regina stated:

> I'm going to tell you, this is a little thing that relates how I'm trying to save the ones that don't know the rocky road we're on. There was a lady in my home, she was…she was of my Nation, my Aboriginal ancestry too and she said "Oh my husband's going to be home in twenty minutes, I have to go and pick him up." And I said "Oh let's get your supper," so I made a quick supper of hot dogs for the babies. I said "Here's the plates." I handed them to her and she put them on the table.

> You just help, you just…you pitch in and you help. Get on
> the path and do the same thing. (Regina Participant)

Leadership in this story is a simple everyday act of building people up and teaching them through actions and example. The path metaphor that this mother uses suggests connectedness and the radical potential of collective action (walking together). These women, both of whom were involved in sex work, are building a mobile community that is physically outside of their home community, but they are bound by shared experience and identity no less. This community is being built through growing children with mutual effort.

Despite dominant representations of Indigenous families as inadequate and dysfunctional, many who spoke with us worked to show their families how, through shared strengths, they could overcome intergenerational struggles together. People worked hard to show their families that their experiences of struggle and hardship generate their own meanings and teachings. Recalling her own experiences with the child welfare system, one woman we spoke to in Edmonton explained it this way:

> When I had my daughter I was like…there's no way I'm going
> to let them do that to my daughter. Because I'm here to stop
> the cycle. So yes it's unfortunate that I had to be exposed to
> those things and this is how my life turned out and but I mean
> down the road I hope that I can be a voice for somebody or
> something and maybe make a change…we can be something
> more and even if we've gone down that rough road that…that
> doesn't matter, we can still be somebody else and be there for
> our children. (Edmonton Participant)

For some mothers whose daughters are in sex work; keeping the family together meant taking primary care of grandchildren to prevent them from being apprehended by child welfare. They maintained connections to their daughters through persistent effort and sacrificed financially in order to provide stable support for their children and grandchildren. One grandmother from Edmonton shared her story:

> Like I said, I'm one hundred percent behind her in supporting her, because I have these two kids, because I adopted the oldest one instead of them going into care…That lifestyle has

to be stopped for this generation...or you know, this generation that I'm keeping now, so they can have a chance in their
life. But if I don't put a stop to it, it's going keep on going if
they keep on seeing that kind of lifestyle.

CHALLENGING CHILD WELFARE SYSTEMS

A piece of the colonial machinery that the mothers and grandmothers who
spoke with us confronted and creatively out-maneuvered is the child welfare system. Because of the lack of data on sex-working mothers, we are
not able to ascertain the impact or level of child welfare involvement in the
lives of the Indigenous women in sex work, aside from the many stories that
were shared with us. The mothers and grandmothers we spoke with were
aware of the injustices and inadequacies of the child welfare system, and
were harsh critics of the cycles of abuse that can be created through these
institutions. One mother we spoke with in Edmonton shared her story of
familial and state violence:

> I had four children, they all went into care and I just contin-
> ued to stay out on the streets. I stopped for a while because I
> thought...my family was a priority; I need to take care of my
> kids. But then it was always a constant battle with my husband
> and fighting and...I had phoned Children Services because I
> really needed support and they came in the home, they saw
> how abusive he was and they said it was not a safe place for my
> kids and took them, and that was my excuse to go back out
> there again.

The right to raise our children in their families and culture is a basic human right and a fundamental issue of reproductive justice for Indigenous
communities. This mother's story sketches the painful reality of how Indigenous mothers are exiled from their families even as they seek to build
up their resources by asking for help (Bennett). We cannot know the real or
perceived threat that her children faced from their father. However, numerous studies have shown that the colonial roots of poverty, displacement,
and violence are obscured by child welfare authorities and the effects of
poverty are mistaken for the effects of neglect (Ashe; Basu and Dutta; Cull;
Kline).

What is known is that the apprehension of Indigenous child in Canada constitutes genocide[2]. That forty percent of the children and youth in state care in Canada are Indigenous, despite Indigenous people comprising less than five percent of the total population, indicates the salience of the racist premises of the ideology of motherhood in determining the outcomes of the court system (Cull 149). As we heard, and as previous research has affirmed, child welfare interventions are also commonplace for sex workers (see Benoit and Millar 225 for more detail). In these women's lives, apprehensions are often rooted in ideological conceptions of good motherhood that preclude sex workers, sometimes regardless of the materiality of their children's lives. The role of extended kinship relations in raising children in Indigenous communities is largely unrecognized by child welfare systems in Canada. As the final arbiters of the ideology of motherhood, courts often ignore kinship relationships and impose dominant ideologies when assessing the mothering practices of Indigenous women (Bennett; Kline).

One grandmother we spoke with, who had been in the sex industry herself, shares her perspective on what needs to change in the child welfare system:

> But I think there needs to be like something where women are more united with their children rather than like apart, you know, because it makes it harder. Everybody has kids you know and then they take their children and then they have...I guess like there's no point in staying out there, there's no point in trying to better yourself you know and find a different life.

Many women we interviewed disclosed that they experienced a profound loss of identity, purpose, and hope as a direct result of having their children apprehended. Child welfare practices must change to reflect this reality by privileging practices that support the family as a whole, and nurturing relationships between mothers and their children—even when it is not deemed safe for the child to reside within the family home.

Child welfare systems are given the privilege and responsibility of raising children, and all too often they fail in this task, tearing apart families, and leaving children vulnerable to abuse. The trauma caused by child welfare involvement was something shared by both the mothers who were in sex work as well as the mothers whose children were in sex work. One mother in Edmonton whose daughter was apprehended critiqued the child welfare system and struggles to overcome intergenerational abuse in this story:

Children Services...it's a different kind of abuse in that system. You know? As a result of me and my history, you know, and in my children being abused in the system, I have a nineteen year old that's out there smoking crack and you know, working, and pregnant and...what do I do? She's not going to listen to me. So there' s a pattern right...The biggest thing I know she needs [is] love.

For this mother and her children, and for all the many mothers, aunties, and grandmas that we spoke with and witnessed, we bear a responsibility to think critically about our assumptions about motherhood and about sex work and to work hard to strengthen, rather than destroy, the family networks of mothers in sex work.

CONCLUSION

We would like to stand up the women (show respect) who supported us in our research and thank them for sharing their lives so open and honestly with us. We would like to stand them up for the role they take on as carriers of culture. For the Hul'qumi'num people of Western Canada, we have a teaching—*Nutsa maat*—which teaches us that we are all one. It does not mean we are emotionally, physically, mentally, or spiritually exactly the same. It simply means that we, the two-legged, are a part of something much larger. We are a part of the four-legged, those that swim, those that crawl, those that fly and all that Mother Earth offers us. This teaching is critical to family and community structure. If we are all one, we necessarily contribute to our family and community in whatever way is required.

Other Indigenous communities also have these teachings about collectivity. In many Plains Indigenous cultures, the term "All my relations" is used to end a statement, teaching or ceremony to remind people in attendance that as Indigenous peoples "we are one big family with 'all our relations' and that nothing we do, we do by ourselves; together we form a circle" (Graveline 56). Many of the sex workers we interviewed, in one way or another, talked about this teaching, albeit in different words. They were practicing the important role as carriers of culture by living everyday acts of leadership. As we were all one, they did whatever was necessary to keep their communities strong. Our hands go up to you with the utmost respect for your acts of leadership—*Huy'ch'qa Siem* (thank you respected one). All my relations.

NOTES

[1]Street sex work is qualitatively different from other forms of sex work and usually involves a combination of sex work for money and the exchange of sex for food, drugs or a place to stay. Street sex work is the smallest sector of the sex industry in Canada, accounting for less than 20% of the overall industry in Canada (Lowman et al.); street sex workers are disproportionately targeted by policing efforts and disproportionately covered by media (Benoit and Millar; Janzen et al.), where negative portrayals dominate.

[2]After decades of pressure from First Nations and Métis communities, the Manitoba government initiated the first Canadian study of Indigenous people and the child welfare system in 1983 headed by Justice Kimelman. Having reviewed the file of every Métis and First Nations child who had been adopted by an out-of-province family until 1981, Justice Kimelman contends in the committee's *File Review Report* that "...the Chairman now states unequivocally that cultural genocide has been taking place in a systematic, routine manner" (Kimelman 51).

WORKS CITED

Ashe, Marie. "Postmodernism, Legal Ethics and Representation of 'Bad Mothers'." *Mothers in Law: Feminist Theory and the Legal Regulation of Motherhood.* Eds. Martha Fineman and Isabelle Karpin. New York: Columbia University Press, 1995. 142–167. Print.

Basu, Ambar and Mohan J. Dutta. " 'We are Mothers First': Localocentric Articulation of Sex Worker Identity as a Key in HIV/AIDS Communication." *Women and Health* 51.2 (2011): 106. Print.

Bennett, Marlyn. "Jumping Through Hoops: A Manitoba Study Examining Experiences and Reflections of Aboriginal Mothers Involved with Child Welfare in Manitoba." *Passion for Action in Child and Family Services: Voices from the Prairies.* Eds. Sharon McKay, Don Fuchs and Ivan Brown. Regina, SK: Canadian Plains Research Center, 2009. 69–98. Print.

Benoit, Cecilia, and Alison Millar. *Dispelling Myths and Understanding Realities: Working Conditions, Health Status, and Exiting Experiences of Sex Workers.* Victoria, B.C.: Prostitutes Education Empowerment and Resource Society, 2001. Print.

Benoit, Cecilia, Leah Shumka, Kate Vallance, Helga Hallgrímsdtóttir, Rachel Phillips, Karen Kobayahsi, Olena Hankivsky, Colleen Reid and Elana Brief. "Explaining the Health Gap between Girls and Women in Canada." *Sociological Research Online* 14.5 (2009). Web. 2 December 2013.

Bletzer, Keith V. "Sex Workers in Agricultural Areas: Their Drugs, Their Children." *Culture, Health and Sexuality* 7.6 (2005): 543–555. Web. March 17 2013.

Castañeda, Xóchitl, Víctor Ortíz, Betania Allen, Cecilia García and Mauricio Hernández-Avila. "Sex Masks: The Double Life of Female Commercial Sex Workers in Mexico City." *Culture, Medicine and Psychiatry* 20.2 (1996): 229–47. Print.

Culhane, Dara. "Their Spirits Live Within Us: Aboriginal Women in Downtown Eastside Vancouver Emerging into Visibility." *The American Indian Quarterly* 27.3 (2004): 593–606. Print.

Cull, Randi. "Aboriginal Mothering Under the State's Gaze." *Until our Hearts are on the Ground: Aboriginal Mothering, Oppression, Resistance and Re-Birth.* Eds. Memee Lavell-Harvard, Memee and Jeannette Corbiere Lavell. Toronto: Demeter Press, 2006. 141–57. Print

Dalla, Rochelle. "Et Tú Bruté? A qualitative analysis of streetwalking prostitutes' interpersonal support networks." *Journal of Family Issues* 22.8 (2001): 1066–1085. Print.

—. "When the Bough Breaks...: Examining Intergenerational Parent-Child Relational Patterns Among Street-Level Sex Workers and Their Parents and Children." *Applied Developmental Science* 7.4 (2003): 216–28. Print.

—. " 'I Fell Off [the Mothering] Track': Barriers to 'Effective Mothering' Among Prostituted Women." *Family Relations* 53.2 (2004): 190–200. Print.

Deisher, Robert, W., James A. Farrow, Kerry Hope and Christina Litchfield. "The Pregnant Adolescent Prostitute." *American Journal of Diseases of Children* 143.10 (1989): 1162–5. Print.

Dean, Amber. "Hauntings: Representations of Vancouver's Disappeared Women." Dissertation, University of Alberta, 2009. Web. 17 March 2013.

Emberley, Julia. "The Bourgeois Family, Aboriginal Women, and Colonial Governance in Canada: A Study in Feminist Historical and Cultural Materialism." *Signs* 27.1 (2001): 59–85. Print.

Gosselin, Cheryl. " 'They Let Their Kids Run Wild': The Policing of Aboriginal Mothering in Quebec." *Until our Hearts are on the Ground: Aboriginal Mothering, Oppression, Resistance and Re-Birth*. Eds. Memee Lavell-Havard and Jeannette Corbiere-Lavell. Toronto: Demeter Press, 2006. Print.

Grekul, Jana, Harvey Krahn and Dave Odynak. "Sterilizing the 'Feeble-Minded': Eugenics in Alberta, Canada, 1929–1972." *Journal of Historical Sociology* 17.4 (2004): 358–84. Print.

Hallgrímsdtóttir, Helga, Rachel Phillips, Cecilia Benoit and Kevin Walby. "Sporting Girls, Streetwalkers, and Inmates of Houses of Ill Repute: Media Narratives and the Historical Mutability of Prostitution Stigmas." *Sociological Perspectives* 51.1 (2008): 119–38. Print.

Hardman, Karen. "A Social Work Group for Prostituted Women with Children." *Social Work with Groups* 20.1 (1997): 19. Print.

Janzen, Caitlin, Susan Strega, Leslie Brown, Jeannine Morgan and Jeannine Carrière. " 'Nothing Short of a Horror Show': Triggering Abjection of Street Workers in Western Canadian Newspapers." *Hypatia* 28.1 (2013): 142–162. Web. May 17 2013.

Kimelman, Erwin and Manitoba. Review Committee on Indian and Métis Adoptions and Placements. *File Review Report*. Winnipeg: The Committee, 1984. Print.

Kline, Marlee. "Complicating the Ideology of Motherhood: Child Welfare Law and First Nation Women." *Queen's Law Journal* 18.2 (1993): 306. Print.

Lavell-Harvard, Memee and Jeannette Corbiere Lavell. "Introduction—Thunder Spirits: Reclaiming the Power of Our Grandmothers". *Until our Hearts are on the Ground: Aboriginal Mothering, Oppression, Resistance and Re-Birth*. Eds. Lavell-Havard and Jeannette Corbiere Lavell. Toronto: Demeter Press, 2006. Print.

Lowman, John, and Chris Atchison. "Men Who Buy Sex: A Survey in the Greater Vancouver Regional District." *Canadian Review of Sociology/Revue Canadienne de Sociologie* 43.3 (2006): 281–296. Web. December 2 2013.

National Collaborating Centre for Aboriginal Health. *The Sacred Space of Womanhood: Mothering Across the Generations: A National Showcase on First Nations, Inuit, and Métis Women and Mothering: Report*. Prince George, B.C: National Collaborating Centre for Aboriginal

Health, 2013. Print.

Native Women's Association of Canada. *What Their Stories Tell Us: Research Findings From the Sisters in Spirit Initiative*. Ohsweken, Ontario: Native Women's Association of Canada, 2010. Web. May 14 2013.

Newell, Robert, and Gabrielle Tracy McClelland. "A Qualitative Study of the Experiences of Mothers Involved in Street-Based Prostitution and Problematic Substance Use." *Journal of Research in Nursing* 13.5 (2008): 437–47. Print.

PACE Society. *Violence Against Women in Vancouver's Street Level Sex Trade and the Police Response*. Vancouver: PACE Society, 2000. Print.

Peled, Einat and Tal Levin-Rotberg. "The Perceptions of Child Protection Officers toward Mothering in Prostitution." *Social Service Review* 87.1 (2013): 40–69. Print.

Phillips, Rachel and Cecilia Benoit. "Social Determinants of Health Care Access among Sex Industry Workers in Canada." *Sociology of Health Care* 23 (2005): 79–104. Print.

Rivers-Moore, Megan. "But the Kids are Okay: Motherhood, Consumption and Sex Work in Neo-Liberal Latin America." *The British Journal of Sociology* 61.4 (2010): 716–736.Web. May 17 2013.

Salmon, Amy. " 'It Takes a Community' Constructing Aboriginal Mothers and Children with FAS/FAE as Objects of Moral Panic in/through FAS/FAE Policy." *Journal of the Motherhood Initiative for Research and Community Involvement* 6.1 (2004): 112–23 Web. March 20 2013.

Shannon, Kate, Thomas Kerr, Shari Allinott, Jill Chettiar, Jean Shoveller and Mark W. Tyndall. "Social and Structural Violence and Power relations in Mitigating HIV risk of Drug-Using Women in Survival Sex Work." *Social Science and Medicine* 66.4 (2008): 911–921. Print.

Sloss, Christine M. and Gary W. Harper. "When Street Sex Workers are Mothers." *Archives of Sexual Behavior* 33 (2004): 329–341. Print.

Sloss, Christine, M., Gary W. Harper and Karen S. Budd. "Street Sex Work and Mothering." *Journal of the Motherhood Initiative for Research and Community Involvement* 6.2 (2004): 102–15. Print.

Smith, Andrea. *Conquest: Sexual Violence and American Indian Genocide*. Cambridge, MA: South End Press, 2005. Print.

Strega, Susan, Caitlin Janzen, Jeannine Morgan, Leslie Brown, Robina Thomas and Jeannine Carrière. (In press). "Never Innocent Victims: Street Sex Workers in Canadian Print Media." *Violence Against Women*.

10.

Motherhood, Policies and Tea

WENDY PROVERBS

the Old one pokes through charred debris
reflections emerge provoking long ago desires
she pauses as ancient tongues whisper daintily
slowly she gently sifts and carefully pulls
one rooted word after another[1]

How do I, as a middle-aged Indigenous[2]—Kaska-Dena—woman, mother and researcher, write about two mothers, one who raised me and one who I never knew? How do I honour two unique individuals—knowing one well and only piecing together scraps of information from government documents and a select few records for the other?

Most Canadians are born into the world without an official personal file; however, many Indigenous children continue to have agency files created detailing intimate aspects of their young lives. My fate was determined for me while I was *in utero*, for I was born to an Indigenous woman who was not legally married to her European common-law husband. Both of my mothers' lives changed forever when, at four days old, I was ushered into the lives of my foster family. What was originally meant to be a temporary stop in my young life turned into a permanent placement for me. My foster family eventually adopted me, and I thrived in a loving home.

This paper highlights the effects of legislation upon Indigenous mothers and their children. I have sometimes thought about how my two mothers would have carried on a conversation about their separate lives over tea. It is likely that I would have been a point of discussion; however, I believe they would have discovered other similarities between their distinct lives. I have incorporated my reflections of the impact of government policies upon Indigenous peoples, overlaid with a "conversation over tea" between my two mothers.

IMPACTS OF LEGISLATION

The impacts of government legislation continue to reverberate throughout Indigenous communities in Canada. Detrimental effects stemming from federal and provincial legislation have severely impacted Indigenous communities.[3] The *1876 Indian Act* had long imposed its power over Indigenous peoples in Canada; social welfare policies during the "Sixties Scoop"[4] era were entrenched in British Columbia and had far reaching impacts on Indigenous families. These policies had a firm grasp on my birth siblings, my birth mother, my adoptive mother and me. It can be argued that these damaging policies still exist and are linked to the coined term "Millennium Scoop"[5] that has since usurped the "Sixties Scoop" era. These policies were tied to the concept of assimilating the First Peoples of Canada. By forcing our peoples to adopt European lifestyles, behaviours and beliefs, assimilation was viewed as an ideal that would raise the "Indian" into being a solid citizen of Canada.[6] Indigenous peoples did not relinquish their own beliefs, cultural practices or ties to their land willingly or easily; thus, processes of assimilation required government policies, legislation and zealous workers to be effective. Assimilative policies included the eradication of Indigenous languages, cultures, traditions and social organizations. These policies were enforced through the Department of Indian Affairs, Indian agents, law enforcement members, social welfare practices, church affiliations and residential schools.

Many Indigenous children were seized indiscriminately from their families; many were put into non-Indigenous homes for temporary or long term foster care and adoption. Some Indigenous children were put directly into residential school from the age of four and stayed until they were sixteen years old. There was little or no consideration given to parents or children respecting culture, family ties, language or homeland. Viewed from the perspective of many Indigenous families, these policies were a complete failure on multiple levels, and communities are still attempting to heal from such discriminatory policies. Opposing viewpoints suggest that policies from this era were for the benefit of Indians, thereby constituting effective and necessary legislation. Indigenous people in Canada have been subjected to a range of policies that have generated ongoing social and economic disadvantages.[7] One needs only to look at the number of Indigenous people incarcerated in Canadian prisons, the murder rate of Indigenous women, Indigenous children still placed in foster care, high drop-out rate of Indigenous students, entrenched patriarchy, Indigenous suicides, drug and alcohol addictions and abject poverty on many reserves and within urban centers that continue to plague Indigenous people in Canada.

When I reflect upon the history of Indigenous people since contact with Europeans—in Canada and in other parts of the world—I am amazed that our population numbers have grown exponentially. The challenges faced by our ancestors were immense. Along with detrimental government policies, missionary zealots, land appropriations and Indian wars, came invisible microbes carrying deadly diseases that took a devastating toll on many Indigenous communities. The resilience of a few ensured that Indigenous peoples and ways of being would continue. Despite devastating impacts experienced by Indigenous people, Indigenous culture was never extinguished, though it may have been forced underground—such as the Potlatch was in some communities—Indigenous culture, in its myriad forms, survived and is celebrated by many communities and individuals in their own distinct way.

My history is not terribly unique. My story can be found among Indigenous communities throughout Canada. There may be different names, dialects and languages associated with the tale of two mothers—one Indigenous and one from a settler background—however, they share a common bond in any language—maternal love and loss.

MY TWO MOTHERS

My Kaska-Dena mother died on November 25, 1976. Her birthday was either on September 17, 1919, or 1921, or December 25, 1924; the former dates are from the 1928 Athapascan Dene Census, while the latter is a date recorded in the Department of Social Welfare records. Holy Family Mission records show that my mother was baptized in the Roman Catholic Church along with her parents and siblings on August 1, 1925 in Lower Post, British Columbia. My Kaska-Dena mother's early childhood name was Beep[8]—though the priest at Beep's Baptism changed this to Martha. Later on, Martha told her sister Agnes (a.k.a. Aggie) that she did not like her new name and out of this came her new name—Mudgy—which I will call her.

The mother who raised me was born to Welsh immigrant parents in Rocky Mountain House, Alberta, on March 24, 1912. My mother was named Lily—just like the lovely flower—yet she preferred to be called Lillian. A Presbyterian missionary hall was built near the Rocky Mountain House settlement in the year of my mother's birth, so I assume that her family attended service there, however, she eventually became a member of the United Church of Canada. My mother passed away on September 18, 2011. I miss her every day.

How does this paper link the above issues into a discussion about Indigenous mothering, family and community? Obviously, government policies had a deep impact on my Indigenous mother, yet they also impacted my adoptive mother—specifically through me and other Native foster children in her care. My two mothers were faced with challenges in life, and each responded to these challenges in her own way. Both of my mothers lacked post-secondary education and lucrative careers, and, similar to many women of their time, *they were women without power*. Being powerless and dependent upon others for financial security was the norm for many women of this era; however, women such as my two mothers employed their own strategies for survival in a changing and demanding environment.

Despite the power imbalance in the lives of my mothers, there were some very positive aspects of their lives. Naturally, I can attest more to the talents of my adoptive mother Lillian than Mudgy. Lillian had skill and finesse in many things. She could make wonderful loaves of bread, and I fondly remember her showing me how to make little gingerbread men, and ladies in bread dough with currants for eyes. Her artistry with needle and thread, sewing, knitting and other crafts was well known. She loved to sing. She always wished she had a greater aptitude for playing the piano or the organ. She had a green thumb and could make a garden bloom with flowers and vegetables despite a short growing season in our northern climate. In another time, she might have made a career where her management skills could be honed and valued within the workforce.

Mudgy's skills are not as well known. The Lejac Residential School[9] curriculum taught Mudgy how to sew and mend garments, as well as kitchen and cleaning chores, prayer and basic academic skills. I suspect Mudgy's sewing skills may have been inherently instilled from early contact with her mother, Yanima. I imagine Yanima showing Mudgy how to craft a well-made pair of moccasins and mitts—a far cry from the constant mending of Lejac school uniforms. My Aunt Agnes[10] describes Mudgy returning to Lejac in the fall of 1934 after a summer home in Lower Post. Mudgy returned with moose hide moccasins and mitts that Yanima had made for the girls. They were very much appreciated for the short time they were allowed to keep them at Lejac.

Despite their different cultural upbringing, my two mothers perhaps had more in common than one would initially believe. Their age difference was not so great that they could not have been friends, and they each had a child born in 1947 who most likely attended the same high school. What would they have said to each other if my two mothers had met? Would it have been an awkward encounter or a relief to finally meet one another? How would they communicate their feelings and share their stories? I believe that by presenting my two mothers having a conversation over tea will enlighten readers to a sliver of Canadian history and a unique perspective of motherhood that has often been overlooked.

TEA AND STORIES

Lillian and Mudgy sit down on comfortable chairs in a cozy corner booth. Tea and biscuits arrive at their table. Lillian takes the initiative and pours tea for both of them. The cups feel warm in their hands. Their eyes furtively appraise each other and then the conversation begins.

Mudgy: Was she a good baby?

Lillian: Yes, she was a good baby, except for the colic. I don't think she liked the type of formula the hospital had her on, and of course most babies prefer breast milk…but we eventually found a formula that she tolerated and her colic lessened.

M: How has her life turned out?

L: I think you will be glad to hear that her life has turned out well. She has always known that she was adopted. My husband and I and our four other (birth) children considered her part of the family from the time she came into our lives at four days old. I remember telling my eldest daughter to come and look in our room, and there on the bed was a wrapped bundle with a pair of dark eyes scowling at us. Perhaps we were enamoured from that moment on.

There were of course times during her teens when she rebelled and wanted her independence, yet considering everything she came through unscathed. It was not always easy growing up in a community where you look a bit different—darker skin—from many of the neighbourhood kids, and your parents are white and older. We told her she was Cree...because we didn't know exactly what her heritage was other than just an Indian baby. There wasn't a lot of information available to us. Prior to our formally adopting her, it troubled her when the social worker would visit our home and ask questions concerning her life with us and also reminding her about having another mother somewhere...

M: You know it wasn't meant to be that way. She was only supposed to be with you temporarily. I tried to make it work but I couldn't...

L: There is no blame here, I only meant for you to know how she felt around the social worker's visits to our home. Perhaps these visits brought out a sense of fear and or feelings of insecurity...anyway I was relieved once the formal adoption was approved and these visits ceased.

M: I can remember signing the adoption forms and my feelings were jumbled up inside...I was deeply saddened that another child of mine was gone forever...and yet I knew that as a young child she could never leave the only family she had known from birth.

Lillian pauses and pours more tea for both of them.

L: She was on the honour roll at High School and after graduation worked for a year and then went south to university. After one year she left university and carried on working. Not long after this, she married a good man and eventually they had a son and a daughter. Later in life, she went back to school and earned her undergraduate degree and followed this with a Master's degree. She works, writes and volunteers her time. She always had an artistic flair and I believe she would be quite content to spend her days painting, writing and visiting galleries.

M: This is good. I am glad to hear this. Tell me, has she ever been in contact with any of her brothers or sisters?

L: Yes, she has. She met three sisters, one brother and her half-sister and brother. Unfortunately, one brother passed on prior to their meeting, and four other brothers have not been contacted. I believe that was all of your children?

M: Yes, I had twelve children. Two from my first relationship with my

American man and ten from my last relationship with a Swiss man. Only my first two and my last two was I able to have a say in raising them...

L: That must have been very difficult for you... to lose so many of your children over the years. I'm sorry... I can't imagine what that must have been like.

My hometown of Rocky Mountain House in Alberta had some large families and I suppose our family of four girls was considered average. We were somewhat isolated as my parents were granted a "free" homestead if it was worked on. I remember local Blackfoot people near us who would occasionally drop by and sometimes trade items with my mother. I could sense their ease within the local environment compared to my mother—my poor mother who left Wales to come to the new country was totally unprepared for her new world. It was a harsh environment for settlers... though as kids we didn't know any different.

What was it like where you were born?

M: My people come from way up north, our territory is located on the British Columbia and Yukon border. We are river people and the Liard River was, and is, a source of food and water for us. We are Kaska-Dena.[11] I was born in a cabin in Lower Post and was the third child in a family of six. My father hunted, fished, and trapped. I don't remember being hungry at home. I remember picking wild berries with my mother and sister and feasting on moose and caribou meat. My mother dried meat and tanned hides to make clothing, moccasins, and such. Our home was small, but comfortable and safe.

Our people were isolated so we didn't really see many white people. At Fort Halkett on Liard River, there was a Hudson's Bay Company trading post where my parents would trade for items like flour and tinned goods. More white people came into our territory during the 1898 Klondike gold rush. These people came by boat and foot, as there was no road into our territory until the Second World War, when the Alaska Highway was built. The gold rush and highway brought big changes into our area; some changes were good—such as new tools—and some were bad, such as alcohol.

Everything changed when that priest took us away to school. I remember my mother was crying, and I did not understand why. I didn't know we were being sent so far away to a Catholic school run by the Oblates—Lejac Residential School[12] near Fraser Lake, BC.

L: Why were you and your sister sent so far away from home? That does not make sense to me! Surely, there must have been a closer school for you to go to?

M: I don't know why we were sent so far away to go to school. There was a residential school in Whitehorse that was closer to our home, but that priest took my older sister Aggie and me to Lejac. Our younger brother Paul was sent to Lejac later on, but was sent back to Lower Post after a couple of years because he was sick—he died from tuberculosis.[13] I was around eight years old when that priest came into our home, and he told my mother that we had to go to school... Yes, Father Allard was a hard man, and we had no way of knowing what lay ahead for us.

L: If there was no road into Lower Post, how did you travel all that way to Lejac?

M: That journey is very clear in my mind. Early in the summer of 1928, Priest Allard told our mother to prepare Aggie and me for the journey to school... no other options were suggested. Many tears were shed the day we were led down to the Liard River. Our two older brothers—Wheegad and Jack—followed us down, as well as our grandmother Gayouse. Our mother stayed at home, I don't think she could take it... our family watched us until the riverboat reached the spot where the Dease River joined up and that was where we lost sight of each other.

L: That must have been very hard for you and your sister... did you have any idea of how long your journey would be?

M: No, not at all, we just were told we had to go to school. In a small way it was exciting to go on a "trip," but it didn't seem right without our family with us. For about the first week we travelled the river by day and camped at night. The two guides hired to transport us made camp each evening, I remember eating fish caught by the guides along the way.

When we reached Dease Lake we said good-bye to our guides and began an overland trek from Dease Lake to Telegraph Creek. We travelled in a mail truck. The road was windy and narrow and it took us a whole day to travel the fifty miles to Telegraph Creek. We had no idea that Telegraph Creek would be our residence for three weeks! The priest was working on the construction of a Catholic Church in Telegraph Creek. It was in Telegraph Creek that we felt the wrath of Allard. After playing outside one day we came in late for dinner... that priest was so angry... he grabbed Aggie's hair and threw her down... I was frozen in disbelief, but he soon threw me down as well and began kicking us both over and over. Our dirty clothes were ripped off and he shoved us into a tub of water…never in our lives had we felt so exposed, naked and ashamed.[14]

L: I know what it is like to feel powerless. I grew up in a home with a tyrant—my father. My father worked in the Welsh mines from the time he was eleven years old and this had to have had an effect on him…Yet other men sent down to the mines as children did not emerge as frustrated adults who took their anger out on their families.

Eventually, our father moved us from Rocky Mountain House to Chilliwack, BC in order to farm in the Fraser Valley. I was sixteen years old and one day I came home to a brutal fight between my father and mother. This time I intervened, and I was thrown out of the house. I left, never to live in the family home again: my closest sister Marion left with me. Two unworldly young sisters out on their own in the big world.

At first I found work as a domestic helper in exchange for room and board: after some time I found work as a waitress. I helped support my sister who went on to earn a teaching degree. I eventually met my future husband and we married. We reached our golden wedding anniversary several years ago. I was fortunate to have my sister along with me when we left our family home…perhaps you were lucky to have your sister Aggie with you.

M: Oh yes, I was very lucky to have Aggie with me, I am not sure if I could have stood that trip and life at Lejac without her!

The day after the beating by Allard, Aggie took my hand and said we were going home. We headed down the main road back to Dease Lake. A ways down the road, we ran into an Indian family heading into Telegraph Creek. The father of the family questioned us about where we were headed…I remember Aggie did the talking and she told the family that the priest was taking us too far away to go to school. The father of the family said that they saw grizzly bears en-route to town and this changed Aggie's mind about us going home alone, as grizzly bears were serious bears. That priest slapped us around when we returned. We didn't try to leave again.

L: You and your sister were very brave.

M: I think you and your sister were brave.

The two ladies order another pot of tea.

M: We left Telegraph Creek aboard a paddle wheel boat—Aggie and I never saw one of those boats before—it operated up and down the Stikine

River. The paddle wheeler took us to the American seaport called Wrangell, Alaska. We were wearing our school uniforms now and we passed through customs with hardly a notice. Everything was strange and it seemed more so when we boarded a steamship destined for Prince Rupert, British Columbia. We stayed overnight at the girl's dormitory at the Prince Rupert Catholic Church. We saw bicycles and noisy vehicles in Prince Rupert—the strange sights and sounds made us laugh!

The next day we boarded a train; giant mountains and valleys passed before us until eventually we were dropped off at Fraser Lake. We walked up a hill with the priest and soon a huge building came into sight—a massive four story red brick building that seemed too imposing for us to enter...

L: Did anyone prepare you for what your new school was like?

M: No, not at all. Aggie and I entered that building as two young naïve Indian girls and, years later, we were released as two vastly different people. We changed physically and emotionally. Family ties were severed...the Indianness in us was erased. We lost who we were. Aggie and I witnessed some unspeakable cruelties against the other children. Those people were supposed to care for us; there were very few acts of kindness there...

L: I am so sorry. No one ever spoke of what went on in those schools. I never knew. Were you ever able to see your family in Lower Post again?

M: Once. I was allowed to go home one summer in 1933. That was the last time I saw my mother—she died not long after.

L: That must have been very hard on you and your sister. Despite my mother's hardships she lived until her mid-90s. There is always a void in one's life no matter what age your mother leaves this earth. How was life after Lejac?

M: Well, I had an accident that injured my spine while at Lejac, so I was placed in the Smither's hospital for several years. By the time my spine was healed, I was of age to leave Lejac and I did. Freedom from that place finally.

I wasn't prepared for the outside world. I had been taught domestic service at Lejac and that did not help me much in the real world.

When I was seventeen years old the Indian Agent sent me to live and work as a domestic with a family near Houston, BC. That lasted for about a year or so. I let people and situations take advantage of me...that is why I could not be a mother to most of my children...I regret that more than anything.

L: Regrets seem to be one of life's constant companions. If it means anything to you, you should know that our family is grateful to you for giving us a daughter that we never anticipated. She is very much loved and has enriched our family. It is hard to imagine our family life without her...thank you.

M: I wish I could have made different choices in my life...I am glad she had you as a mother. I only hope that my other ones found as good a home as you provided...all my children who I was forced to give up—I left them unwillingly...they ended up being left to scatter like seeds in the wind...

Mudgy and Lillian say their goodbyes with an embrace and go their separate ways.

REFLECTION

Lillian and Mudgy faced many life challenges. They made choices in their lives, some they regretted and some not. Major life changes were forced upon them that changed the direction of their lives forever. Lillian was forced to leave the family home at an early age when she was unprepared to make her way in the world alone. Mudgy was forced to leave her family home at an even earlier age and taken to an alien environment at Lejac Residential School that forbade use of her language, culture and Indigenous ways of being. Indifferent and hostile caregivers contributed to Mudgy's feelings of inadequacy and shame of being Native. Lillian did not have forces such as the *1876 Indian Act* or Lejac Residential School dictating her life, and, because of her ethnicity, Lillian had more rights and was not subjected to colonial laws and racial intolerance. Lillian and Mudgy each had to conform to BC Provincial social welfare policies, though from different perspectives. As a result of the accepted social welfare practices and policies of the day-Mudgy's loss was Lillian's gain.

It is incomprehensible to imagine having eight children apprehended, yet legislative powers in place resulted in this for my Indigenous mother, and for many other Indigenous mothers throughout Canada. The majority of seized Indigenous children during the "Sixties Scoop" era were put into foster care and deliberately adopted into non-Indigenous homes where native culture and language were absent. This is not a reflection on foster homes or adoptive parents, but simply an acknowledgment of the overt acceptance of these placements as the norm in a process to ensure assimilation. Social welfare policies have evolved over the years, and placement of Indigenous children is now actively sought in First Nation homes. Some First Nation communities now have the resources and capacity to manage their own social services agencies and care for their community children. While this is a step forward, figures show that the numbers of Indigenous children in foster care are still proportionately higher than those of non-Indigenous children. Statistics[15] also reveal that incarceration of Indigenous people remains high, and that poverty still plagues Indigenous families across Canada. Social problems, lack of adequate housing, lack of education, systemic racism, patriarchy, poor health, addictions and suicides remain a constant in many Indigenous communities. There remain many negative perceptions of both historical and contemporary Indigenous people throughout Canada.

While acknowledging ongoing challenges, it is important to recognize the many positive influences stemming from Indigenous communities. Visual arts, stories, dance and song highlight expressions of beauty within Indigenous culture. Indigenous knowledge, history and way of life enrich all communities. Some Indigenous communities have recovered are culturally vibrant, and have prospered economically; however, many Indigenous communities are still in the process of recovery and healing.

When we acknowledge and welcome women into equal positions of power within our homes, communities, and outside communities, then the process of healing and further enrichment will truly advance.

Sógá senenla' Mudgy
Sógá senenla' Lillian[16]

NOTES

[1]Verse by Wendy Proverbs
[2]Multiple definitions are used to depict Indigenous people—including First Nations, Metis, and Inuit—in Canada. I prefer the term Indigenous, and where possible I acknowledge the individual's Nation, however I also use the term Indian, Native, Aboriginal, First People, and First Nation interchangeably.
[3]For an in-depth look at colonial and contemporary policies and Indigenous people, see Andrew Armitage's 1995 *Comparing the Policy of Aboriginal Assimilation: Australia, Canada, and New Zealand.*
[4]The term "Sixties Scoop" was coined by Patrick Johnston in his 1983 report *Aboriginal Children and the Child Welfare System.* It should be noted that "Sixties Scoop" was not an official policy but rather a term used to reflect

the era of apprehending "scooping" newborn Indigenous children by social workers from the 1960s until the mid-1980s.

[5] The term "Millennium Scoop" reflects current child welfare statistics involving Indigenous children who are overly represented within todays foster care system. See Raven Sinclair's 2007 article *Identity Lost and Found: Lessons from the Sixties Scoop*, 66–68.

[6] Lisa Salem-Wiseman's 1996 article *Verily, the Whiteman's Way Were the Best: Duncan Campbell Scott, Native Culture, and Assimilation* offers a thorough look at policies directed toward assimilation of Indigenous people in Canada.

[7] Cora J. Voyageur's 1998 article *Contemporary Aboriginal Women in Canada* offers a comprehensive overview of legislation affecting First Nation women in Canada.

[8] According to the 1928 Athapascan Census my maternal grandmother's Native name was Neschoot, her baptized name was "Sophie," however, her family called her Yanima. My birth mother's Native name—Beep—is recorded in the 1928 Census beside her baptized name "Martha."

[9] Lejac Residential School was operated by the Roman Catholic Church and the Federal Government. The Missionary Oblates of Mary Immaculate ran the mission school from 1890. In 1922 a new school building was erected until its closure in 1976. Lejac was razed after its closing, all that remains is the cemetery and the Rose Prince Memorial.

[10] Mudgy's older sister Agnes (Aggie) had her memoir of her life and time at Lejac transcribed prior to her death in 2001, facts related to the sisters' time at Lejac are from this memoir.

[11] For an early ethnographic record of the Kaska-Dena see John J. Honigmann's 1949 *Culture and Ethos of Kaska Society*.

[12] For further information on Lejac Residential School see Bridget Moran's 1988 *Stoney Creek Woman* and Jo-Anne Fiske's 1981 Masters' Thesis *And Then We Prayed Again: Carrier Women, Colonialism and Mission Schools, and Fiske's 1989 Gender and the Paradox of Residential Education in Carrier Society*.

[13] Tuberculosis plagued many Indigenous children while attending residential school. A report to R.H. Moore, Indian Agent, from Lejac principal states the following

> Paul Shorty, registration number 306, was discharged from Lejac on September 1937, Age on Discharge: 11 years old, Number of Years in School: Two, Trade or industry learned:

Chores, Principal remarks: Very good conduct, very willing but not much energy. Returned in a sick state and rapidly got worse at Liard Post, was under care of the R.C. Mission but died November 14, 1938. (B.C. Archives File 881-23 RG10 V6446)

[14] Agnes's memoir states that this is the first outright sense of racial injustice, prejudice and violence that she and Mudgy were exposed to.

[15] Statistics Canada www.statcan.gc.ca highlights statistics on Indigenous people in Canada taken from the 2006 Canadian census.

[16] Kaska-Dena (Liard) Dialect: Sógá = good, happy; senenla' = you made me; together = thank-you

WORKS CITED

Armitage, Andrew. *Comparing the Policy of Aboriginal Assimilation: Australia, Canada, and New Zealand.* Vancouver: UBC Press, 1995. Print.

Fiske, Jo-Anne. *Gender and the Paradox of Residential Education in Carrier Society.* Women of the First Nations of Canada: National Symposium, 1989, 131–145. Print.

—. *And Then We Prayed Again: Carrier Women, Colonialism and Mission Schools.* Masters' Thesis, Department of Anthropology and Sociology: University of British Columbia. 1981. Print.

Holy Family Mission. Roman Catholic Church Baptismal Records of Kaska Dene Families. Lower Post, BC. 1984. Print.

Honigmann, John J. *Culture and Ethos of Kaska Society.* London: Yale University Press, 1949. Print.

Johnston, Patrick. *Native Children and the Child Welfare System.* Toronto: James Lorimer and the Canadian Council on Social Development, 1983. Print.

Kaska Language Website. "Kaska Language Lessons: Liard Dialect." Eds. Pat Moore and Mida Donnessey. First Nations Languages 100K, University of British Columbia. (2003) Web.

Moran, Bridget. *Stoney Creek Woman: The Story of Mary John.* Vancouver: Arsenal Pulp Press Book Publishers Ltd., 1988. Print.

Principal, Lejac School. Follow-up report on residential school graduate submitted to Indian Agent R.H. Moore, May 1939. RG10, Vol.6446, File 881-23, British Columbia Archives (BCA). Print.

Salem-Wiseman, Lisa. "Verily the White Man's Ways Were the Best: Duncan Campbell Scott, Native Culture and Assimilation." *Studies in Canadian Literature/Etudes en litterature canadienne* 21 (1996): 120–142. Print.

Sinclair, Raven. "Identity Lost and Found: Lessons From the Sixties Scoop." *First Peoples Child and Family Review* 3 no.1 (2007): 65–82. Print.

Stolz, Agnes. Personal Memoir. Pages 1–168. Print.

Voyageur, Cora. "Contemporary Aboriginal Women in Canada." *Visions of the Heart*. Eds. David Long and Olive Dickason. Scarborough: Thompson Canada Ltd., 1998. 81–106. Print.

11.

The Power of Ancestral Stories on Mothers & Daughters

STEPHANIE A. SELLERS

As a woman with an identity founded in multiple ancient ethnicities, who is also a Native American Studies and Women & Gender Studies scholar, my very existence has created an opportunity that has informed me about the larger contrasts between Euro-western and Christian patriarchal approaches to women and Indigenous traditions. Since my birth, I have occupied a borderland that has offered me the privilege of the long view of human cultural experience that is often denied and ignored, and almost always rendered invisible. From this firsthand account, I can make observations as a scholar who has lived it, witnessed the culture clash deeply wound the women around me (and myself), and suggest ways women can emerge healed from this colonial, cataclysmic breach. Though the woman-centered traditions may be invisible to ourselves at times, they remain ineffably embedded at the cellular-level of our being, just as all ancient stories of the cultures to which we are born are part of us.

The story of Eve, from the patriarchal culture of the Euro-American invaders, is my mother's ancestral story and thus partly my story. My story is also the story of Selu from my father's Cherokee ancestors. I am also deeply influenced by the Haudenosaunee Sky Woman story, along with the buried story of the Hebraic goddess Lilith (Adam's first wife who rejected him) of my mother's lineage, from which I drew the strength and healing to survive my mother's inability to love me. As a mixed blood Jewish Indian, I turned to the richness of my Native community to disentangle messages of the confusing family I was born into. This abuse stemmed more obviously from my mother's lifelong blaming of me for her teenaged pregnancy to my father. But far more than that, the gendered, intergenerational abuse my mother experienced as a girl at the hands of her parents and sisters is what broke our bond long before my birth. As I struggled to make sense of and heal the legacy of my own and my mother's abuse, I began to wonder about the impact of patriarchy on mother-daughter relationships. Over several decades, I have come to realize that the oppression of women in western culture powerfully impacts the mother-daughter bond, and that the Origins Story that places into western consciousness the concept of women's subjugation is the story of Eve.

The knowledge of Eve's original pain is carried in the atoms of every woman of her lineage, and that includes me. This mostly unconscious knowledge is acted out, like all unresolved trauma, in the lived experience of the current generations, feeding the bonds of mothers and daughters with psychological wounding from their literal conception. The story of Eve was brought here with Columbus in 1492, and it has been disseminated over Turtle Island, affecting mothers and daughters of all ethnicities, for the past 500 years. But there were hundreds of other Creation stories on Turtle Island before the European settlers arrived, and it was the power of this legacy that sustained me through decades of loss and confusion. I am also a daughter of Selu, and the knowledge of her original creation is also carried in my atoms. Connecting with the Indigenous community in Pennsylvania revived that ancestral story within me, and through those connections to the living cultures of the land where I was born, I was able to recover, heal and forgive. Through the love of my ancestral community, I was able to play some part in bringing healing to a lineage of women from whom I had to absent myself in order to survive—to not drown in that legacy of misogyny.

A fundamental investigation of the legacy of mothering in both cultures, European invader and matrilineal Indigenous nations, offers significant insight into what happened to my mother and to me, and how I recovered from a family system of gender-specific abuse. In the Indigenous cultural worldview, there is no separation from the events of the past and of now—these Origins Stories and their images of women are as real and connected to mothers living today as we daughters are. Unfortunately, my experience is not unique, as the trauma inflicted upon daughters at the hands of their mother is common in patriarchal cultures. This reality is seldom openly interrogated in terms of gender-specific emotional violence in our contemporary times. What is uncommon in my case is how ancestral stories expressed in Indigenous ceremony and the everyday life of my community created an opportunity for me to heal wounds of the Euro-settler legacy I was also born to. That legacy, held by both the Indigenous people in my neighborhood and the Native academics across Turtle Island, sustained me during frightening, dark times after all the women relatives on my mother's side shunned me and demanded my sibling and cousins do the same. Through these Native women, I discovered I still have a mother and I still have women relatives—indeed, they were with me all along the way!

HAUDENOSAUNEE CREATION STORY: SKY WOMAN

As Paula Gunn Allen recounts in her award-winning anthology, *Spider Woman's Granddaughters* (Fawcett 1989), Sky Woman is the divine creatrix of the Haudenosaunee nation and is part of their creation story. In this story, the young Sky Woman lies beneath a beloved tree of light and "a blossom fell on her vagina…touching her with sweetness…soon after she knew she was pregnant" (66). From this sexual-spiritual encounter with the sacred tree, Sky Woman becomes pregnant and falls to the blue planet below her that becomes Turtle Island (Planet Earth). Here she gives birth to a daughter and together they create land and name every creature on the planet. This ancient story goes on to recount a beloved relationship between mother and daughter as the first humans of earth, human women who are deities and shape the course of life on our planet. Based on this foundation, all Haudenosaunee women were understood to be progenitors of life—human, spiritual and environmental—and thus were central in all socioeconomic structures within their nations. Haudenosaunee women have their own governing councils, appoint and depose chiefs, are judges, marriage counselors, and lawmakers and control use of the land (Mann 116–17). These rights have been passed from mother to daughter in matrilineal fashion from Sky Woman to Haudenosaunee women living today building a web of women's power with each new generation. Indeed, woman-centered deities in creation stories are present in many Indigenous nations like Corn Woman [or Selu] from the Cherokee, Thought Woman from the Laguna Pueblo, Hard Beings Woman from the Hopi and White Buffalo

[Calf] Woman from the Lakota (Allen 13–16), as well as Nokomis, or First Grandmother, from the Ojibwe (Child 30).

The message of this Indigenous story is the wholeness of women, the sanctity and primacy of mothers and daughters and the centrality of women's agency. Indeed, some of the highest offices of Indigenous nations were women's offices: like Jigonsaseh of the Haudenosaunee (Mann 36–38) and Beloved Woman of the Cherokee (Allen 1992; 36). Such beliefs are fundamentally distinct from, if not outright opposed to, the promulgation of Christian constructions of Eve/woman, as made from, lesser than, and subordinate to man, and man's dominion over all the earth, including woman. Haudenosaunee married, divorced, determined gender identity, reproduced and lived by their own life trajectory, all within the parameters of an ethic of communal ethics and personal responsibility to one's people. Indeed, as women from many Indigenous nations did, Haudenosaunee women saw their own image within the image of their deity and enjoyed all the privileges of life that such spiritual constructions would engender: wide latitude in sexual expression, personal appearance, self-determination and freedom from violence, particularly sexual violence. A key consideration is the fact that Haudenosaunee women owned the means of production and the products of their own labor (Mann 212), much like Ojibwe women held property rights and "controlled the entire social organization of the harvest" (Child 25).

With women's agency and sanctity as the bedrock of matrilineal and matriarchal Indigenous nations, the mother-daughter relationship is established and nourished within an environment that allows its fullest and healthiest expression. Indeed, a woman birthing a daughter in such a society can only mean that she has created a life that will be held in the highest regard—an experience that was surely spiritually ennobling and psychologically fulfilling. To the contrary, birthing daughters within a male-dominated culture, where fear of gendered violence and economic poverty are the norm, would be, at its core, psychologically distressing, regardless of the mother's own personal experiences or lack thereof. In other words, the threat of those experiences is always present in such a system, and, thus, undergirds a woman's self-conceptualization.

TWO CULTURES OF MOTHERING

What mothering means today in mainstream America is radically different from its social expression and legal definition in Eastern Woodland Indigenous nations before European immigrants arrived on Turtle Island. Among these nations, the time of the Mother in a female's life was defined by the cycles of her own body. Woman/Motherhood was begun with a girl's menarche, and her Grandmother years began when her bleeding times ended. These stages of life were not dependent upon heterosexual relationships with men, but merely with the cycles of a female's body. For example, Ojibwe girls were honored with puberty traditions that are still referred to as the Berry Fast (Child 5), and the Navajo people hold a lengthy and elaborate Kinaalda ceremony for girls honoring their first menstruation (Carr).

Haudenosaunee women held political status as clan mothers and they alone nominated women and men to office (Mann 172). Many Indigenous nations held and still practice matrilineal descent in determining identity; they hold girls' coming of age ceremonies, structure society around women's full participation and recognize a Divine Creatrix. All these cultural components that were in place for millennia deeply nurtured the mother-daughter bond, as they promulgated by belief and practice the notion that being female has worth, that Woman, and therefore Mother, are sacred. Of course, this did not mean that all mother-daughter relationships were problem-free or that all Indigenous mothers were effective. It simply demonstrates that there continues to be a cultural pattern where women and mothers were valued, thereby setting the stage for a strong opportunity for healthy mother-daughter relationships. Indeed, women were solely in charge of rearing and educating children, and the history of Haudenosaunee mothers' tenderness and generosity toward their children is legendary (Mann 271).

European invaders brought different cultural practices to North America based on entirely different belief systems. Unlike the Indigenous peoples who honored a female creator and recognized the strength of all women, the imported religion recognized a single-male deity, imposed the authority of man, and reinforced submissive (often condemned) females in their Origins Stories. In this creation story, Adam is created as the first human, and he alone names creation (Genesis 2: 19–20) and has dominion over the earth (1: 26–27). Eve, as the second human created, who was to specifically be the man's "help meet" (2: 18), is condemned by God for the downfall of humanity, particularly of men, for not submitting to both. God says to Eve after he discovers Adam has eaten from the Tree of Knowledge, "I will greatly multiply thy sorrow and thy conception: in sorrow thou shall bring forth children; and thy desire shall be to thy husband, and he shall rule over thee" (3:16). A further rebuke comes from God to Adam: "Because thou hast hearkened unto the voice of thy wife...cursed is the ground for thy sake; in sorrow shalt thou eat of it all the days of thy life" (3: 17). Though apologist theologians sensitive to the oppression of women like to argue that there are multiple meanings to this story, and that its archaic messages have no application in today's society, statistics on violence against women at the hands of husbands and male intimate partners demonstrate otherwise. Indeed, this is the story that has over millennia legitimated the subjugation of women and reinforced a hatred of femaleness in every new generation, creating significant barriers to women's safety and self-esteem and, thus, a healthy mother-daughter bond.

The punishment of Eve by the Judeo-Christian god in Genesis of the Bible set the stage for generations of women's oppression. Centuries of biblically-sanctioned misogyny culminated in events like the European witch burnings circa 1400 to 1700. The Roman Catholic Church's witch burnings, where perhaps up to several million women were tortured, then burned at the stake, were in full swing when the Pilgrims arrived on our shores. In Mary Daly's work, *Gyn/Ecology: The Metaethics of Radical Feminism* (Beacon 1990), she recounts the history of the European witch craze and its devastating impact on mothers and daughters at the time. In her work, she notes how daughters were forced to watch the torture and murder of their mothers who were accused of practicing witchcraft, and how this intergenerational, psychological wounding of the mother-daughter bond continues up to today (Daly 196).

English Common Law, instituted in the Euro-American colonial states, created significant challenges in the mother-child relationship as well. As neither women nor children were defined as persons under the law, they were deemed property of either their father or husband, and women, therefore, had no legal rights to their own children. Violence against children was common, as the adage "spare the rod, spoil the child" brought with the Europeans demonstrates. Newspapers from the 19th century are filled with Runaway Wife ads, where Euro-colonial men sought the return of their wives who fled, like runaway slaves, intolerable home lives. Fear, then, was actively present in colonial women's lives, and birthing a daughter into an environment of fear surely engendered internalized conflict about being female.

These historic events of Euro-American invaders laid the groundwork for damage to the mother-daughter bond that is embedded in the structure of the American family systems where the needs of men and boys are still privileged. The family is a microcosm and reflection of a culture's values and beliefs where indoctrination into social values begins. With its lack of nurturing girl or woman-centered ceremonies and absence of a Divine Creatrix in its religious practices, Euro-American culture struggled with its mother identity and thus the mother-daughter bond was, and continues to be, deeply challenged. In a social system where being female is understood as organically flawed, conflict and psychological wounding are embedded in the mother-daughter relationship. Feminist scholars such as Adrienne Rich (*Of Woman Born*) and Demetra George (*Mysteries of the Dark Moon*), and renowned psychotherapists such as Harriet Lerner (*Women in Therapy* and *The Mother Dance*) and Alice Miller (*Drama of the Gifted Child*) have written pioneering works on this topic.

Due to the cultural genocide policies enacted through Indian Boarding schools and the relentless efforts of Christian missionaries, patriarchal beliefs and practices in Euro-American culture came to be expressed as hegemonic, colonial intrusions upon many Indigenous nations' matrilineal systems. These systems had formerly been structured around women defining themselves from an image of wholeness and female sanctity. Over time, government programs and Christian missionaries attempted to replace the Indigenous clan structures with nuclear family systems, and the clan matrix that created, by design, "many mothers" was hit hard, but not obliterated. The European immigrants' heteronormative approach not only spawned restrictive expressions of mothering, but it simultaneously poisoned the mother-daughter bond, as the woman-cum-mother psychologically recognizes her subjugated role in a patriarchal social structure and, thus, the world in which she has birthed her daughters. At its core and foundation, Euro-American definitions of Woman have sabotaged the mother-daughter bond and set-up significant roadblocks to a healthy expression of this fundamental relationship in a female's life.

BELATED INDIGENOUS MOTHERING

My mother was raised in a home where males were held in high esteem and girls were treated as unworthy. To compound this gendered problem, her family openly denied their Jewishness, going to great lengths to say "We're not Jewish." This is another oppression brought by the European invaders that not only valued men, but Christianity, and therefore reinforced another component of her identity that was understood as unworthy.

At nineteen years old, I began to spend time with the local Indigenous people here in Central Pennsylvania, and this played a profound role in helping me recover from the trauma wrought by my mother and her side of the family. Actually, the local Indigenous grandmothers are the ones who found me and took me in. When I was just a teenager, visiting a Native friend, I participated in a Round Dance she was hosting. While I danced, I felt totally out of place, especially because I noticed the grandmothers kept watching me. I was certain I was offending them and did not belong there because I am a mixed blood, so afterwards I stayed in the house and did dishes. Before I left for home that day, I was told that the grandmothers said I was to be brought to the ceremonies from then on. That was how my traditional education began and how I returned to my Indigenous community. From that day forward I encountered something totally different about being a woman and about being a daughter. I was amazed that I belonged to a people because of something important they saw within me, without my asking or naming it, and that they loved me for it.

Connecting with my Indigenous family grounded me for the profound psychological work ahead to unravel the devastation from my birth home. Sitting with Native grandmas and beading, cooking and preparing for the next ceremony gave me a sense of belonging that I did not have with the women of my mother's immediate family, where I was required to be the family scapegoat like my mother had been. In ceremony, I first experienced a sense of deep connectedness, not only to kind people, but also to the earth, in a more conscious and mature way than I had throughout childhood. I began to better understand what it meant to be Native, especially a Native woman, beyond the simple transmission of fact my father offered me about our identity. With people I only knew for a short time, I felt deeply and immediately connected and valued. They talked to me about my spiritual purpose, about speaking up for my people even though I was a mixed blood and had been raised as a middle-class white person. They did not shun me, but treated me like a daughter—many grandmas and grandfathers call me "daughter." This was a wonderful new experience for me and by doing this they gave me some internal permission to finally admit I was abused by my mother. In particular, my Pap, Bill Robertson, grandson of the famous Nellie Robertson from the Carlisle Indian School, told me, "Your family would sell you down the river for a dime, but here with your People, you are home." That was on the first night we met, and I had not mentioned anything about my family problems.

I learned about what it means to be a treasured daughter, from merely being in community with the People, watching the white-haired chiefs eat last at our huge suppers, and the generosity of the grandmas. Since we do not have a clearly-defined geographic community here in Central Pennsylvania as other Indigenous nations do throughout the country, we come together at each other's homes and at fire halls, much like urban Indians do. Here in Central PA, the Natives learned generations ago the importance of keeping a low-profile in an area of conservative, white, Christian folks, who may be friendly on the surface but are quick to tell us we are "idolaters" who need to be saved, or that we are not Indian enough. So, though our people are scattered across the countryside, our bonds are strong and close.

Being in relationships with Indigenous women friends and elders is when I first noticed something about myself that showed me how little mothering I had received. I felt shocked that an older woman was taking so much time talking to me—actually taking time showing me how to do something important, and with so much love in her voice. I kept saying, "Oh you don't have to help me so much" and then profusely thanking her like she just pulled me out of a burning car. At first I was embarrassed to recognize how unloved I had been by my mother and how obvious it was to my new Native community. I also felt like I was betraying my mother by acknowledging that other people loved me like family, since it seemed akin to openly admitting she had failed me. Second, I began to understand that these Native women saw that lack within me, and were deliberately reaching out to offer me their kindness and love in order for me to heal. I felt self-conscious about how vulnerable and, admittedly, how needy I was. I was also extremely grateful because, in reality, I was grieving for the mother I never had, and struggling to come to terms with her rejection. She was an upper-class, educated woman, a psychotherapist, and she told me everything was my fault. Though I wince writing this, I had to work hard for many years to undo all that brainwashing. To my mother, my biggest crime, the act that warranted her rejection of me more than anything else, was loving my Native father and being too much like him.

If I had been raised in my traditional community, my mother's unplanned pregnancy outside of marriage would not have been a sin for which she would be shunned and abused for the rest of her life. Her father died just a few months after my birth, and her mother and siblings repeatedly told her that, because she caused so many problems in the family, she had hastened his death, if not outright killed him, because of her pregnancy to a poor Indian man. These statements preceded her first suicide attempt, and I have struggled to let go of my rage at them for what they did to my mother. Indeed, if I had been raised traditionally, there would be no Christianized society to condemn my mother for her pregnancy, and she would have had no need to target her ineffable anguish at me as the source of her pain. Thanks to my Native family, and the ancestral stories from which our worldview originates, I have found a space to heal my wounds.

To me, my mother's suffering, and hence my own, is a direct legacy of the Eve story, the legacy of a culture that denigrates women. The level of sickness in my mother's family did not come in only one generation and was not created by them, but by larger cultural mores concerning women.

EPILOGUE

My mother was psychologically damaged by her birth family by nothing less than American acculturation to the multiple supremacies of whiteness, maleness, Christianity and heteronormativity. Her parents wanted sons, and she was first in line to reap their frustration over producing four daughters. Her un-owned shadow side is what I came to embody—and a woman's un-owned shadow in the cultural presence of patriarchy is the hidden presence of the Divine Creatrix. Within me, she simultaneously placed all that she hated about herself and all that she was never allowed to be: the true legacy that is the Great Mother. Though she raised me to be a feminist, she could not love what she was taught to hate: herself/being female. My mother spent our entire relationship emotionally stabbing me to death, then desperately resuscitating me: killing her split-apart daughter self and pulling her other self above the waters for air—her one hand continually at my throat and the other one reaching out to rescue.

Six thousand years ago when knowledge of the Divine Feminine was forced underground by the military takeover of the goddess-worshiping nations of the Mesopotamia and their temples were destroyed, my relationship with my mother was broken. When the tribes of the solar gods brought their iron and bronze down upon the heads of the moon goddess people and replaced the Great Mother's story with Eve's story, our mother-daughter bond was broken. It took the unexpected ancestral turn of a Jewish girl falling in love with a Cherokee man to break that chain in one family, in one generation. It took one daughter, (me), to reconnect with a lineage that honors women to break the intergenerational wounding and come out of the dark spiral of abuse. Without knowing it, my mother gave that strength to me. Perhaps without intending it, she set us both free. In my adult life today, I have reclaimed all my identities: the sanctity of being a woman, of being Jewish, and being a culturally-identified, mixed blood Cherokee woman. I have also forgiven my mother, but will never forgive or stop fighting the culture and religion that broke her and millions of women before her.

I will always carry for my mother, from this safe vantage point, an image of her wholeness, blessing her life with my love. In the lodge, I have prayed for the healing of my mother's lineage and to its female deities, Lilith and Hera, and sent healing to all my Euro-settler grandmothers. This is my spiritual purpose. This is what the Native Grandmothers taught me, what the Ancestor Spirits showed me. This healing was never just for me.

WORKS CITED

Allen, Paula Gunn. *The Sacred Hoop: Recovering the Feminine in American Indian Traditions.* Boston: Beacon Press, 1992. Print.

—, Ed. *Spider Woman's Granddaughters: Traditional Tales and Contemporary Writing by Native American Women.* New York: Fawcett, 1989. Print.

Carr, Lena and Aaron Carr, directors. *Kinaalda: A Navajo Rite of Passage.* Indian Summer Films, producers. New York: Women Make Movies, 2000. Video-recording.

Child, Brenda J. *Holding Our World Together: Ojibwe Women and the Survival of Community.* New York: Viking, 2012. Print.

Daly, Mary. *Gyn/Ecology: The Metaethics of Radical Feminism.* Boston: Beacon, 1990. Print.

Mann, Barbara Alice. *Iroquoian Women: The Gantowisas.* New York: Peter Lang, 2004. Print.

The English Standard Version Bible: Containing the Old and New Testaments with Apocrypha. Oxford: Oxford University Press, 2009. Print.

12.

Rebirth and Renewal

Finding Empowerment through Indigenous Women's Literature

JENNIFER BRANT

> A couple of winters ago, on a journey that took me half way
> around the world, the vibrant, tenacious spirits of two won-
> derful old Koochums (Grandmothers) came to me in a dream
> and directed me back to my home communities and, most
> importantly, my sense of self. Throughout most of my life,
> I've felt those very distinctly maternal energies although con-
> sciously I paid little attention to them. This time, I responded
> to those energies, whose spiritual directives prompted my
> journey home. When at last my feet touched the earth from
> which I came, I felt the spirits of Kah' Ki Yaw Ni Wahko-
> makanak (all my relations) welcome me home. (Acoose 17)

I chose to start with these words for two reasons. First, Janice Acoose's
book, *Iskwewak Kah' Ki Yaw Ni Wahkomakanak: Neither Indian
Princesses Nor Easy Squaws* is the first book I use in the Aboriginal women's
literature course that I teach at Brock University, and which I discuss
throughout this paper. The book's connection to Indigenous maternal
pedagogy will thus become evident throughout the chapter. Second, I feel
the words capture the essence of empowered Indigenous mothering in a
way that connects all Indigenous women, regardless of their status as mothers, or their relationship with their birth mothers. This includes an understanding of mothering that moves beyond "biologically-defined identities"

(Bédard 66) towards community-oriented understandings, in which "raising children is understood as the creation of a people, a nation, and a future" (Bédard 66).

We all have a connection to the maternal energies surrounding us as Indigenous women, and have written about this connection for years. Sylvia Terzian draws attention to this "maternal legacy" by reflecting on the mother figure in Native women's literature "as the site at which all things are interconnected" (147). Moreover, describing the mother figure as a "web of continuity," she suggests that "the mother's web functions as a survival mechanism, a perpetuating force of female agency that enables the resilience of Native peoples and the continuity of Native cultural traditions" (147). Emma LaRocque also writes about the interconnectedness between mothering, Aboriginal women's literature, and cultural continuity. "In the tradition of our grandmothers and mothers, Aboriginal women have continued to work for the preservation of our families, communities, and cultures, and, in so doing, are keeping our peoples and cultures alive and current. Writing is one such expression of both creativity and continuity" (155).

The maternal theories present in Indigenous women's writing stand in contrast to the patriarchal forces that have severely altered that maternal legacy within Indigenous communities. Lina Sunseri draws attention to one point of disruption, the Indian Act, which legally removed the maternal line among the Haudenosaunee. As Sunseri advises "this led to a devaluation of Indigenous womanhood and is at the heart of the unequal gender relations that currently exist in our communities" (60). Acoose describes the patriarchal forces that disrupted the maternal authority within her own family, with the first point being at birth:

> After nine long months of being nourished and loved inside my Nehiowè-Métis mother's womb, I was delivered into a cold and sterile white eurocanadian patriarchal catholic hospital[1]. Immediately imposing their patriarchal authoritative discretion disguised as christian duty, the nuns who were then the hospital administrators, stole my mother's right to name me. Thus, just like my three older sisters, I was named Mary, becoming the fourth nominally indistinguishable female child in my immediate family to be so named. (20)

Acoose names the subsequent disruptions: the second when she was only a few days old and was registered as a treaty Indian; the third, her baptism into the catholic church at only a couple months old, and finally, the fourth, at five years old, her "imprisonment behind the drab and dreary walls at the Cowessess 'Indian' Residential School in Saskatchewan" (23).

Despite the patriarchal forces that have left a significant imprint on Indigenous Motherhood, our women continue to write stories reconnecting us with that maternal energy. The stories shared in my Aboriginal women's literature class at Brock give testimony to our varied experiences as Indigenous women and mothers who are on our own journeys to reclaim the ways that were lost amongst the many points of disruptions we faced. It is through these stories that Indigenous motherhood can be understood, and Indigenous women can begin their journeys home. With this understanding, Aboriginal women's literature becomes a site of cultural continuity for the rebirth and renewal of our maternal legacies.

Aboriginal women are often considered the backbone of our communities. Their strength and resilience, however, is less apparent when we see the disheartening social and economic realities that Indigenous women, many of whom are young mothers, face within our communities and across our nations. This chapter describes how these realities can be transformed through culturally-specific and maternally-based educational opportunities. Drawing on an Indigenous women's literature course, I describe the transformation that takes place when students connect with the maternal energies described above. By sharing the words of women who have completed the course, I present Indigenous maternal pedagogy as a site of empowerment for the rebirth and renewal of Indigenous motherhood.

MATERNAL PEDAGOGIES

Maternal pedagogies are not new to the study or application of education, but are becoming more popular through motherhood studies. The work of Sharron Abbey and Andrea O'Reilly advances understandings of "Maternal Epistemology" offering the following definition, "to know, understand or claim a particular authority and knowledge based on experiences of mothering" (330). Kim Anderson contributes to the study of maternal pedagogies by presenting Indigenous ideologies of motherhood, where she draws attention to the lack of literature on Indigenous mothers within motherhood studies, outlines the distinctiveness of Indigenous ideologies of motherhood and considers strategies for reclamation and empowerment. Her work, along with the anthology, edited by mother and daughter, Jeannette Corbiere Lavell and Memee Lavell-Harvard reveals the depth of Indigenous maternal pedagogy, while simultaneously contrasting mainstream feminist approaches to motherhood studies with those that are Indigenous by virtue of reality, shared histories and lived experiences.

My first engagement with maternal pedagogies was during a Motherhood studies course that I took. Although the course was not inclusive of Indigenous content, I made my own connections as an Indigenous student familiar with the importance of the "Motherline." As a Haudenosaunee woman and mother, maternal connections and the importance of the maternal line are part of my birthright; these differ from western patriarchal models of naming, birthrights and so on. This, however, is complicated by the fact that my mother is not Haudenosaunee and I draw on my paternal Grandmother for those connections. Beyond this familiar instinctive knowing, and connection with the maternal pedagogies in this course, was a deeper appreciation as a daughter. The course helped me to develop a better understanding of the tensions in my relationship with my mother, and prompted a deeper sense of understanding my experiences as her daughter and her experiences as a mother; it was a transformational experience. I left this class with a renewed sense of my own daughter-mother relationship, much of it being understood through a reflection of my experience of becoming a mother. While the course was not Indigenous-based, I took away these cultural values, and applied them for my own healing. Thus, the course was much more than just another university elective. It left a significant imprint.

I connect this to both the healing power of story and life narrative that I consider foundational to Indigenous maternal pedagogy. I recall this experience because, as an Indigenous educator, I have a strong desire to empower and leave an imprint on the students I teach. I know I am not alone in doing this, and so, I draw on the stories of the many Indigenous women who collectively bring maternal energy and keep that power alive within our communities. In a recent article I co-wrote with Kim Anderson we refer to this as the power of "the eachother" that connects us to a "greater web of relationships that has been critical to rebuilding an empowered Indigenous motherhood" (202).

THE ABORIGINAL WOMEN'S LITERATURE COURSE

My words are a colourful tapestry. They are my art. My struggle is to recover the identity that allows me to walk in the way of beauty. (Monture-Angus 152)

I draw on one of the courses offered in the Gidayaamin Aboriginal Women's Program,[2] *Reclaiming Aboriginal Women's Literary Traditional and Educational Aspirations* to illustrate the delivery of Indigenous maternal pedagogy and the impact the course had on Aboriginal mother's empowerment in education and community contexts. The course is guided by Indigenous maternal pedagogy, and delivery is based on Kim Anderson's theory of identity formation. Anderson presents her theory of identity formation within the framework of a Medicine Wheel with four components: Resist, Reclaim, Construct and Act. Anderson explains this as a journey of "resisting negative definitions of being; reclaiming Aboriginal tradition; constructing a positive identity by translating tradition into the contemporary context; and acting on that identity in a way that nourishes the overall well-being of our communities" (15). Drawing from Anderson's model, the course is divided into four interconnected sections: *Resist, Reclaim, Construct* and *Act*. There are consistent themes that traverse throughout the course material, given the integrated nature of Aboriginal women's literature; namely, the maternal legacy, lessons of resiliency, survival and Indigenous women's agency.

The course material involves a balance of academic and non-academic literary works authored by Indigenous women. The rationale for incorporating non-traditional sources in such a course can be best described in the following quote from Patricia Monture-Angus who illustrates the connections among Indigenous culture, identity and personal experience by expressing the importance of reclaiming Aboriginal women's identities by looking inward to our own teachings and personal experiences.

> "It is *only* through my culture that my women's identity is shaped. It is the teachings of my people that demand we speak from our own personal experience. That is not necessarily knowledge that comes from academic study." (29)

In honour of the above words, the literature course incorporates a variety of sources that include literary criticism, narratives, autobiographies, poetry, memoirs, as well as audiovisual material. Her words reiterate the role culture has in shaping Aboriginal women's identity. According to Indigenous worldviews, we learn and gain understandings through experience. Thus, our cultural experiences, such as that of mothering, teach us about our identities as Indigenous women. Through Indigenous women's writing, teachings about mothering, as gained through personal experiences, are passed on. For example, stories that embed women-centered creation stories, traditional to many Aboriginal nations, remind us of the maternal energies and reconnect us to the vibrant and powerful role women once held in our communities. The title of Sandra Laronde's anthology, *Sky Woman: Indigenous women who have shaped, moved or inspired us*, is evidence of this connection. As Laronde advises:

> Since Sky Woman, millions and millions of Indigenous women have inherited her legacy. As Indigenous women, we have been resourceful, resilient and remarkable in our will to keep falling and moving forward. We fall to better ground because of the many women who have gone before us, breaking our fall, and inspiring us from the shining example of their own incandescent lives. (Laronde vii)

In this way mothering extends to ideas about nurturing the nation and those who follow us in the next generations. It is about continuing that maternal legacy. Laronde's words also remind us of the importance of acceptance and compassion for those who hit the ground, perhaps even in their experiences as mothers, and the role other women play in reaching out to help those women find their footing once again. It is with this in mind that the literature course features the narrative of women who serve as these examples by sharing their beautiful stories of survival, resiliency and rebirth.

These stories, however, are not always the most settling for the students, especially during the first section of the course that focuses on the element of resistance. This makes sense if we think of the theory of identity formation (Anderson) as a decolonizing and healing journey. Before we can begin such a journey, things tend to get messy. Healing is not an easy or painless process. The students must first learn, or perhaps be reminded, of the stereotypes of Indigenous women from which negative definitions of being arise. Throughout mainstream literature and media Aboriginal women have been portrayed as promiscuous, drunk, lewd, licentious, prostitute, easy, available, willing, dissolute and dangerous (Acoose; Anderson; & Carter) and of Aboriginal mothers as unfit and uncivilizing (Cull). Students learn to deconstruct these stereotypes, reflect on the purposes they serve, and consider the implications on Aboriginal women, families and communities. It is these contexts that must be understood as part of the resistance phase before students can move towards the next phase and begin reclaiming the beauty of Indigenous women's identities that are shaped through our cultures (Monture-Angus).

As Morningstar Mercredi author of *Morningstar: A Warrior's Spirit* points out during her keynote at the Missing and Murdered Indigenous Women's Conference, "The issues we talk about make some people uncomfortable, well I'll tell you what: Get uncomfortable!" (Mercredi "Honouring the Warrior Within") Her story, however, much like Maria Campbell's biography *Half-breed*, is one of survival, resiliency and rebirth. It is a narrative of personal triumph. She shares her history of abuse, prostitution and the hardships she faced as a young woman and her journey to recovery (included in her story is how all of this affected her relationship with her son). Her story, much like the stories shared by Beatrice Mosioner in *In Search of April Raintree*, can serve as a mirror that allows Indigenous women to see their own stories reflected in text and know that they are not alone. For others whose stories are not reflected, it allows for a deeper understanding of the sociocultural and historical context of the ways in which colonial history has impacted the lives of many Indigenous women.

Adding to the messiness of the stories shared during the *Resist* section of the course, the women learned about policies such as the eugenics movement and the sixties scoop that were justified by the negative definitions of Indigenous womanhood and further implicated women's rights to literally give birth and mother their own children (Anderson; Cull). With the help of Acoose, the course provided a forum for discussion of the patriarchal forces that gave rise to the power relations that imprisoned Indigenous women. Acoose points out that literature is a powerful political instrument serving not only to perpetuate ongoing stereotypical constructs of Aboriginal women, but also to justify numerous legally sanctioned initiatives with the overall goal of assimilation.

Literature becomes a powerful tool that moves beyond resistance through the words of Indigenous women who reconstruct and *Reclaim* positive definitions of being. Writers like Janice Acoose, Beatrice Culleton, Lee Maracle, Beth Brant, Emma LaRocque, along with many others, reclaim literature and draw awareness to not only the pervasiveness of negative images that persist, but also to the power, resilience, and beauty of Aboriginal womanhood. In this way, Aboriginal women are rewriting themselves and reconstructing positive definitions of being (Anderson). The act of writing and sharing these stories moves us from the *Construct* phase to the *Act* phase of Kim Anderson's theory of identity formation. Students gain access to different literary resources that showcase the power and the creative processes of Indigenous women's words. In writing about the cultural contributions of Indigenous women, LaRocque so eloquently captures the process of identity formation through Indigenous women's literature in a way that brings together all of the elements resist, reclaim, construct and act:

> Not only have they confronted colonial history and misrepresentation, which I would argue is a "positive" response to colonial realities, they have drawn deeply from the well of their cultural memories, myths, and mother languages. And, as artists, Aboriginal writers form bridges in areas Western thinkers traditionally thought unbridgeable: many, perhaps especially poets, move easily from the oral to the written; all move from the ancient to the post-colonial and from historic trauma to contemporary vibrancy. Some form bridges from personal invasions to personal triumph. Native women have moved far beyond "survival"; they have moved with remarkable grace and accomplishments right onto the international stage. These writers not only retrieve our histories and experiences, a process that is both necessary and painful, but they also collect and thread together our scattered parts and so nurture our spirits and rebuild our cultures. (152)

LaRocque captures the maternal essence present in both the words of Indigenous women and also in the act of writing the words. Much like the act of mothering, Indigenous women's words nurture and strengthen our spirits. Beth Brant writes about the power and strength gained from women heroines such as Pauline Johnson. Brant's reference to Pauline Johnson as "a spiritual grandmother" connects her to that maternal energy that empowers us as Indigenous women:

> Pauline Johnson's physical body died in 1913, but her spirit still communicates to us who are Native women writers. She walked the writing path clearing the brush for us to follow. And the road gets wider and clearer each time a Native woman picks up her pen and puts her mark on paper. (195)

In honour of this legacy, the course is not only about the study of Indigenous women's literature but also about empowering women to pick up that pen and begin writing themselves. Because writing is such a personal and powerful process, students are encouraged to journal and to write for themselves but are also reminded that they do not have to share their words unless they are comfortable in doing so.

I end this section with another powerful quote from Beth Brant to reaffirm the maternal legacy—the gift—of Indigenous women's words.

> I look on Native women's writing as a gift, a give-away of the truest meaning. Our spirit, our sweat, our tears, our laughter, our love, our anger, our bodies are distilled into words that we bead together to make power. Not power *over* anything. Power. Power that speaks to hearts as well as to minds. (195)

VOICES FROM THE WOMEN: STORIES OF REBIRTH AND RENEWAL

To fully describe the impact of culturally specific and Indigenous maternal pedagogy on the empowerment of Indigenous mothering, I documented voices from two women who have completed the literature course. I held a sharing circle with the women and a community Elder who provided guidance as they reflected on their experiences in the course. While I hoped to gather the experiences of the women, I could not have anticipated the power of the sharing circle. The words of the Elder affirmed the very maternal energy that I discussed above, and we could feel that energy in the room, in our hearts and in the shared stories. The sharing circle was a wonderful way of bringing this work full circle, and, in this way, it provided me with a deeper understanding of my own role as an educator and a writer. Reflecting on the circle, I can see that, much like my experience of mothering my own children and the reciprocal relationship in which my children teach me how to be a mother as I teach them through my mothering, the women teach me how to be an educator. A reciprocal learning exchange happens between us and I can only understand the power of that exchange as one guided by maternal energies. The words I chose for the title, "Rebirth and Renewal," have now taken on a new meaning for me, in that they also capture my experience of the sharing circle. It is not just the students who I can describe as going through a process of rebirth and renewal, but I felt that for myself in the circle as well.

I present the discussion by listing the questions asked in the gathering and selecting pieces that demonstrate the responses of the participants.

Many of the quotes are lengthy. I have chosen to leave them in this format to honour the women's voices and fully capture their experiences not only in the course but in the exchange with the Elder during the gathering.

Can you share a bit about your overall experience in the Aboriginal Women's Literature course?

In response, one woman stated that she liked the course because it gave her a deeper understanding of the traumas we faced as Aboriginal women. She noted that *In Search of April Raintree* was an enjoyable book for her because she learned a lot from it: "You're not holding anything back in that book—it's like, out there" (Jessica). Another woman said she liked the course because she found it relevant:

> Everything that I learned in that class I had gone home and implemented in my family structure and that was exciting too because I was able to leave the class and talk to my children and my husband about what I learned in the class and then come up with a plan of how I was going to implement it in my family so I looked forward to coming to class because I was always learning something new and something useful to me and my family so I really enjoyed it. (Roxanne)

Roxanne's contribution provides evidence of the connection between Indigenous maternal pedagogy and the role of mothering as she looked forward to learning new lessons useful to her family. Roxanne also noted a connection with *In Search of April Raintree* and *Sweetgrass Basket*:

> Those are sad stories and I know they're reality because I face that in my family, like that's my family, you know so they weren't really like shocking to me, they didn't have that shocking effect, it was kinda like well it's out there now like and other aspects like where I would never be able or I would never consider telling my story in that kind of context but because it was out there it kind of made me feel a little bit more safe with my feelings, my own feelings. So I learned a lot and I really enjoyed it. (Roxanne)

Here we see how the curriculum can draw on Indigenous women's narratives to connect with students and bring a sense of security to their own realities. In this way, cultural identity formation takes place by students learning to come to terms with their own experiences, by understanding collective trauma and reflecting on community healing.

How has this course shaped your understanding of the connection between Aboriginal Women's literature and Aboriginal Mothering?

Roxanne noted that her father began his own reclaiming journey into her adulthood. She explained that, while she did not grow up with the culture, it has always been there for her children. She described being pregnant with her first son, and just starting to connect with the Drum. She shared the following experience that took place while she was eight months pregnant with her first son:

> He was in my stomach and I can just sort of see his feet going because of the drum right so and then when he was born he was at that drum and he's been at that drum ever since so my children were always in a position of privilege when it came to culture and traditions and I never really had the understanding.

Roxanne continued by sharing how she has been able to implement the knowledge she gained from class into her role as a mother. For example, she expressed a deeper understanding of cultural protocol—within a historical and colonial context—that has empowered her to explain to her children why cultural practices are done in a certain way as well as the value of continuing and holding on to their family traditions:

> Everything that I was learning in class about the residential school, and then thinking back on my own history like with my grandfather being in residential school, and how that affected my dad and how that affected me, and then this reclaiming stage. So everything I learned in your class it kind of like backed up what I was saying to the kids. So instead of me saying "because I said so" I actually had the knowledge and my stuff to be like this is why we do it. Everything in my house is based on that Kim Anderson's theory resist, reclaim, construct and act...It's everywhere, so I'm really actually thankful for that, being able to understand and know that theory, because I can use it in so many different contexts and it's a lot for

me. It's a better line of communication when I can tell them the history of it and the reasons why we do it... With everything I learned in that class, it's easier for me to explain it in a healthier way.

Jessica agreed, noting that she used Kim Anderson's theory to begin reclaiming herself, and was then able to apply it at home and with her children. Listening to Jessica talk about her own reclaiming journey prompted Roxanne to express a new feeling that she was having a hard time articulating. Roxanne asked Jessica if she felt different through this journey of reclaiming. Jessica explained:

> I do. I'm still trying to locate myself. I'm going to say locating because I had to find out who I was, what clan was I from, all that kind of stuff. So I'm trying to locate and I still find it's still a journey for me. It's not done yet. I'm not done learning about who I am. Do I feel a difference within myself? Yea I do because now I can start applying that stuff in my home and with my kids and with my life just and with my community. So if I go back home or even here I can have conversations with Elders and actually understand what they're talking about and understand what things mean. I didn't understand any of that before so now I'm still learning but I feel a difference.

Roxanne asked the Elder if she knew the feeling she was having trouble articulating. The Elder responded:

> It's coming home. And right now listening to you it's just like a prayer to all those grandmothers. That their daughters have wandered off and now, that maternal energy, it's been, you've been knowing, but not knowing, and the desire becomes stronger. And so when that desire becomes stronger you're starting to listen to that mother instinct that mother intuition. "I need to know more, I need to know more." And so in a sense, it's like coming home. Coming home to your spirit, you're coming home to Indigenous knowledge that has been ingrained in all of us, every part of our physical, mental, emotional, and spiritual, they have had all this memory that's just waiting there... and now it's time to go back... and find

out all that information and that's what it feels like. Coming home!

This was such a powerful moment in the gathering because it connected all of us to that first story that began this chapter, that describes Janice Acoose's journey home, and the maternal energy that guided her. In hearing those stories throughout the literature course and applying Kim Anderson's theory of identity formation within themselves and with their families the women were able to recognize this feeling that the Elder described as "coming home." Roxanne agreed:

> I'm like comfortable now in my own self…but I never had a way to verbalize those feelings. And even when I try to explain to my kids or husband and I can't verbalize it properly I'm like *IT JUST FEELS RIGHT!* That's how I feel! I can't explain it! They notice a difference in me to so we've all learned together.

Connecting us to that maternal energy, the Elder told us that she could see "all the grandmothers are just kicking up their heels right now!" The Elder continued by talking about the importance of returning home and reclaiming our identities as Indigenous women:

> It's knowing that power, as a woman, that you have. You're reconnecting and it's so powerful because they've been wanting it for a long time, because they see so much and all of them have been guiding. The ancestors are saying "go here, go here, go here" and they're hearing your words it's just like I can see them just kicking up their heels and saying yes they got it! They got it!

The Elder continued by describing the power of Indigenous womanhood:

> Our strength comes from within us and within our Mother the Earth we have the ability to heal. We wore many hats, we weren't just women, we were leaders, we were teachers, we were doctors, and we were healers. All of us have that inside of us, and it's so nice to hear the different women coming forward. Pauline Johnson was a woman before her time. She spoke out and that's the most important thing. She's teaching those women.

The Elder reaffirmed the role Indigenous women have in empowering one another. Her words were so powerful, and we could feel the energy in the room. Feeling that energy pass through us in the room was a gift. Roxanne expressed that "I almost cried like four times already" and the Elder responded "now you gotta tell your body it's okay to cry." At this point during the circle, the Elder shared a teaching about the importance of crying, and connected this to the importance of learning to say no. The Elder told us that " 'No' is one of your most important protectors, 'no' is to help you have boundaries." This was an important lesson that was also connected to a teaching about "taking care of our healthy seeds." By sharing these teachings, the Elder connected us with our maternal role as protectors of our future generations. Her words affirmed Roxanne's comment about "feeling different" by linking it to "coming home" as a way to strengthen herself and her family.

Has your experience in the course impacted your understanding as a student or as a mother pursuing university and the need to balance those roles?

Much like Roxanne had stated in response to her overall course experience, Jessica responded by noting the ability to take the knowledge she learned in class and apply that in her role as a mother:

> I've learned a great deal as a student…and being a mom to be able to apply that knowledge down to my children just sitting here listening to [Elder] I'm learning from her. So it's like a non-stop learning environment. I'm gaining all this knowledge. Even though we're not in a classroom setting, I still feel like a student here, listening to you [the Elder] speak. So I think this knowledge that I'm gaining I can apply that to being a mom and I can apply that to my children and I can apply that to my children who have children. I think it has impacted my learning environment and my understanding of issues.

Jessica's acknowledgement of the non-stop learning environment also highlights the importance of having Elders and Traditional Knowledge Keepers work with the students. Bringing their teachings into the learning environment is bringing Indigenous knowledge to the students, and should be integral to any classroom that adopts Indigenous maternal pedagogy.

Roxanne's response brought a new aspect to the discussion that acknowledged the holistic approach of honouring the whole family in a mother's learning journey:

> I'm on this healing journey. I'm thankful for a lot of things along the way. I'm thankful for what I'm being taught, but I'm also thankful that my husband and my children allowed me to go on this journey. I was able to step out of the role…and it was not a happy job but that's what I did to provide for my family. And I say all the time I recognize the sacrifices they made because they were so used to me being one way and then all the sudden I go on this journey and I'm somebody totally different. They're excited about the changes but at the same time I never would have been able to do that if they weren't supportive and encouraging of me. So it's kind of like a balancing, like I'm really happy for what I'm learning in school but I'm also really happy that I've been given the chance by my family to take that journey.

Roxanne's acknowledgement of the reciprocal exchange that takes place between mother and family during a mother's education journey led the Elder to share a deeper understanding of the gift that Mothers give to our families by taking time for ourselves:

> This going to school is just like your moontime, where you would go to a women's lodge and learn all about all life skills so when you went back the absence would make your partner and your children appreciate you more…Now you have passion and when you talked about your job you were (dissatisfied) and the children felt it and your partner felt it. So now you got that, your fire, it's been burning now…and everything is affected by it. You're even maybe singing and humming around and cooking and baking and they're looking at you, but they're feeling it, and it's like they benefit more than you benefit by it you know it's just like it's a gift you receive and you give it, and you receive and you give it. And because you went away and you give them the gift of being independent, and the gift to appreciate you more, and you give them the gift to know that when you are away that things can still

continue…So what you are reading…when you go to class and what you are getting is almost like a teaching lodge. You're getting time away. You're getting time to mature your seed and so they are just so happy because they feel that happiness from you.

The Elder's connection between going to school and going to a teaching lodge brought more clarity to the interconnectedness between the Indigenous mothering, education and literature, and cultural continuity. By going to school, these women are able to nourish their own seeds by gaining new insights through meaningful and relevant curriculum and bring this nourishment back to their families. The final question asked in the sharing circle considers how this nourishment can then be brought back to their communities.

Has your experience in the course impacted your understanding as a community member?

When asked this question, Roxanne noted that she was just beginning to recognize her advocacy skills and use them in her new position on the board of directors for two community organizations. She noted that she now has the knowledge to back up her statements, and urges the organizations to "decolonize our thought processes." Roxanne advised us that, through this approach, she is "bringing back the holistic to my community." Roxanne also pointed out that she still feels unsure of what her role is on the boards, because everyone has a professional background, while she only brings a student perspective. The Elder reminded her that as a mother and community member she has an important role to bring. The Elder expressed that "Mother…was once held the highest because [Mothers are] the first teacher[s] of life." This comment adds to the empowerment of Indigenous mothering by making the connection back to that role of being the first teachers to our future generations. As the first teachers, Indigenous women hold an essential place in our communities that must be recognized. Jessica contributed by noting the development she has had in understanding her role as a community member:

I think for me it's the same thing. I have that advocacy spirit in me just to create awareness or to stop the hurt in our community…I think that's where my journey has brought me just to say enough is enough.

When asked if the women had anything else they would like to share, Roxanne brought more clarity to the connection between the power of Indigenous women's literature and empowered motherhood. She pointed out that she has her children journal every summer and noticed "that their journaling this summer has been a lot different than past summers." She was not sure why this was the case but stated "It means more to me seeing how they felt throughout the day rather than what they did throughout the day." She also noted that, part way through the literature course, she had purchased three notebooks, one for each of her children, and began to write their birth stories (including what everyone was feeling) on the day they were born. Roxanne thought that watching her fill out these birth journals may have been what prompted a change in the way her children now journal.

A PERSONAL REFLECTION

I have been taught that the prophecy of the seventh generation is common among many Indigenous nations across Turtle Island. As a Yakonkwe-hón:we (*Mohawk woman*) I have come to know this prophecy over the years, and been reminded of its meaning more recently.

During the time that I was working on this chapter, I attended the Kaha:wi dance theatre's production *The Honouring*. The performance was held at the Old Fort in Fort Erie, Ontario, and depicted the Haudenosaunee role in the War of 1812. The production was presented from a holistic perspective that touched on the experiences of the warriors who went to the battlefields, the women and families who prayed for the safe return of their men and the community that mourned for those who did not return home safely. Interwoven throughout the piece was a mixture of Mohawk and English narration that spoke of the connection to our Mother Earth, our first mother, who endlessly sustains, nourishes and nurtures us. As I watched the performance, I gained a deeper understanding of the Haudenosaunee role in the war and the intentions to protect our Mother Earth.

The performance ended with a reminder of the prophecy of the seventh generation. According to this teaching, after seven generations of living in close contact with Europeans, the Onkwehonwe would see the day that the Elm trees would start to rot from the top, that we would see animals that were born deformed with twisted limbs, that the earth would be torn open by huge stone monsters, that the rivers would burn aflame, that the air would burn our eyes, that the birds would start to fall from the sky, that the fish would start to die in the waters and that we would grow ashamed of the way we treated the earth.

The prophecy also tells us that during this time, people will turn to the Onkwehonwe and look for direction. It is the children of the Kanien'kéha:ka who will have the answer; they are the seventh generation. *The Honouring* was such a strong and beautiful reminder of this prophecy. The performance ended with one of the men echoing "the answer will come from our young ones."

As a mother, the prophecy gives much deeper meaning to my role and responsibilities to nurture my children. I must nurture them emotionally, physically, spiritually and intellectually. But I also feel that they must be nurtured politically and understand their roles as young Haudenosaunee boys who are among the seventh generation. If the answer will come from our youngest, and it is those who will lead our people into the future, mothering them, sustaining, nourishing and nurturing them, takes on a whole new meaning. We must ensure they have strong roots, and that as mothers we support their cultural identity development. I am so thankful that my Eldest son was able to experience this message delivered in *The Honouring* while my youngest slept on my lap.

The next day we attended the Fort Erie Spirit of the Youth Powwow. I was there to recruit for the Gidayaamin program so was not planning to bring my regalia. As I packed up my children's regalia, my son told me he really wanted me to dance. He said it was important and that I need to be out there dancing because it's my culture and I should be proud of who I am. My son is a constant reminder of the direction that will guide me into the future. Both of my children continue to teach me new lessons every day. In this way, my relationship with them is reciprocal; they teach me how to mother them in a way that honours their spirit and, in return, I mother them in a way that allows them to choose their own paths and take ownership for their growth and development. In mothering them, I learn more about myself as an Indigenous mother, thus my cultural identity is shaped and gifted through my children.

FINAL WORDS

The purpose of this chapter was to look at the impact of culturally specific and Indigenous maternal pedagogy on the empowerment of Indigenous mothering within an academic and community context. To clarify what I mean by the term empowerment of Indigenous mothering, I considered the connection between educational aspirations as they relate to, and may be motivated by, one's role as a Mother, and how these aspirations extend to one's role as a community member and influence the work that may be aspired toward, within a community context. The voices of the women describe how the delivery of the course, based on Kim Anderson's theory of identity formation, provided them with something relevant and useful that they were able to apply at home and within the community. The women described being inspired by the curriculum, coming to a deeper understanding of the traumas Indigenous women have faced, and finding their own voices to continue on their own reclaiming journeys. Perhaps what was most profound was that the women were able to connect with that maternal energy that inspires Indigenous women's literature. For example, both women identified with that new feeling Roxanne described and shared about the impact this transformation has on their families and communities. The rippling effect of this impact extends the process of rebirth and renewal connecting us as Indigenous women.

I began writing this piece with the words of Janice Acoose who writes about the maternal energies who prompted her journey home. I will now end with a story shared by Beth Brant in *The Good Red Road: Journeys of Homecoming in Native Women's Writing*:

> In Mexico, a story is told of La Llorona. It is told that she wanders throughout the land, looking for her lost children. Her voice is the wind. She weeps and moans and calls to the children of her blood. She is the Indian, the mother of our blood, the grandmother of our hearts. She calls to us. "Come home, come home" she whispers, she cries, she calls to us. She comes into that sacred place we hold inviolate. She is birthing us in that sacred place. "Come home, come home" the voice of the umbilical, the whisper of the placenta. "Come home, come home." We listen. And we write. (205)

NOTES

[1] In honour of Janice Acoose's explanation of why she refuses to capitalize these institutions in her book, I have also chosen not to capitalize them here where I share her story.

[2] I have described the development of the Gidayaamin program elsewhere (Brant, 2012) and since have had the opportunity to work with the deliv-

ery of the program at Brock University. Here I briefly describe the foundation of the program in honouring the role of Aboriginal women as the first teachers of our future generations. The Gidayaamin program was built on the premise that supporting the educational success of Aboriginal mothers would, in turn, support and enhance the well-being of their children. I draw from this perspective to highlight the importance of nurturing women and mothers through education that promotes cultural identity and empowerment to support the well-being of women so that they are prepared emotionally, mentally, spiritually and physically to nurture and support themselves and their children. By encouraging a holistic educational environment that honours and supports familial realities, the intended outcomes of Gidayaamin are to empower Aboriginal women as a way to strengthen their families and by extension their communities (Brant, 2012).

WORKS CITED

Abbey, Sharon, and Andrea O'Reilly. *Redefining Motherhood: Changing Identities and Patterns.* Toronto: Second Story Press, 1998. Print.

Acoose, Janice (Misko-Kìsikàwihkwè). *Iskwewak Kah'Ki Yaw Ni Wahkomakanak: Neither Indian Princesses Nor Easy Squaws.* Toronto: Women's Press, 1995. Print.

Anderson, Kim. "Giving Life to the People: An Indigenous Ideology of Motherhood." *Maternal Theory: Essential Readings.* Ed. Andrea O'Reilly. Toronto: Demeter Press, 2007: 761–781. Print.

—. *A Recognition of Being: Reconstructing Native Womanhood.* Toronto: Sumach/Canadian Scholars' Press, 2000. Print.

Bédard, Renée Elizabeth. (Mzinegiizhigo-kwe) "An Anishinaabe-kwe Ideology on Mothering and Motherhood." *"Until our Hearts are on the Ground" Aboriginal Mothering, Oppression, Resistance and Rebirth.* Eds. D. Memee Lavell-Harvard and Jeannette Corbiere Lavell. Toronto: Demeter Press, 2006: 65–75. Print.

Brant, Beth. "The Good Red Road: Journeys of Homecoming in Native Women's Writing." *American Indian Culture and Research Journal* 21:1 (1997) 193–206. Print.

Brant, Jennifer, and Kim Anderson. "In the Scholarly Way: Making Generations of Inroads to Empowered Indigenous Mothering." *What do Mothers Need? Motherhood Activists and Scholars Speak out on Mater-*

nal Empowerment for the 21st Century. Ed. Andrea O'Reilly. Toronto: Demeter Press, 2012: 201–216. Print.

Brant, Jennifer. "A Vision of Culturally Responsive Programming for Aboriginal Women in University: An Examination of Aboriginal Women's Educational Narratives." *Well-being in the Urban Aboriginal Community.* Eds. David Newhouse, K. Fitzmaurice, T. McGuire-Adams and D. Jetté. Thompson Educational Publishing, 2012: 131–152. Print.

Carter, Sarah. "Categories and Terrains of Exclusion: Constructing the 'Indian Woman' in the Early Settlement Era in Western Canada." *In the Days of our Grandmothers: A Reader in Aboriginal Women's History in Canada.* Eds. Mary-Ellen Kelm and Lorna Townsend. Toronto: University of Toronto Press, 2008: 146–169. Print.

Carvell, Marlene. *Sweetgrass Basket.* Dutton Children's Books, 2005. Print.

Cull, Randi. "Aboriginal Mothering Under the State's Gaze." *"Until our Hearts are on the Ground" Aboriginal Mothering, Oppression, Resistance and Rebirth.* Eds. D. Memee Lavell-Harvard and Jeannette Corbiere Lavell. Toronto: Demeter Press, 2006: 141–156. Print.

Culleton, Beatrice. *In Search of April Raintree.* Winnipeg: Pemmican Publication, 1983. Print.

LaRocque, Emma. "Reflections on Cultural Continuity through Aboriginal Women's Writings." *Restoring the Balance: First Nations Women, Community, and Culture.* Eds. G. G. Valaskakis, M. D. Stout and A. Guimond. Winnipeg, MB: University of Manitoba Press. 2009: 149–174. Print.

Laronde, Sandra. *Sky Woman: Indigenous Women Who Have Shaped, Moved or Inspired Us.* Penticton, BC: Theytus Books, 2005. Print.

Lavell-Harvard, D. Memee, and Jeannette Corbiere Lavell. *"Until our Hearts are on the Ground" Aboriginal Mothering, Oppression, Resistance and Rebirth.* Toronto: Demeter Press, 2006. Print.

Maracle, Lee. *Daughters are Forever.* Vancouver: Polestar, 1992. Print.

Mercredi, Morningstar. "Honouring the Warrior Within." *Missing Women: Decolonization, Third Wave Feminisms, and Indigenous People of Canada and Mexico Conference.* 2008. Luther College, University of Regina. Regina, Saskatchewan. Keynote address.

—. *Morningstar: A Warrior's Spirit.* Regina: Coteau Books, 2006. Print.

Monture-Angus, Patricia. *Thunder in my Soul: A Mohawk Woman Speaks.* Halifax, NS: Fernwood, 1995. Print.

Sunseri, Lina. "Sky Woman Lives On: Contemporary Examples of Mothering the Nation." *First Voices: An Aboriginal Women's Reader*. Eds. Patricia Monture and Patricia McGuire. Toronto: Inanna, 2009. 54–62. Print.

Terzian, Sylvia. "Surviving my Mother's Legacy: Patriarchy, Colonialism, and Domestic Violence in Lee Maracle's 'Daughters are Forever.' " *Journal of the Motherhood Initiative for Research and Community Involvement* 10.2 (Fall/Winter 2008): 146–157. Print.

IV: Building on the Past to Create a Future

13.

Māori Mothering

Repression, Resistance and Renaissance

HELENE CONNOR—TE ATIAWA, NGATI RUANUI IWI
(TRIBES); NGATI RAHIRI AND NGATI TE WHITI HAPU
(SUBTRIBES)

INTRODUCTION

This chapter explores the experience of Māori[1,2] mothering in *Aotearoa*/New Zealand by weaving together a brief overview of the literature on Māori women's maternal bodies and Māori mothering, with autobiographical material about my Māori grandmother, Lulu Skelton (nee Coulter) (1909–1986), her *tupuna* (ancestors') and her *aitanga* (descendants') experiences of birthing and mothering. The articulation of Māori women's narratives and ways of knowing can be framed within *Mana Wahine* theory, a theory which acknowledges and affirms the *mana*, the status and prestige of *wahine*, (Māori women) (Pihama ix). *Mana wahine* theory remembers our *tupuna wahine* (female ancestors) and our *atua wahine* (female deities) and affirms Māori women and our *her*stories within Māori society and within *iwi* and *hapu* (Pihama ix). *Mana wahine theory* is also referred to as Māori feminist discourses, a theoretical and methodological approach that explicitly examines the intersection of being Māori and female and validates *mātauranga wāhine* (Māori women's knowledge) (Simmonds "*Mana wahine*: Decolonising politics" 11).

My grandmother, Lulu, had *whakapapa* (genealogy) links to *Te Atiawa iwi* (tribe) and *Ngati Rahiri hapu* (subtribe). Her husband, my grandfather, Lesley (known as Mick) Skelton (1902–1980) had *whakapapa* links

Figure 1: Unknown Photographer. Lulu Skelton (nee Coulter) aged approximately eight months, seated on a chair draped with two *whanau* (family) *korowai* (cloak). Circa 1909.

to *Te Atiawa* and *Ngati Ruanui iwi* and *Ngati Te Whiti hapu*. Lulu and Mick had their first *taitamaiti* (child), Tui Ramare Skelton, in 1930; the first of eleven *tamariki* (children). Of the eleven *tamariki* Lulu gave birth to between 1930 and 1944, seven were born at the homestead on the family farm in the small settlement of Motunui in Northern Taranaki. The remaining four were birthed at maternity centres in either New Plymouth or Waitara[3].

This chapter has been organised into three sections. Section one examines Māori mothering within traditional Māori society and discusses the importance of *tupuna wahine* and *atua wahine*. The second section discusses the impact of colonial and European influences on Māori society and culture and consequent repression of traditional mothering. The final section introduces the Māori Renaissance and the resurgence of Māori mothering and birthing practices within the postcolonial context. Within this context, many of the *aitanga* of Lulu and Mick Skelton have created a space for engaging with the complex intersections of colonization, post-colonization and gender and are attempting to re-define the Māori maternal body and birthing practices as well as mothering *tikanga* (culture), which was eroded during the colonization period.

TRADITIONAL MĀORI MOTHERING

One of the central principles of traditional Māori child rearing was the conviction that children were gifts from the *atua* (spiritual beings). *Tupuna* were also viewed as being intrinsic to the *whanau*, and the elders were revered members of the *whanau*, the *hapu*, and wider *iwi*. The socialisation and nurturing of children within traditional Māori society was shared amongst many family members (both kin and non-kin), and the notion of a nuclear family was anathema. Whanau organisation was modelled on the cosmic *whanau*, where *Papatūānuku*, the Earth Mother and *Ranginui*, the Sky Father, were considered to be the primal parents, although, not necessarily the sole caregivers (Jenkins and Harte xi). Knowledge about the primal *whakapapa*, beginning with *Io*, the Supreme Being, and the cosmic realms of the *atua* (deity) would have been well engrained in both Lulu and Mick's *tupuna*, and they would have been familiar with Māori mythology creation stories about *Ranginui* and *Papatūānuku* and their children.

For Māori, and other first peoples, the earth is sacred and considered a precious gift. In *te reo Māori*, (Māori language) it is no coincidence that the word, "*whenua*" means both land and placenta. The land offers both nourishment and sustenance, just as the placenta does to the developing foetus. After a child was born and the *whenua* expelled, it was returned to *Papatūānuku* as a sign that the child would continue to grow and develop, just as he or she did inside the mother's uterus. In traditional Māori society, the *whenua* would be buried in a specific area of land that served to legitimate the child's *turangawaewae* (place to stand) within their *iwi* and *hapu*. From a Māori perspective, the land and the people are intimately connected. "*Te whenua ki te whenua*. The body and the land are one. There is no separation" (Potiki & Kahukiwa 62). The close, spiritual relationship with the land stemmed from the traditional concept of the origins of humankind having derived from the union of the Earth Mother, *Papatūānuku*, with the Sky Father, *Ranginui*(Sinclair 86).

The creation stories and the intimate connection to *Papatūānuku*, as both Earth Mother in the cosmological sense, and as *whenua* in the secular sense, had a profound impact on traditional birthing and mothering. As Wikitoria August (120), notes, there are a number of cultural practices, or *tikanga*, associated with women's bodies and the birthing process that have traditionally been handed down from the creation narratives connected with *Papatūānuku*. From *Papatūānuku* came life, and the first woman *Hineahuone*, who was part atua and part human (Jenkins and

Harte xi), and from this association between *Papatūānuku* and her daughter, *Hineahuone, tikanga* was put in place to protect the life-giving properties of women.

In traditional society, the maternal body was perceived as being in a state of *tapu* (sacredness), where there were certain restrictions put in place to protect the *hapu* (pregnant) woman and her unborn child. The removal of *tapu* would take place approximately one week after the child had been born via *tohi*, a ritual ceremony performed in flowing water, where the child would be dedicated to a particular *atua* by immersion in the water or by sprinkling him or her with water (Papakura 113).

When the time came for the mother to *whakamamae* (go into labour) her mother, grandmother and other relatives were with her, especially if it was her first child (Papakura 114). *Karakia* (sacred chants) would be performed during childbirth and after the labour. Many of the traditional *karakia* were associated with *Hine-te-iwaiwa*[4], the *atua* associated with childbirth, and the Moon (Potiki and Kahukiwa 91). *Oriori* (lullabies) were chanted to the infants to welcome them into their *whanau* and *hapu*. The *oriori* were commonly composed by the child's *whanau*.

After the baby was born, it would be very gently shaken, with its feet up and its head down, to loosen the *nanu* (secretions) in its mouth and nose. If a child did not cry when it was born, it was firmly but gently shaken to make it cry. If anything was needed to soften the *pito* (umbilical cord), a piece of softened flax or soft cloth was soaked in the oil from the kernel of the *Titoki* berry[5] and placed over the *pito* (Papakura 115). While one of the birthing supporters would look after the new born baby, others would support the mother until she was ready to expel the *whenua* (placenta). The *whenua* would then be buried in an area significant to the *hapu*, a practice that reinforced the relationship between the newborn infant and the land. Newborn babies fed from the breast soon after birth, and were generally breast fed until the child was two years old. After the first trimester, the *hapu* woman's *ū* (breasts) and *matamata* (nipples) were massaged during the remaining months of her pregnancy to ensure the *wai-ū* (milk) flowed easily and readily (Papakura 117).

Lulu and Mick's *tupuna wahine* would have been familiar with the traditional birthing practices and rituals associated with labour and the care of newborn infants. While there is little written history of their *tupuna wahine*, my grandfather's great grandmother Ngapei Ngatata (born circa 1811), who was the fifth child of the *rangatira* (chief) Ngatata-i-te-Rangi[6] and Whetowheto of Ngati Ruanui, is mentioned in the memoirs of her En-

glish, common-law husband, John George Cooke.[7] Ngapei had two children with John George Cooke: Te Piki Ngatata (1844–1932), also known as
Mary Ann Cooke, and George Gray Cooke (1848-1865). As both of these
children were born in the mid-1840s, there can be little doubt that Ngapei
birthed them in a traditional manner. It is also highly likely that she chanted
traditional *oriori* to her children within John George Cooke's hearing. Indeed, the 19th century novelist, Geraldine Jewsbury, records visiting him
and his English wife, Margaret, in London and hearing him singing lullabies
in *te reo Māori* (probably learned from Ngapei) to their first born daughter,
Harriet Marcia Cooke (born 20 March 1869).[8]

Mothering within traditional Māori society was carried out within the
context of the wider *whanau*, with children being raised by multiple "parents;" including biological parents, grandparents, uncles, aunts, cousins
and siblings (Jenkins and Harte xiii). My grandparents, Lulu and Mick Skelton, raised their *whanau*, incorporating many traditional Māori parenting
practices within an extended *whanau* environment, where Lulu's mother
Ngakuru Rona (1878-1943), and Mick's step-mother, Tangiora Rona (1874-
1937) lived with the *whanau* and assisted with child birthing and child rearing. Ngakuru also maintained her own home, and would often have one
or two of her grandchildren, nieces and nephews stay with her. Ngakuru
was an industrious woman who maintained a large garden, and she enjoyed
teaching the children how to grow vegetables, how to gather *kai moana*
(food from the sea) and she would also take them whitebaiting[9] using the
traditional nets made from stripped flax to catch these small fish. Having
Tangiora and Ngakuru live with the *whanau* was one of the ways my grandmother was able to incorporate traditional mothering within the wider extended *whanau*, providing the children with multiple carers and first teachers, which was invaluable when it came to passing on traditional knowledge and *tikanga*. At the same time, though, many of the traditional Māori
methods of child-raising were being eroded, as, by the early twentieth century, not all Māori had access to land, and were not in the fortunate position
of being able to have extended *whanau* live within a communal family home
setting. Racial amalgamation and interracial marriage also eroded much of
traditional Māori kinship practices and family structures. Indeed, as Wanhalla (68) asserts, racial amalgamation can be viewed as an instrument of
colonization.

REPRESSION OF TRADITIONAL MĀORI MOTHERING

The colonization period of *Aotearoa*/New Zealand had a profound impact on identity and cultural, as did Christianization. Christian missionaries, through such organisations as CMS (Church Missionary Society),[10] encouraged "regular" marriage between *Pākehā* and Māori converts to Christianity as a way of "civilizing" and controlling, and Christian marriage was put forward as a model of appropriate gendered behaviour within the domestic sphere (Wanhalla 45). European wives of the missionaries had a significant role in encouraging Christian marriage, both interracial and between Māori men and women. The missionary wives viewed themselves as "saving" Māori women from what was perceived as their "natural promiscuity" and immorality. "Saving" would take the form of the missionary wives teaching Māori women Christian values, domestic chores and "mother-craft" from a European perspective, all of which insidiously eroded traditional Māori mothering and child-care practices (Connor *Ko te hononga mauri* 21).

Māori culture and identity was further eroded after The Treaty of Waitangi[11] was signed on 6 February 1840 between the British Crown and the *tangata whenua* (Māori Indigenous peoples). The Treaty of Waitangi considered all inhabitants of *Aotearoa*/New Zealand to be under British sovereignty. The Treaty had originally given the British Crown the exclusive right to purchase Māori land. However, in 1844, Governor Robert FitzRoy gave in to demands from both Māori and settlers and waived this right, and, consequently, private land purchases were allowed. Where the Māori view of the land was a deeply spiritual one, closely connected with *Papatūānuku*, European settlers viewed land as a commodity. These starkly different attitudes towards land were to cause many misunderstandings and conflicts between Māori and the settler population, together with a systematic processing of legislation which eventually eroded Māori land ownership significantly (Connor *Ko te hononga mauri* 4). As Māori land was sold or confiscated, or passed to the ownership of European husbands, traditional ways of living gradually eroded. Over time, the spiritual connection to the land became less powerful, as many Māori took up European religious beliefs and learned the English language and European methods of agriculture, as well as learning new trades.

A further impact on Māori cultural erosion, as previously alluded to, was racial amalgamation. This belief permeated settler society during the colonization period and was based on Governor Hobson's much quoted phrase at the signing of the Treaty of Waitangi, "*He iwi tahi tatou,*" we are one people. Becoming "one people" ultimately translated as Māori becoming brown *Pakeha* (European), living under British rule, law and culture.

Within the context of my grandparent's family lives, remnants of the colonization period were clearly in evidence. Both my grandparents spoke English to their children, although they would *korero* (speak) in *te reo Māori* with older *whanau* members. Christianity had also replaced traditional spirituality. My grandfather's great grandmother, Ngapei Ngatata, converted to Catholicism in the 1860s following the lead of her brother, Wi Tako Ngatata.[12] The conversation to the Catholic faith may have been influenced by some parallels between Catholicism and Māori spirituality. For example, the saints, who are predominant features of the Catholic Church, can be likened to the atua. As there was a different saint for practically every aspect of life, so, too, was there an atua. Similarly, as there were various blessings and prayers for a number of aspects of every-day life in the Catholic Church there were also parallels with Māori spirituality, where prayers or *karakia* were also offered for the daily mundane tasks.

Catholicism, however, was not the only Western religion the family took up. Ngapei's daughter, Te Piki Ngatata (Mary Ann Cooke) became an Anglican when she married Sergeant George August Skelton in 1868, and their descendants tended to belong to the Church of England. Ngakuru Rona, my grandmother's mother had some affiliations with the Māori Mission Chapel at Waitara and followed the leaders of the Parihaka[13] non-violent movement, Te Whiti o Rongomai and Tohu Kākahi, who drew on both ancestral and Christian teachings to offer spiritual and political leadership to their followers.

While Western religion has replaced some of the traditional spiritual beliefs within my *whanau*, their cultural identity as Māori was very much reinforced by their hold on traditional land. This land provided a subsistence livelihood as it supported a small dairy farm and produced milk and cream. The family also had access to *kai moana* (seafood) at Turangi beach, which was within walking distance. Family dynamics were played out in *tuakana* and *teina* relationships, where the older children, the *tuakana*, looked out for the younger children, the *teina*. As there were fourteen years difference between my grandmother's first child and her last, the *tuakana-teina* principle was well utilized and the older children had the responsibility of both caring for and teaching younger children. One of my aunts, Pam Bruce, recalls the *tuakana-teina* principle she grew up with:

I enjoyed my childhood; we had responsibilities beyond our years heaped on us and we were disciplined… There were jobs to do and we knew that. We knew what each of us was responsible for and we got on and did it. The big kids would help the little kids. We had a coal range which seemingly never went out; the heart of the family centered around the fire place in the kitchen and everything happened there. The older children would help bath the babies in front of the fire. The endless meals were cooked there and it provided warmth and comfort for the whole family and we all became adept at lighting it and judging the various temperatures required for baking and cooking. We had rosters to milk the cows and the older children would teach the younger ones how to help with the cows and to help in the garden and especially to help with household chores, dishes, getting meals and cleaning. My mother always did the washing but we girls always did the ironing. My mother had a huge vegetable garden which kept us and all our town friends who visited supplied with vegetables. We had lots of chooks (chickens) so we never wanted for eggs and poultry and of course we had milk and cream and butter from the cows. We also lived about a mile from the beach and we were able to go and collect seafood, pipis, mussels and paua and of course fish. There were special places to catch flounder and always there was snapper.

Gathering food, whether it were from the garden or the sea, was always done together as a family. One of my grandfather's nieces, Kura Taylor, who spent a lot of time at the farm with my grandparents and their children (her first cousins), can remember my grandmother's mother, Ngakuru, preparing and eating traditional Māori fare: Old Ngakuru had a pot for cooking what she called *kol dol dos* (sea anemone)… They were beautiful colours; red and blue and orange. There was a special method for cooking *kol dol dos*. They used to take about three days (Connor *Kura: A life history* 6).

Kura can also remember Ngakuru cooking Karaka berries. Again, there was a special method for cooking these berries, which were poisonous unless cooked in the correct way. Both Kura and Pam can recall how Māori conservation methods were put into place. Gathering *kai moana*, for example, was carried out only two days before or after the full or new moons. Families would only ever take as much as was required and they never ate on the beach to ensure debris was not left to pollute the remaining shellfish. If the children looked like they were about to stumble into an area that was *tapu* or out of bounds, Ngakuru would call out, "There's a *taniwha* (mythical water creature) over there" and the children would quickly retreat.

My grandmother and her extended *whanau* were able to continue with many of the traditional child rearing practices because they lived in a rural area and had their own land, which was a huge boon during the Depression years, allowing them to be self-sufficient. Nevertheless, my grandmother was not immune to the discourses of biomedical baby feeding and the medicalization of childbirth, which impinged on the majority of mothers in the early 1900s in New Zealand with the advent of the Royal New Zealand Plunket Society, established in 1907, by Dr Frederic Truby King. King aimed to promote the health of infants and reduce infant mortality, through the education and guidance of mothers, by nurses trained in "mother-craft" (Bryder 184). The "mother-craft" instruction provided by the Plunket nurses included baby nutrition regimens for both breastfed and formula-fed babies. Babies were to be fed at four hourly intervals with no more than five feeds per day, and overnight feeding was expressly prohibited. These rules remained in place for 40 years, mirroring Truby King's belief in a standardised, scientific approach to baby feeding (McBride-Henry and Clendon 184). As my grandmother and the majority of Māori lived in rural areas in the early to mid-1900s, Māori infants were not usually visited by Plunket nurses during this period. Nevertheless, the Plunket Society's sphere of influence and ideology on "mother-craft" spread to the rural areas. Prior to 1920, there was considerable concern about the high mortality rate for Māori children and babies, with approximately half of all children dying before the age of four. The majority of the deaths during this period of time have been attributed to infectious diseases, such as tuberculosis, but also to malnutrition and birthing difficulties (McBride-Henry and Clendon 5). To address the high death rate amongst children, many mothers and *whanau* members began to imbibe the discourses of "mother-craft" which expounded that success at raising and feeding healthy babies required specialty language and knowledge within the domain of maternity health care professionals, such as registered midwives, doctors and Plunket nurses. In effect, traditional Māori maternal knowledge was eroded as these values and beliefs were undermined by twentieth century discursive constructions of childbirth and childcare.

When her first child was born in 1930, my grandmother, Lulu Skelton, had a home birth with her mother and aunt in attendance. The placenta was taken away and buried and her mother recited some traditional *karakia* to welcome the new infant into the *whanau*. The newly born infant was breastfed and was looked after by her mother, grandmother, aunties and cousins. My grandmother's next six children were also birthed at home. However, by the time her eighth child, Janet Erina, was born in 1940, over 80 per cent of child births in *Aotearoa*/New Zealand were occurring in maternity hospitals. My grandmother was encouraged to have this baby and also her last three children, in maternity hospitals. I can recall a conversation with my grandmother about her experience of giving birth to her youngest child in hospital. She spoke with indignation at how she had been treated. She was made to take a bath on admission, even though she told the medical staff the baby was on its way. However, the staff insisted she take the bath and the baby was born in the bath. My grandmother would say she was one of the first women to have a water birth. She always believed, however, that she was told to have a bath because they saw her as a "dirty Māori." Her new baby was taken away to be cleaned and weighed and to my grandmother's horror, she was only allowed to see the baby at feeding times. Her memories are in alignment with the regimes of maternity hospitals of the 1940s and the influence of the Plunket Society. Women generally stayed for fourteen days after giving birth, and, during this time, they were allowed only limited access to their babies in order to establish regimental feeding times and to assess the amount consumed by babies, who were weighed after each feed.

My grandmother negotiated her way through traditional Māori mothering practices and the twentieth century discursive constructions of childbirth and childcare espoused by the Plunket Society. When her own daughters married and had children of their own during the 1950s, 1960s and 1970s, all gave birth in maternity hospitals or maternity annexes. Of my grandmother's twenty eight grandchildren (born between 1954 and 1975), over half were bottle fed. Not one of these grandchildren had their *whenua* returned to the land. However, as the grandchildren began to have children of their own, within the context of post-colonization and the social movement known as the Māori Renaissance, many of the traditional birthing practices have been revived.

Figure 2: Unknown Photographer. Mick and Lulu Skelton with their eleven children. 1947. Back Row: Mick; Pamela Mereaina; Lesley Tangiora; Chloe Ropa; Tui Ramare. Front Row: Melvin; Raewyn; Elaine Pikitu; Robert; Elspeth; Lulu; Janet Erina; Anthony

RENAISSANCE OF MĀORI MOTHERING AND BIRTHING PRACTICES

The Māori Renaissance is a social movement which began in the 1970s and promoted the retention and revival of the Māori language and Māori culture. One of the most influential and significant initiatives to come out of the Māori Renaissance was the establishment of the *Kōhanga Reo* movement[14] (language nests) in 1981. Maori elders from all over the country who could speak *te reo Māori* were encouraged to teach the language to *tamariki* in the newly established *kōhanga*. My grandmother found she had retained considerable knowledge of *te reo Māori* and began speaking it again in her sixties. She would spend several mornings a week at *Kōhanga o Waitara* at our *marae* (meeting place), *Owae Waitara Marae*, helping with the revitalisation of the language and culture. Her involvement in the *Kōhanga Reo* also enabled her to model traditional mothering and grand-mothering, which was carried out in the context of the wider *whanau*, with children being taught *tikanga* and language by multiple "parents," who were not necessarily blood kin. Ensuring *te reo Māori* does not become an extinct language has been paramount for many Māori *whanau* over the last several decades, and parenting, for many, has been heavily involved with the *Kōhanga Reo* movement and other Maori education initiatives, where mothering, parenting and grand-parenting have been contextualized within an extended *whanau*.

The Māori Renaissance also created a space for Māori to develop uniquely Māori theoretical perspectives, such as *Kaupapa Māori* and *Mana Wahine* Theory. *Mana Wahine* theory was also influenced by several feminist theories, including Black feminism and Women of Colour feminism. Under the lens of *Kaupapa Māori* and *Mana Wahine* theory, the complex intersections of colonization and gender have been scrutinised in an attempt to re-define the Māori maternal body and to revive traditional Māori birthing and mothering *tikanga* (culture).

Kaupapa Māori theory has been enormously influential in *Aotearoa/* New Zealand and has enabled Māori and non-Māori to carry out research from a Māori perspective. *Kaupapa Māori* theory has four central features:

1. Is related to "being"

2. Is connected to Māori philosophy and principles

3. Takes for granted the validity and legitimacy of, and the importance of, Māori language and culture

4. Is concerned with "the struggle for autonomy over our own cultural well-being" (Smith 185)

Each of one of these four central features is related to the Māori Renaissance in which the resurgence of Māori mothering and birthing can be located. The personal narrative of my grandmother can also be contextualized within the Māori Renaissance and *Kaupapa Māori* theory. Her story discusses "being Māori" and having a Māori cultural identity across an historical time frame dating back to the times of her *tupuna*, through to the present day. The construction of "being Māori" within differing historical and social contexts demonstrates the evolving place of Māori within

Aotearoa/New Zealand, from pre-European contact, through to colonization and the relative cultural suppression during the years of assimilation
and amalgamation polices, through to the reclamation of Māori cultural
identity during the Māori Renaissance, and beyond.

While colonization eroded many of the traditional Māori narratives,
the Māori Renaissance has been instrumental in reviving them, and there
has been a resurgence in Māori spirituality and a greater acknowledgment
of traditional mythology in recent times. A return to ancient mythology
is not an uncommon response when a society is in transition, as with contemporary Māori society and its movement of cultural reclamation. The
reconnection with Papatūānuku has been part of this response on both a
spiritual level and a symbolic one. Naomi Simmonds, (Mana Wahine geographies) argues that Māori women's maternal bodies are intimately tied
to Papatūānuku in a way that challenges the oppositional distinctions between mind/body and biology/social inscription. She states:

> The colonization of Māori women's bodies and bodily
> tikanga has denied many women this relationship. Further-
> more, Māori women have had to adopt Western practices
> and spaces of birth and afterbirth. Despite this, many Māori
> women are regaining a degree of control over their materni-
> ties. By re-positioning Māori bodily tikanga, they are entering
> into discourses of critique about dominant birthing practices
> and ideologies (Simmonds 5).

This is certainly the case for myself and many of my cousins within our
extended whanau. Many have sought out a Māori midwife to facilitate pre-
natal care and birthing within a framework which acknowledges the validity
and significance of whanau and reaffirms Māori maternal epistemology and
knowledge of whakapapa.

Wikitoria August (117) argues that Kaupapa Māori theory can produce
research that respects and nurtures Māori practices and she advocates a
Māori perspective that constructs Māori women as being connected to the
Atua as powerful, sacred and life giving. Within the Māori Renaissance and
postcolonial period, Māori artist, Robyn Kahukiwa, has been instrumental in creating August's call for reconceptualised constructions of Māori
women as powerful and staunch. In the 1980s, Kahukiwa created a series
of paintings and drawings based on the Māori myths which make up a collection entitled Wahine Toa (women of strength). Kahukiwa's interpreta-

tions of the female deities can be viewed as a feminist reading of traditional mythology where she reinterprets and portrays the female atua in the series as being just as powerful and equal counterparts to the male atua. The Wahine Toa series of paintings depicted by Robyn Kahukiwa can also be read as symbolic of Mana Wahine Māori and Māori feminist ideals which have striven to reinvigorate Māori women's mana and aspirations and self-determination. Self-determination for Māori women affirms mana wahine and is achieved through connection to our land, language and culture. The right to self-determination was, for many Māori women, an impossibility. For those women, (and indeed, men), who lived through assimilationist policies of the early twentieth century, the right to speak our own language, practice our own spiritual beliefs and live our own tikanga was frequently denied. The Māori Renaissance has provided a space to address these issues.

For Māori feminists the colonial history of *Aotearoa*/New Zealand has served as a force against which an anti-colonial Māori identity has been defined, based on traditional constructions of selfhood and dependent upon "difference." Implicit in Māori feminist politics is the confrontation and exploration of colonialism. One of the most insidious ways colonization has impacted upon Māori women has been through the notion of embodied oppression where the differential ciphering of the Māori body, through racializing and sexualizing discourses, transformed gender roles and relations, eroding and destabilizing Māori women's bases of power. One of the agendas of Māori feminism is to re-inscribe the Māori female body and re-establish bases of power for *wahine Māori*. Discourses around the body as articulate and transforming are situated within notions of decolonization. Autobiographical research into both historical and contemporary Māori figures can demonstrate the impact of colonization on Māori women's lives so that the often abhorrent events of our colonial past are not forgotten. It can also promote the resurgence of *mana wahine* by raising awareness of the accomplishments of Māori women and providing revisionist her-stories which demonstrate the power and status of Māori women prior to colonization. One example is *The Old Time Māori*, originally written in 1930 by Makereti Papakura, a rare example of an ethnographic text researched and authored by a Māori woman of that era. Reprinted in 1986 with an introduction by Māori scholar, Dr. Ngahuia Te Awekotuku, it is now celebrated as a classic reference for information on traditional Māori society, particularly with regard to matters pertaining to women such as childbirth, menstruation, marriage and child rearing.

Māori women have always had *mana*. The historical experiences of colonization, with its tiers of patriarchy, racism and capitalism, resulted in a temporary suppression of *mana* for many Māori women, but by no means for all. The resurgence of *mana wahine Māori* evident in contemporary society is indicative of decolonization and the collective resistance of all indigenous people who are attempting to dismantle power structures that marginalized and eroded our cultural identity.

Women's *her*stories and personal narratives offer a space for Māori to reclaim cultural identity and mana within the context of *Mana Wahine* theory. *Mana Wahine* theory, as Pihama suggests, affirms Māori women's *mana* and uplifts the status of Māori women. The snippets of my grandmother, Lulu Skelton's, personal narrative, which have been woven through this chapter, have not only provided some insights into her life as a mother, they have also affirmed her life and her *mana* as a Māori woman.

Soon after my daughter, Carabelle Tangiora Connor, was born in 1998, I took her *whenua* back to an area of Ngati Rahihri *hapu* land at Motunui in Taranaki, where traditionally, the placenta would be buried. Invoking ancient *karakia* her *whenua* went back to *Papatūānuku*, literally and symbolically cementing her relationship to her *tūrangawaewae* and her home space. It is my hope that she, in turn, will take the *whenua* of her children, yet to be born, back to this same sacred place.

He ira tangata, He ira atua

A human life force, A source of the divine

GLOSSARY

Māori term	English translation
Aitanga	Descendants
Aotearoa	Māori name for New Zealand (meaning the land of the long white cloud)
Aroha	Love
Atua	Spiritual beings, deities
Atua wahine	Female deities
Hapu	Sub-tribe; pregnant
Io	The Supreme Being
Iwi	Tribe
Kai moana	Food from the sea

Māori term	English translation
Karakia	Sacred chants
Kōhanga Reo	Language Nest
Korero	Speak
Korowai	Cloak
Mana	Prestige, status
Mana Wahine	Prestige and status of women
Māori	Indigenous people of *Aotearoa*/New Zealand
Marae	Traditional Māori meeting place
Matamata	Nipples
Mātauranga	Māori knowledge
Nanu	Secretions
Noa	Ordinary, free from restrictions
Oriori	Lullaby
Pakeha	People of European descent
Papatūānuku	Earth mother
Pito	Umbilical chord
Ranginui	Sky father
Taitamaiti	Child
Tamariki	Children
Tangata Whenua	Māori indigenous peoples of *Aotearoa*/New Zealand; literally means "people of the land"
Taniwha	Mythical creatures that live in rivers and the sea
Tapu	Sacred, taboo
Te reo Māori	Māori language
Teina	Younger kin or non-kin family member
Tikanga	Cultural practices
Tohi	Ritual ceremony over a child in flowing water while petitioning the *atua* (deity) to endow the child with the desired mental and physical qualities.
Tuakana	Older kin or non-kin family member
Tupuna	Ancestors
Tupuna wahine	Female ancestors
Turangawaewae	A place to stand
Ū	Breasts
Wahine	Women
Wahine toa	Women of strength

Māori term	English translation
Wai-ū	Breast milk
Whakapapa	Genealogy
Whakawhanau	Giving birth
Whanau	Family
Whanaugatanga	Extended family
Whenua	Land; placenta

NOTES

[1] Māori terms are used throughout the chapter and in-text translations are supplied the first time the Māori word appears. A glossary is also provided at the end of the chapter.

[2] The term Māori refers to the Indigenous people of *Aotearoa*/New Zealand. *Aotearoa* is the Māori name for New Zealand, which means the land of the long white cloud.

[3] Taranaki is situated on the west coast of the lower half of the North Island of *Aotearoa*/New Zealand. The province of Taranaki takes its name from the spectacular volcanic cone, Mount Taranaki, which dominates the region. New Plymouth is the largest city within the Taranaki province. Waitara is a small town in Taranaki.

[4] *Hine-te-iwaiwa* was the deity associated with the Moon and childbirth, and work associated with women such as weaving. http://nzetc.victoria. ac.nz/tm/scholarly/tei-BesAstro-t1-body-d1-d5.html

[5] The Titoki tree is indigenous to *Aotearoa*/New Zealand. Oil from the Titoki berries were frequently used by Māori for the skin and hair. Refer to: http://www.arbortechnix.co.nz/tree-botanics/s-z/titoki

[6] Born around 1790, Ngatata-i-te-Rangi was the son of Te Rangiwhetiki and Pakanga. Through his mother, Pakanga, he was an influential *rangatira* (chief) in the Ngati Te Whiti hapu of Te Atiawa. He was a signatory of the Treaty of Waitangi and signed the Henry Williams copy on 29 April 1840, aboard the schooner, *Ariel*, at Port Nicholson, Wellington (Orange 148).

[7] John George Cooke (1819–1880) was the son of Christopher Cooke and Elizabeth Austen (who was related to the English novelist, Jane Austen, through her father, Francis Motley Austen). He came to New Zealand in March 1841 aboard the *Amelia Thompson* and returned to England in 1850. He married Margaret Townsend Ward (1837–1912) in 1868 and had four children with her. He had friendships with a number of 19th century authors

including Geraldine Jewsbury, Charles Dickens and Thomas Carlyle and his wife, Jane Welsh Carlyle.

[8] As an aside, it is pertinent to note that the interracial "marriage" between Ngapei Ngatata and John George Cooke was sanctioned within the colonial period of the 1840s in which they cohabitated. Interracial marriage was never legally prohibited in New Zealand and as Wanhalla (47) points out racial amalgamation was a fundamental aspect of the colonial project during the 1830s and 1840s. Indeed, New Zealand's marriage laws were fostered by a philosophy of racial amalgamation with an underpinning discourse of creating a nation of social intermixing where Māori and non-Māori could become "one people." Racial amalgamation was also connected to the civil rights and sexual freedom of the male European colonizers, especially control over marital property, land ownership and inheritance and eventually had serious implications for Māori communities and traditional Māori culture.

[9] Whitebait are small fish (about 5 centimetres long) that swim upstream from the sea, each spring.

[10] Samuel Marsden was one of the key figures in establishing the CMS in New Zealand. He gave his first sermon on Christmas Day, 1814. He believed Maori would convert to Christianity through teaching them useful trades and agriculture. His methods were relatively unsuccessful as there were no Maori baptisms before 1830. http://www.nzhistory.net.nz/culture/missionaries/marsden-and-cms

[11] Approximately 40 Māori chiefs signed the Treaty of Waitangi on 6 February 1840 and by September 1840 another 500 chiefs around the country had signed. Almost all of the chiefs signed copies of the Māori text of the Treaty. http://www.nzhistory.net.nz/politics/treaty/treaty-timeline/treaty-events-1800-1849

[12] Wi Tako Ngata (?–1887) was a well-known Te Atiawa leader. In 1872 he was appointed to the Legislative Council, one of the first Maori to be a member. http://www.dnzb.govt.nz/en/biographies/1n10/ngatata-wiremu-tako

[13] Parihaka is a small Taranaki coastal Māori settlement, located 55 km south west of New Plymouth. Its leaders, Te Whiti o Rongomai and Tohu Kākahi were committed to non-violent action in order to resist the invasion of their estates and to protect Māori independence. http://parihaka.com/

[14] Te Kōhanga Reo was initiated in 1981 by the Department of Māori Affairs in response to Māori concern to ensure the continuing survival of the Māori language. Te Kōhanga Reo was also behind the Māori Language Act of

1987 which established the Māori Language Commission and saw Māori becoming an official language in *Aotearoa*/New Zealand.

WORKS CITED

August, Wikitoria. "Māori women: Bodies, Spaces, Sacredness and Mana." *New Zealand Geographer* 61 (2005): 117–123. Print.

Bruce, P. "My Childhood". Unpublished essay. 2004. Print.

Bryder, Linda. "The Plunket Society: Part of the New Zealand Way of Life?" *Australian Historical Studies* 1.6. (2008): 183–198. Print.

Cooke, John G. *Reminiscences of John George Cooke. Vol 2, 1839–1850*. MS-Papers-0605-08, Alexander Turnbull Library, Wellington, New Zealand. 1876. Print.

Connor, D. Helene. "Kura: A life history." Unpublished research project, Massey University, Palmerston North, New Zealand. 1992. Print.

—. "Ko te hononga mauri, ko te hononga wairua, ko te hononga mana o te wahine: The Resurgence of Mana Wahine: A Response to Prisonization: Histories, Reflections and Stories". Unpublished Master's thesis, University of Auckland, Auckland, New Zealand. 1994. Print.

Establishing the Church Missionary Society. Ministry for Culture and Heritage. 20 December 2012. Web.

Hine-te-iwaiwa. 20 August 2011. Web.

Jenkins, Kuni and Helen Mountain Harte. *Traditional Māori Parenting: An Historical Review of Literature of Traditional Māori Child Rearing Practices in Pre-European Times*. Auckland: Te Kahui Ririki, 2011. Print.

McBride-Henry, Karen and Jill Clendon. "Breastfeeding in New Zealand from Colonization until the Year 1980: An Historical Review". *New Zealand College of Midwives Journal* 1.11 (2010): 5–9. Academic Search Premier. EBSCO database. Unitec Lib. 23 April 2013. Print.

Kahukiwa, Robyn, and Patricia Grace. *Wahine Toa Women of Māori Myth*. Viking Pacific, Auckland. 1984. Print.

Kōhanga Reo Movement. Te Kōhanga Reo National Trust. 2013. Web.

Ngatata, Wiremu Tako'. 30 October 2012. Web.

Orange, Claudia. *An Illustrated History of the Treaty of Waitangi*. Wellington: Allen and Unwin, 1990. Print.

Papakura, M. "The Old Time." New Zealand Electronic Text Collection

- Te Pūhikotuhi o Aotearoa, part of Victoria University of Wellington Library. Web. 11 July 2013.

Parihaka. http://parihaka.com/. Web.

Pere, Rangimarie Rose. *Te Wheke: A Celebration of Infinite Wisdom*. Gisborne, NZ: Ako Ako Global Learning, 1991. Print.

Pihama, Lionie. "Tīhei Mauri Ora: Honouring our voices. Mana Wahine as a Kaupapa Māori Theoretical Framework." Unpublished Doctoral thesis. University of Auckland, 2001. Print.

Potiki, Roma and Robyn Kahukiwa. *Oriori: A Māori Child is Born*. Auckland: Tandem Press, 1999. Print.

Simmonds, Naomi B. "Mana Wahine Geographies: Spiritual, Spatial and Embodied Understandings of Papatūānuku." Unpublished Master of Science thesis. Waikato University, 2009. Print.

Simmonds, Naomi. "Mana wahine: Decolonising Politics." *Women's Studies Journal* 25.2 (2011): 11–25. Print.

Sinclair, Douglas. "Land: Māori View and European Response." *Te Ao Hurihuri: Aspects of Māoritanga*. Ed. M. King. Auckland: Longman Paul. 1981. Print.

Smith, Linda, T. *Decolonizing Methodologies: Research and Indigenous Peoples*. Otago: University of Otago Press. 2001. Print.

Titoki tree. Web. 11 July 2013.

Treaty events 1800–49—Treaty timeline. Web. 11 July 2013.

Wanhalla, Angela. *Matters of the Heart: A history of Interracial Marriage in New Zealand*. Auckland: Auckland University Press. 2013. Print.

14.

Nimâmâsak

The Legacy of First Nations Women Honouring Mothers and Motherhood

LORENA FONTAINE, LISA FORBES, WENDY MCNAB, LISA
MURDOCK AND ROBERTA STOUT

This chapter is dedicated, in memory, to our dear friend and sister digital storyteller, Claudette Lizette Michell (1966–2012), "Rattle That Glows in the Dark" and "Turtle Shooting Star Woman." Claudette was an exceptionally beautiful woman who shared many precious and valuable moments with all of us, individually and together as a group. She was an excellent mother and grandmother who clearly demonstrated that children truly are our gifts from the Creator, our little teachers, intended to be loved, nurtured and cherished. Claudette was our symbol of strength, courage and resilience. She inspired us with hope—for our future generations of children, for the unity of our families and for Mother Earth to heal. Claudette, like all of the teachable moments she shared with us, will be forever remembered with love, honour and respect.

INTRODUCTION

In the fall of 2010, Prairie Women's Health Centre of Excellence (PWHCE) gathered a group of six First Nations women whose mothers had survived

Canada's residential school system. They were asked to participate in a research project entitled, *kiskinohamâtôtâpânâsk:*[1] *Intergenerational Effects on Professional First Nations Women Whose Mothers are Residential School Survivors.* The aim was to determine how they had been affected by the legacy of residential schools. With an understanding that Aboriginal people's stories are intellectual traditions, and to ensure the research remained grounded in the women's life stories, digital storytelling[2] was used.

Each produced a digital story depicting how they had experienced the intergenerational effects of residential schools[3]—one woman chose to keep her video private. Their videos also reflected the stories that had been passed on to them from their mothers who had, collectively, attended eleven residential schools: All Saints, Birtle, Blue Quills, Elkhorn, Guy Hill, Lebret, Merival, Sturgeon Landing, Saint Albans, Saint Henry's Mission and Saint Joseph's Roman Catholic Residential Schools.

In addition to generating information on the intergenerational effects of the schools, the project served a therapeutic purpose for the women. They discovered a sense of healing, as they journeyed through the project together. The women's stories called attention to their emotional detachment from their mothers and their reconnection with them; their own journeys into motherhood; their reconciliation of childhood and adulthood trauma as intergenerational survivors; their strength, determination and resilience transmitted through mothers; and their move toward spiritual healing for mothers, families and all community people who have been affected by the residential school legacy.

Recognizing the importance of sharing their stories with others, this chapter is about how Indigenous mothering has been disrupted by residential schools but also how Indigenous women are reclaiming motherhood.

LORENA FONTAINE'S STORY: MY JOURNEY INTO MOTHERHOOD

Initially, when I found out I was pregnant with my daughter, I did not think I had anything to give a baby. I wondered what I could possibly bring to a child's life. I did not feel as though I could nurture a baby, I did not know very much about my people's culture and history. I can't speak my language. All these thoughts made me question my ability to be a mother. Then a part of me became afraid that someone would see my fear, and then my child would be removed from my care.

Although my journey into motherhood was not easy, the digital story project allowed me to make connections between my fear and the legacy of the residential school system. Participation in the project also provided me with new insight into the way I chose to raise my daughter. Before I go into more detail about my experience of becoming a mother, I will briefly talk about my grandmother and mother's experiences in the residential school system that took them away from their mother at a very young age. I will then go on to talk about how their experiences ultimately impacted my role as a mother.

My maternal grandmother, the late Elizabeth Jane Young, grew up in a northern Indigenous community of the Opaskwayak Cree Nation, located adjacent to the Pas, Manitoba. Although I don't know a great deal about her experience in the residential school system, I do know that she attended an industrial school at a very young age, where she was taught to work. Later in her life, she became a mother to fifteen children (three sets of twins). She raised her children with my grandfather (also a former student of an industrial school) in a four-room home with no running water. In the home, she enforced a strict language policy, allowing her children only to speak Cree. Her adamant connection to the Cree culture and language is very powerful testament, considering the abuse she endured for speaking our language in the residential school system.

My grandmother was also gifted with the knowledge of the plants and medicines in our territory. However, she did not pass on this knowledge to her children, likely from fear that she would be sent to jail. The Canadian government outlawed our ceremonial practices and anything associated with our ceremonies during this period. During this period, many of the women from my community were informed that they could no longer use our traditional medicines. Although the medicinal knowledge was not passed onto my mother and aunties, the language was kept alive in my mother's generation.

My mother also attended residential school. She was removed from our community at the age of three, along with her twin sister. For sixteen years, she was without the care and influence of a mother. She did not have her parents to protect her or to provide her with affection or love. Instead, she experienced a great deal of abuse and loneliness. On many occasions, she was physically beaten for speaking Cree. She also witnessed other children being abused for speaking their language.

In spite of my mother's childhood experiences, she went onto to complete her master's degree, and was the first president of an Indigenous women's organization in Manitoba. When she became a mother, she did the best that she could. I now recognize that becoming a mother was not easy for her because she also did not have a good foundation to draw from. As a result of the alcoholism that plagued our family, my mother endured further violence in our home as she was raising her children.

Later on my mother sought help from a counselor and went on a quest for a healthy place where our family could connect with spiritually. She attended a few different churches over the years. Then one day, she started attending our traditional ceremonies. My brother and sister and I were invited to go with her, but we did not choose to accompany her until later in life. I became keenly aware of how important ceremonies are to the life of my people when I had a child.

When I found out I was going to become a mother, terror engulfed me. After the shock of my pregnancy wore off, my instinct told me that I needed to have a home birth. The first battle I faced was that home births were not yet legal in the province that I was living in at the time. In fact, the doctors refused to see me after I informed them that I was contemplating a home birth. I decided to conceal my decision about home birthing so that I could obtain the services of a doctor. After I did a bit or research on midwifery, I made the decision to have my baby on our reserve where my mother currently resides. I also arranged to have two Indigenous midwives present during my delivery. It was legal in Manitoba to have a baby at home, if there were two certified midwives present. After I made arrangements with the midwives, Sarah's birth fell into place.

Two weeks prior to her due date, my partner and I packed up our car and drove to my mother's place located on the Opaskwayak Cree Nation. We spent the next fourteen days walking amongst the trees, the water and the rocks that surrounded my family for generations.

What occurred over the next three weeks was pivotal. I reconnected with the land that my family had lived on for generations. During my daily walks, with my partner, I thought a great deal about my grandparents. I tried to envision their life raising fifteen children. The steady flow of the river comforted my spirit, as pictures of my family swept through my mind. All the doubts and fear I carried with me for eight months were brushed away. The power of the land reassured and encouraged me to keep moving forward. My spirit was nourished by the life of the land. I became stronger in that environment. The regular sightings of a small muskrat gracefully swimming by on the side of the road was a sign that my partner and I were not alone.

In my mom's home, I was fed traditional soups and meat dishes. The next-door neighbours shared duck. My mom and aunties made muskrat soup (no, it wasn't my little friend). Other nights we feasted on pickerel, moose, and bison meat.

On the morning of Sarah's due date, one of my midwives requested a sweat-lodge ceremony. Sometime during the sweat, I started to have contractions. Later on, after twelve hours of intense labour, I didn't think that I was going to be able to deliver Sarah on my own. I felt so weak. Then I noticed a picture of my grandmother hanging on the wall. The image of her standing beside fourteen children, while pregnant with her fifteenth child, gave me the burst of energy I needed. I thought to myself, if my grandmother could give birth fourteen times, I could get through this one. Right before Sarah was born, my Auntie put out tobacco for the sacred journey we were experiencing.

After Sarah was born, my mother held her while greeting her in our sacred Cree language. When it was my turn to hold Sarah, I looked at her and felt so much awe. Her big beautiful brown eyes stared intently into mine. My family prepared a bath of cedar water to bathe her and then the bath water was poured outside alongside the house. A few days later, her placenta and umbilical were buried in a sacred place so that she would always feel connected to our land.

For the next week, my family and community members greeted Sarah. Her birth was celebrated with gifts, food, and conversation. It was a happy time for everyone. I was informed that Sarah was the first baby born in the community in over fifty years, and therefore her birth was extremely political.

I then left the Opaskwayak Cree Nation, just after Sarah turned a week old. I felt good about her birth, but as I drove away from my mother's house, a deep sadness took hold of me. The sadness remained with me for the next three years. As the days turned into months, I experienced a deep depression. I would often stare into Sarah's deep brown eyes and wonder how she came to be my child. I wondered how I was supposed to love her. I eventually coped with my fear in silence, while carrying on with what I thought was necessary for her care. It was a very hard period of my life, but I was not consciously aware that something was wrong with me. Eventually, I lost all connection with the identity I had before Sarah came into my life.

In some way, the power of Sarah's birth gave me strength that I did not think I had. Although I struggled with depression, it was the first time in my life that I allowed myself to feel pain, sadness and fear. Her presence gave me the courage to walk towards those feelings and sit with them for a few years. I was finally diagnosed with postpartum depression. I had no idea that I had been living with that illness for the first few years of Sarah's life.

The digital storytelling project provided me with the opportunity to reflect back on this period realizing that I had focused on the depression and not the beautiful start in life that my family, partner and I were able to provide Sarah. I was also able to make connections between my postpartum depression and the legacy of the residential schools

The other women who participated in this project also went through a process of self-reflection. Knowing that others were going through this process made me feel safe. For the first time in my life, I did not feel alone. Prior to this project, I was never provided with an opportunity to share my experiences or express my feelings with others. As I listened to the other women speak during our sharing circle and throughout the project, I related to their stories.

After our sharing circle was complete, I felt a great burden had been lifted. I was then asked to write a one-page script that captured one memory I had. But most importantly, writing was another avenue for me to break silence. For most of my life, I stuffed my feelings and memories inside because this is what I was taught to do in order to survive.

Another realization I had during this project is that the knowledge about birthing was carried by my grandmother and mother's resilience. My grandmother kept the language and culture alive as well as the knowledge of our medicines. My mother kept determination and her connection to our ceremonies rooted my brother, sister and me into our traditions. Collectively, they gave me the tools I needed to prepare for Sarah's birth, in spite of my fear. The experience taught me that, as Indigenous women, we collectively carry knowledge of mothering in our heart and spirit. The residential school experience did not destroy that part of our life.

LISA MURDOCK'S STORY: I AM MY MOTHER'S DAUGHTER

When I accepted the invitation to participate in the digital storytelling project on the intergenerational impacts of residential schools, I felt somewhat apprehensive, in the sense that I would not have anything of value to contribute to the research, given that my mother rarely talked about the time she spent in residential school. When my mother did talk about her childhood experiences, it generally was in the form of comments rather than stories. "If it wasn't for residential school, I would have starved," she said on a number of occasions. I remembered her saying something about the Grey Nuns, but I really could not remember what she said. That was it. There was nothing else; only brief comments, with little or no detail. As I walked in to our first of three project sessions, I thought to myself, "Oh my gosh! What am I doing? I don't know anything about the intergenerational effects of residential schools. What could I possibly contribute to this project? Surely, I'm going to waste everyone's time." Indeed, I was mistaken.

Six First Nations women, including myself, showed up to participate in the project. Our first session together began with a learning circle. We were asked, "How do you feel having been parented by a mother who went to residential school has had an impact on you?" Until that time, I really had not thought about the ways in which I was parented, nor did I think about the ways in which my childhood experiences of being raised by a residential school survivor had affected me. In fact, until then, I did not think about my mother as being a residential school survivor.

Growing up, I did hear the words "residential school" being muttered now and then, but I did not begin to know the whole story about residential schools until I started attending university. It was there that I first learned about the dark history surrounding Canada's Indian Residential School system. From time to time after that, I would ask my mother a thing or two about residential schools. For the most part, however, she remained silent on the issue.

Still, I learned that just before her fourth birthday, my mother was taken away from her family and community and interned in residential school. Aside from a two-week visit at home when she was almost six years old, my mother was kept in residential school for eleven years; "until they had no use for me anymore," she said. I learned that my mother experienced all forms of violence and abuse throughout the entire duration of her internment. I learned that she was deprived of a nourishing diet, and as a result, lost all of her teeth at the age of twenty-one years, and today, is plagued with osteoporosis and diabetes. More importantly, I realized that my mother carries with her an overwhelming degree of pain as a result of her residential school experience. But she is resilient.

As a participant in the digital storytelling project, I was expected to create a short video about how my mother's experiences in residential school had affected me. To find my story, I thought about my mother's experiences as a child in residential school. I reflected on my own childhood and adolescent experiences. I thought about my own children and the childhood I am providing for them. Going through this process of finding and telling my story proved to be extremely difficult for me, given the rollercoaster ride of emotions involved with this healing journey.

Reflecting on my own life experiences, I remembered all the good times I had as a child, the special times that I grew to cherish. My favorite memories were the ones that involved my family, laughing, eating and engaging in some sort of carefree adventure together. I remembered all the times we spent at the beach on cold and windy days, wrapped in blankets and eating cold baked potatoes, after what seemed like a joyful eternity of wave-jumping on the shores of the chilly waters. I remembered all the road trips we took, sleeping in the back of the station wagon or on the Greyhound bus, counting train cars, playing punch-buggy, and eating dried moose meat along the way. I remembered playing on the monkey trees at the park, going to Christmas concerts at school and visiting my mother at her places of employment. I remembered my mother baking bread, pulling taffy, ironing and beading, curling my hair and hiding Easter treats.

I also remembered the not-so-good memories; the unfortunate times of forgotten birthday and Halloween parties, of being locked out of the house, of hanging wet clothes on cold winter days, and of being punished for not knowing. I remembered times of being hungry, embarrassed and ashamed. I remembered the anxiety of having to get my siblings into the house before 6:00 p.m. and the stress of getting them up and off to the school breakfast program each morning, without notice. I remembered the unpleasant sound of the drinking parties, the stench of their aftermath and the misery of having to restore a clean and tidy home environment. And sadly, I remembered the weight of my mother, and the fear I felt as I longed for her to wake up.

The experience of being taken from her family and community and of being raised in the cold, unfamiliar and harsh environment of residential school had deeply affected my mother. She spent a good portion of her life being angry, and she coped with the pain she carries through hard work, alcohol use, violence and self-harm. My mother trusted no one and hustled many to survive. She struggled to make sense of her own identity, to value her own self-worth, and to find her sense of belonging.

The video that I created reflects the impact that my mother's life experiences had on me. Each image in my digital story represents a series of underlying stories about what it was like to grow up feeling lonely and alone, worried and afraid, abandoned and unwanted, and struggling to find some sense of belonging. The message that I send through my video is that although my life experiences have taken a different form than my mother's experiences, they are very much similar to and rooted in my mother's experiences as a residential school survivor.

My mother did not know what it was like to be nurtured, protected and loved as a child should be, growing up. She was deprived of the natural teachings of motherhood. Still, through her parental shortfalls as a mother, and her recuperation as a loving and caring Grandmother, my mother taught me how to be an excellent mother to my own children. As a mother, I know the value of being open and honest with my children, of listening attentively to their seemingly trivial stories, of respecting their feelings and relationships, of hugging and kissing them often and of tucking them into bed each night. More importantly, I understand the significance of their cultural identity, their belonging, and their resiliency.

Recently, I was asked the question, "What was the best thing to come out of your digital storytelling experience?" Looking back, I would have to say that the best thing to come out of my participation in the *kiskinohamâtôtâpânâsk* digital storytelling project was being able to reclaim my relationship with my mother, and hear her response to my video: "I just watched your video. Honey, I love you very, very much. Do you know that? I love you, my girl."

WENDY MCNAB'S STORY: NIKÂWIY EKWA NIYA

In 2010 when I was invited to participate in this project, I quickly discovered it was like no other project I'd ever participated in. Our circle turned into a circle of women sharing, supporting and quietly embracing each other as we explored something we had never done before. We shared our experiences of being mothered by mothers who had been torn away from their own mothers when they were a little more than toddlers. They were taken and placed in environments where the underlying goal was to enforce silence and fear.

Together we created an opening through a viscous wall of silence around residential schools, which had been debilitating and disrupting us, our families and our communities, through emotional, mental, physical and spiritual pain. We explored how the residential schools were to separate and ensure detachment from the self, parents, family, siblings, community and language.

Looking for you? Looking for me? Looking for each other.
Finding you. Finding me. Finding each other. (Excerpt from
Wendy's Digital Story: nikâwiy ekwa niya)

Residential schools could have "killed the Indian in the child." Many of
us have experienced the loss of our language. Our languages hold our culture, our systems of kinship, community governance and the connection to
our ancestors and the spirit world. Our languages are the key to everything.
With the loss of language, compounded with the residential schools, enforcement of silence and fear impacted our ability to accurately and authen-
tically communicate emotions and feelings. Our language has profound descriptions and meanings in relation to our relationships with each other.
For example, the word used for "family" in Cree is "wakotawin," which
doesn't only describe one or two people responsible to a child. The child
is the responsibility of the entire extended family. Although neither my
son nor I speak our language, my son refers to all my mother's siblings as
Mosoom or *Kookum* (correct spelling *nimosôm* and *nôhkom*), and he refers
to all my first cousins as Auntie or Uncle. Kinship is another small act of
reclaiming who I am, as a mother and family member, and to my community.

My mother demonstrated her own act of reclaiming her parenting. In
her silent protest against the churches, my mother never baptized me, or
my brother, because she wanted us to be able to decide our own preferred
path of religion or spiritual belief. My appreciation didn't surface until I
was in my 20s. I am grateful to my mother that I wasn't formally indoc-
trinated within any of the Christian or Catholic beliefs, or any religion for
that matter. I am Cree and Salteaux. My ancestors originally came from
the Maple Creek area, before they were moved to the Qu'Appelle Valley
and surrounding area. Those are our people, our connection to the land,
and thus, the connection to our ancestors. My conviction is, and will be,
who I am as a mother, working towards re-learning and re-claiming, so that
my son knows his people. My son has the same choice for his faith that my
mother has provided her children.

My mom was born in 1952, and is one of fourteen children (two were
taken in and adopted by my grandmother). My grandmother raised these
children all on her own, without the luxury of running water or electricity.
My grandfather was ill in the hospital, and my grandmother, at home with
the little ones, couldn't visit him. My mother's father passed away when
she was twelve years old. I don't recall ever hearing about how the passing

of my grandfather impacted my mother, nor hearing about how she was impacted by the forced separation from her mother and siblings when she was placed in residential school. My mother was taken away at the age of six and she attended two residential schools until she was sixteen.[4]

> Two primary objectives of the residential school system were to remove and isolate children from their home, families, traditions and cultures. Indeed sought, as was infamously said, "To kill the Indian in the child." All were deprived of the care and nurturing of their parents, grandparents and communities. (Prime Minister Stephen Harper, June 11, 2008)

Imagine my mom and my grandmother being separated because the churches and the Government of Canada believed my grandmother wasn't a good mother. I feel a sense of immobility, followed by terror, fear, and grief. Those feelings came out sixteen years ago, in combination with a sense of intense panic, immediately after learning I was pregnant. I felt that someone would come to take my child away. These are feelings that remain with me. Is that fear mine? Or is that my grandmother's fear? Or my mother's fear? What I understand today is that it's not my fear. It is one of the intergenerational impacts of residential schools. This sense of fear has impacted the ability for me and my mother to become our authentic selves and to fully mother our children. Imagine always parenting with the sense of paranoia that if you make a mistake, and someone finds out, your child will be taken away.

My son has taught me to begin to release that cumbersome fear. It happened one morning as I was driving him to school. He was about nine years old and I discovered that he didn't bring the inner piece of his winter jacket. As the paranoid mother, I scolded him to the point that he was in tears. It was then, he reminded me of something I would always say to him. "Who cares what people think? That's what you always tell me!" In my panic and paranoia, I proceeded to tell him that the school would call Child and Family Services and take him away from me. I had never said such things to him before, but I had always functioned from that frame of mind. He said, "No one will take me away; it won't happen." It seemed so simple, and that's all it took to begin to slowly let go of my mind's vice-grip hold of my fear, panic and paranoia that someone would take him away.

There are many of us, as adult children of survivors today, who are consumed profoundly with the fear of losing our children. I'm still dealing with my fear of loss. It's still there, just not as overwhelming as it was when I became the mother of my son.

> The darkness inside my heart and soul moved outside of my body to become my self-comfort and my self-embrace. I learned to laugh at myself. I forgive myself for the mistakes I make. I'm not bad. I'm not horrible. (Excerpt from Wendy's Digital Story: nikâwiy ekwa niya)

Since giving birth to my son, I have always felt such an enormous honour and privilege. I cannot recall how old he was when I learned about how children choose who they want to assist them on their journey in the physical world as their parents. Immediately after learning that story, I've shared it with him and have always thanked him for choosing me. This for me is another act of reclaiming my Indigenous motherhood. So now he always tells me he loves me more than I do, because he knew me before I knew him. My son has been my greatest teacher, and sometimes he leaves me speechless. He has been influential in my determination to reclaim my authentic self, my motherhood; to be self-observant and present; to be able to move forward and function from a place of peace, safety and sharing of voice.

> In a garden of fresh smelling flowers sits a young lady with dreams and aspirations in a world full of chaos. She does not quiet her thoughts, she gratefully screams her arguments and ideas in deafening blasts of truth and conviction. Does she see her beauty? The soft, quiet one who resides within the blooming rose, in the sweet-smelling perfumes and protective cocoons of the soft petals. (Excerpt from Wendy's Digital Story: nikâwiy ekwa niya)

LISA FORBES' STORY: MARY-LOU AND ME

My mom became a young woman in Birtle, Manitoba where she went to residential school for senior high school. She didn't tell me details about her time there, but I know that she made friends, played hockey, and sang in the choir. What I know, I learned from pictures, innuendo and scattered comments. I see photos of her and my grandmother in regalia. Then, her, at the same age—an older teenager, dressed in 1960s ladies fashion—stilettos, a pencil skirt, blouse and holding a cigarette. Those residential school years for me are these photos—my mom, in a rec room or cafeteria in the 60s ladies wear, a Coke machine and a picture of an Aboriginal man wearing a headdress on the wall. Photos of her as an Indian woman, of culture, outside of residential school, but inside, there's just a symbol of native culture—hanging on a wall. My mom's, and my story, is not so much about the abject failure of Canadian society's attempt to assimilate Indian people, but that my family shows degrees of how we assimilated, and the hidden but real, and devastating effects on her health, and on mine. There are two parts of my mom; the girl who got her education and became a young woman in residential school far from home, a place where she would never live again; and the other, a cultural Indian woman from the reserve, who loved her family, did traditional sewing, had a mooshum.

She left one part of who she was and married my dad—a non-Native man. Together they made their own life. She worked hard as she coached our sport teams, made sure we had music lessons, and made our clothes. She drove us in the dark winter mornings to sport practices and then stayed up late into the night sewing costumes and clothes. In the day she went to work. She was a dedicated supervisor, working in a field she loved—interpreting local history. Her co-workers she treated like family. She was dedicated, and hard-working, taking files home every night. She worked too much and the stress contributed to the illness she died from.

My role as a child was to study hard, be a good girl, and achieve. I grew up to be my mother's daughter. I am an extraordinary worker, meaning I work extraordinarily hard, and long. Working too much is socially acceptable, praiseworthy. However, my approach to work has had a devastating impact on my mental health. Now, I struggle to balance my family and work life, keeping my unhealthy habit, my excessive work in check.

I became a woman and will become a mother with the guidance and love of my mom, in spirit. Who I am is borne of the memory of her in my blood and being, as well as the love of my family and friends in this life.

I was loved and cared for by my parents as a child. Yet, despite this, I feared becoming a mother. I knew that members of my parents' families had been affected by violence, and, I had thought that because of this, the chance of that violence continuing in a family that I would create was too great to leave to chance. But later, as a woman, I dreamt of becoming an adoptive mother. That dream was trapped until I became a part of the circle of digital storytellers that I call "The Crying Wagon Girls." Fear of mothering, or of having children taken away, came up in our stories. When I started to consider that being a bad mom was not inevitable, that, perhaps I had been externally influenced through our collective legacy as Aboriginal people in Canada, I allowed my heart to open further to the idea. Now my partner and I are actively pursuing parenthood through the foster child adoption process with a local Aboriginal agency.

ROBERTA STOUT'S STORY: RESILIENCE

My mother, Madeleine Dion Stout, is a residential school survivor. Before then, she was *kêtêskwew* ("Ancient Woman" or "Child with an Ancient Spirit"). She hasn't really talked about her childhood years spent at Blue Quills Residential School in Alberta, nearly 50 kilometres from Kehewin First Nation, her home community. In some ways, I believe this is now a closed book for her, with good reason.

The little I know is based on what she has chosen to share publicly. These stories cluster around the profound need of a seven year old girl to experience love, to shun the depth of separation from brothers, sisters, and her mom and dad and grandfather. I often wondered how my mother and the other children in the residential schools found the wherewithal to make it through the day-to-day, month-to-month and year-to-year stretches of motherlessness.

My mom tells me that she had three mothers: Sarah Dion, Billy Dion and Solomon Youngchief. Her mother, father and grandfather. These three mother pillars bestowed onto her a moral compass, an emotional intelligence and a deep curiosity and respect for the sun, the stars and the universe. Seven formative years of speaking and thinking Cree, of love immersion, of tailing behind her patient mothers gave her the wisdom and determination to "get along, get through and get out" of Blue Quills Residential School intact. Yet, like other children of her time, something in her was forever altered by the unwanted institutionalized care she experienced. kêtêskwew morphed into Madeleine.

Since as far back as I can remember, I knew my mother went to a residential school. For many years though, I believed that these years had been primarily positive for her, quite possibly because she never spoke of any physical and sexual horrors as having occurred. As a young girl then myself, I didn't understand what it was like to cry for my parents because I had them without interruption. It also didn't occur to me that one could be affected by the removal of love, because throughout my childhood, I was unconditionally surrounded by it. I ate around a table with my family every night, I was protected from all forms of abuse, I played with my sister,

I was free, as a child, to be a child. I was fully and lovingly mothered and fathered.

The first time I heard specific stories of my mother's childhood at Blue Quills was in the summer of 2004 at the Aboriginal Healing Foundation's National Gathering in Edmonton, Alberta. Surrounded by hundreds of strangers, I listened to my mother and wept. The visuals she spoke of transformed my understanding of her childhood. I also felt the depth of impact the residential school system had on all of my mother's family members. Stories of needless suffering of children and parents, and the human resilience they must have drawn upon to adapt to and push back against the systems which were so heavily and hastily placed upon them.

I realized, that day, that though my mother didn't personally witness any direct abuse, this didn't mean that her experience was positive. Indeed, there have been lifelong scars. I see now that childhood trauma, such as that which was experienced by my mother and other residential school survivors, has more complex and insidious outcomes. Amongst some of these are: early onset bodily aches and disease; chronic adulthood loneliness; a longing for that which can never be found; emotional disabilities; an all-out need and readiness to work and clean—faster, longer and evermore perfect; the struggle to trust and communicate pain and loss.

It has been through this project of bonding with a group of kindred First Nations women, that I've been able to explore my mother's childhood and of parenting as an Indigenous mother. It has been liberating for me to see my story, my mother's story, and my daughter's story in all of the other women's stories. Just as it has been liberating to laugh and weep together at the commonalities in our upbringings and in acknowledging that our mothers' behaviours, like ours, are deeply rooted in a history none of us had control over. Certainly what I've seen is that through the very vulnerable process of sharing of stories, we have the power to "move forward without looking back."

CONCLUSION

Following the conclusion of the project, the *kiskinohamâtôtâpânâsk* storytellers continue to meet independently to explore and discuss the legacy and intergenerational experiences of residential schools and what they can do to encourage more public dialogue and understanding around these issues. The storytellers have formed a unique bond with each other as a result of their involvement in the project. As a group, they have offered guidance, support and mentorship to three subsequent digital storytelling projects with other women and men focused on the intergenerational effects of residential schools; they have played an instrumental role in the creation of a digital storytelling education toolkit intended to contribute to Aboriginal people's emotional, mental and spiritual well-being; and they have made a point of sharing their videos and stories with other Aboriginal survivors, intergenerational survivors and non-Aboriginal peoples from the general public, education institutions, scholars and those working with Aboriginal communities across Canada and internationally.

NOTES

[1] *kiskinohamâtôtâpânâsk* is a Cree phrase that means "school bus," but has various other nuanced meanings when looking at each of the root words individually. The root word kisk means "to learn," mâtow is a verb that, on its own, means "to cry," and otapanâsk is the word for "wagon." Through this particular morphological interpretation, crying is part of the school bus experience.

[2] Digital storytelling, the art of combining oral tradition with digital technology, is a community-based, learner-centred approach to generating knowledge. It involves using digital storytelling computer software to blend voice-recorded, first-person narratives with a collection of still images, music and sound effects to create a 3-5 minute video to illustrate a personal story.

[3] The digital stories can be viewed at http://www.pwhce.ca/program_aboriginal_digitalStories.htm.

[4] My mother and I feel it is important to acknowledge our gratitude to my Uncle Peewee (1955–1977) and my mom's Uncle Dingy for doing everything possible to ensure the safety of mother during her time in residential school.

WORKS CITED

Stout, Roberta and Peters, S. *kiskinohamâtôtâpânâsk: Intergenerational effects on professional First Nations women whose mothers are residential school survivors*. Winnipeg, MB: Prairie Women's Health Centre of Excellence. Web. 2014.

15.

Indigenous Principles for Single Mothering in a Fragmented World

DAWN MARSDEN

INTRODUCTION

This paper is a reflection upon the challenges that arose when I tried to guide my children according to Indigenous principles for a good life (Figure 1) in today's fragmented society. The period reflected upon was between 1994 and 2012, as a single, off-reserve, low-income, pale-faced, urban-dwelling mother. I am Anishinaabe and French and a member of the Mississaugas of Scugog Island First Nation.

The principles being used for this reflection were derived in the summer of 2013 in a retrospective analysis of the Elder teachings shared with me over my lifetime, towards developing educational materials for Indigenous youth resilience, and as a response to a call by space scientists to design a sustainable intergenerational starship community. Most of the Elder teachings informing the Indigenous principles came from my father and grandmother who were raised by their Anishinaabek grandmothers, from my early childhood with extended family in a cabin, from Anishinaabek people living on the west coast, from Coast Salish and Kwakwakuwak people, and from Elders of other Nations attending Elders gatherings, pow-wows and conferences across Canada.

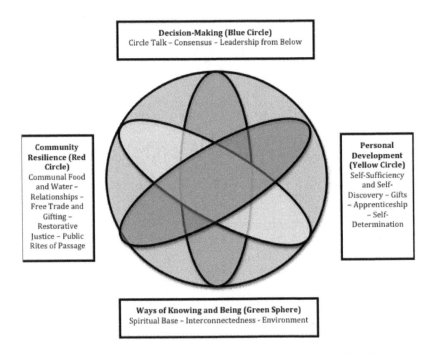

Figure 1: Indigenous Principles for Enviro-Cultural Sustainability (first presented at the 100 Year Starship Society 2013 Symposium, Houston, Texas. Credit: Dawn Marsden, First Nations University of Canada).

The courage to do this reflection comes from the Seven Fires Prophecy, which instructs us to light the Eighth Fire, towards world balance and harmony, by sharing the wisdom of the Elders. I am convinced that the increase in social and environmental issues over the last 500 years is directly related to increasing fragmentation of personal and collective connections to the earth and to sustainable ways. Conversely, the more people experience the natural world, the stronger their spirit and desire for good relationships with the natural world, other people and other species. Many Elders still carry the multi-millennial wisdom of these good relationships, which provide guidance and resilience in the face of adversity. In an effort to start developing educational materials for youth, I tried for a year to summarize the teachings about living a good life given to me; it seemed impossible. Through a sideline interest in space exploration, the opportunity came to focus my reflections, by answering a call for papers on how to build a sustainable intergenerational starship society. After some prayers, I was able to summarize key principles within a week. The principles that are applied in this paper were first presented at the 100 Year Starship 2013 Symposium held in Houston, Texas.

A limitation of this motherhood reflection is that it's one person's perspective, from a single-parent point of view, located far away from Indigenous community. The other limitation is that as a pale-face, I am offered more privileges than browner skinned Indigenous mothers, which makes my experience of single parenting with Indigenous principles unique; it also makes me the target of people who think I'm squandering my privilege, since I could "pass as white." The goal of this paper is to highlight some of the areas of friction created by trying to live according to Indigenous principles while parenting as a pale single mother, and to offer both individual and societal recommendations for overcoming these barriers, for the benefit of future generations.

SPIRITUAL-BASED LIVING

I raised my children, alongside their natural exploration of the world, to conceive of and recognize the spiritual essence of reality through physical and emotional sensations, intuitions and visual attention, to identify the experience of all-knowing, sentient and loving light as the source of that reality, and referred to it as the Creator. When my daughter was four, I discovered her showing her friends how to pray properly on their knees with palms together. In bewilderment I asked where she had learned the behaviour and was told that the daycare had taught her, after I had received assurances that the daycare was not promoting Christianity. Later, during play with other children, it became apparent that my children weren't Christian; some mothers refused to let my children play with theirs, or would only allow my children to play at their house, or come to church with them. Our ideas about ancestors, spirits and other sentient beings were labeled dangerous influences, flaky and evil, which I usually found out about when my kids came home and shared their experiences. Initially they were upset, so I had to teach them about diversity and respect for other spiritual traditions at an early age. After years of the same kind of responses, they seemed to become immune and learned to censor their words. In an ideal world, knowledge would be shared about Indigenous and diverse metaphysical traditions throughout the public education system and during public events, to reduce spiritual ignorance and prevent discrimination against Indigenous and other ways of thinking and being and to put the divine back into diversity.

INTEGRATING INTERCONNECTEDNESS

This concept arises naturally from a belief in a spiritual universe, where everything is literally connected by a spiritual essence. Spider webs, circles, dream-catchers and the entire natural world make ideal teaching aids for imparting this concept. Other than the spiritual base to this concept, the scientific side of interconnectedness was readily accepted by my children's peers, their parents and teachers, and gave my children an advantage when learning the sciences, because of its similarity to ecology. However, the word itself—interconnectedness—was an alien word to most of my children's peers and given the eyebrow by their parents. I speculate that the hippy and later new age movements—though commendable and important exploratory shifts—may have tainted the concept through superficiality, and what Chogyam Trungpa calls spiritual materialism. Of course, this kind of discrediting would serve long-standing efforts to disempower and assimilate Indigenous people. Given shifts towards more wholistic thinking, the concept of interconnectedness has become less threatening and could easily be integrated into school and community programming as a scientifically sound way of thinking about ourselves in relationship to each other, other species and the planet, especially if integrated into science lessons and relevant applications.

ENVIRONMENT-CENTERED THINKING

The concept of interconnectedness is most readily applied to the environment, which is the literal ground of our being, from which we are made; this relationship is sometimes described as humans being the children of, and dependent upon, Mother Earth. This concept is extended even further with the idea of interdependence between all living cycles and systems. While conceiving of an environment distant from ourselves is the norm in Canadian society, conceiving of humans as environmentally-embedded animals is on the margins. While not often verbalized, the centrality of the earth and environmental cycles is in direct conflict with Christian teachings of human domination over the earth and the need to be separate from our "baser" natures. Because these are complex concepts, they didn't cause friction until my children were older and started making connections between business, industry, profiteering and the destruction of the environment and, consequently, human health. These ideas were perceived as radical, tree-hugging, conspiratorial, unscientific, flaky and even anti-social. With guidance and introduction to critical thinking, evidence and basic arguments, my children were armed to challenge the disbelief, if needed. As my children get older and seek to act upon their convictions, their lives and livelihoods will become endangered by the labels and by the people who make a living off of environmental destruction, to the point of being criminalized and threatened with jail time for publicly pointing out such offensive connections.

Environmental issues are already being taught in schools, and students learn all about life cycles, food chains and the need to recycle, but this doesn't go far enough. When my son went to kindergarten at Curve Lake, the students were taken into the bush and for boat rides on a daily basis, so they could experience the natural world first hand. Consciousness of our deep dependence upon the environment should be mentored throughout public education by taking students out of the classroom and into the natural world, through fieldtrips, camping trips and programs like Rediscovery. Only by raising personal awareness of the connections between societal practices, environmental impacts and our health, will our societies have the understanding necessary to repair and protect our damaged world.

SELF-SUFFICIENCY AND SELF-DISCOVERY

From babyhood, I aspired to teach my children to acquire the skills to become independent contributors to the household. I told them that they should have all the knowledge needed to live on their own by the time they were fourteen, which meant cooking, cleaning, doing laundry, making money and guarding their own safety. I have several regrets in this area. One was that having a single parent with scattered family and friends, my children didn't have community or male role models for contributing their labour to the wellbeing of the household or community. While they learned to cook, clean, find work, learn self-defense and do their own laundry, they did not have the role models for the real teachings of self-sufficiency: hunting, fishing, gathering, gardening, making clothes and shelter.

Self-discovery arises naturally from opportunities to learn and practice self-sufficiency and leads to the knowledge and skills required for self-determination. To improve self-sufficiency without the support of a community, I developed mini-gardens to augment our diet, shopped at local

and organic markets (when finances allowed) and developed a food cooperative with friends and family to share and prepare wild or organic foods;
my children were involved and learned about these processes. I also encouraged them to learn sewing, basic first aid, swimming, babysitter training
and how to use the survival kits I had prepared. This included teaching
about basic threats like hypothermia, dehydration, starvation, stranger attack and heat exhaustion. Consequently, they learned the basics of where
to get food or where it came from, how to prepare it, how to stay warm
and cool and what to do in emergencies. Surprisingly, this kind of training
was met with incredulity by the parents of my children's peers, who either
did all the household work themselves, or challenged the usefulness of such
training in a modern stable society where you could buy all your needs in
a store. They also suggested that teaching about potential societal or environmental dangers—which are a regular part of human history—might
frighten or damage my children. My response was that those teachings were
age-appropriate, dependent upon how much the children wanted to hear
and could comprehend, and increased my children's resilience in the face
of adversity. The emergency training, in particular, became a source of embarrassment for my children and subject of jokes among adults, including
family members. What does this say about our society, when making sure
our children can provide for themselves is ridiculed?

With self-sufficiency comes self-discovery and awareness of the value
of community effort and cooperation. Traditionally, youth would be given
teachings and guided opportunities to test their self-sufficiency and discover
themselves, through independent hunts, vision quests, sweat lodges, survival tests and initiations. These teachings are invaluable for the growth
and maturation of children into whole adults, who learn the disadvantages
of isolation and benefits of collaborative effort and respect. These lessons
for self-sufficiency and self-discovery should be initiated in age appropriate stages, perhaps in combination with environment-centered training, or
through community-supported programs, so that, by the time youth are in
their teens, they are already confident, self-aware and understand the benefits of being responsible and contributing members of society. Without
this training, youth seem to be lost, to become perpetual children, without
healthy orientations to society. The challenges involved with organizing
such training and events in urban areas, as a single mother, with few appropriate Elders around, and with multiple moves for work and school meant
that my son's training was fragmented. I encouraged him to spend time
with male role models, like my father and other healthy men, but his train-

ing was always being counteracted by societal promotion of misogyny and self-centeredness. When my son was a teenager, I was able to rent a property with a garage, so we cleaned it up, painted and carpeted it so my son could have his own space; while this was a minor test of self-sufficiency, it was a good transition for learning to be independent. The impact of my fragmented training and any real tests of self-sufficiency come when our children leave home. When I made a move to Saskatchewan, my son decided not to come with us and—surrounded by extended family and friends—has been able to make a successful transition to self-reliant adulthood.

GIFTS

One teaching I received, repeatedly, was that everyone has gifts, that nurturing them was important to developing adults who were fulfilled in their lives, and that this was the wealth of the community. As a homeschooling mother, it was easy to identify and encourage the gifts that my children displayed. They showed aptitudes for diverse talents in multiple domains: mental, emotional, physical and spiritual. Both my children enjoyed dancing at powwows and wanted to be traditional and jingle dancers. My daughter could speak full sentences at eleven months and was composing and singing songs all day long. My son had a photographic memory and could remember every detail about every collection he made, and was doing square root equations in his head at five years old. I know that these weren't the extent of their gifts, so I strove to find opportunities for them to learn in any area of interest. Some of the challenges to nurturing gifts include adequate finances for supplies or lessons and the social sanctions around practical careers, being realistic, not being proud, or raising your head too far above the crowd. How much money could an artist make, after all?

They also learned that, whenever they were in public school for a term, to keep their heads down, and not speak about any of their gifts. My daughter stopped composing and singing because of both the positive attention and ridicule she was getting at school and in public, and my son was permanently scarred by a kindergarten teacher who told him in the first week, with annoyance, that there was no place for square roots in kindergarten and that he had to learn basic addition like everyone else. My daughter lost her confidence, not just with singing and composing, but also with her ability to speak up among her friends and teachers. After encountering stereotyping in school projects and realizing the status of Indigenous people in society, both children went from wanting to be traditional dancers to hat-ing the suggestion of it, as if I was ridiculing them for mentioning it. My son struggled with his math for years, and resisted having to repeat concepts in homework even after he'd learned them. This transferred into a resistance to do any homework and to miss classes. Though he was a fast learner and could ace tests if he wanted, he was branded a troublemaker and lost marks for not doing homework. In a similar way, I was branded a troublemaker for advocating for student-directed learning. In principle, inherent gifts are supported in mainstream society, but the actual nurturing of them is very limited in the public school system. Because of the strong educational conditioning to "fit" into society, not "standing out" is sought by our youth, who then hide or "dumb down" their talents. With cuts to any programs other than the 3 R's (reading, writing, math), opportunities to explore talents is even more limited. Attempts to support gifts outside of the school system is severely limited by finances, especially for single parents or other unemployed or working poor. Homeschooling and alternative schooling are good options, but are costly and unaffordable for stay-at-home contract workers like myself. The constraints of society requires single mothers to choose between staying home and nurturing their children's gifts, in poverty, or giving up the raising of children to strangers with Euro-Canadian worldviews and little time or interest in nurturing our children's gifts. Community consciousness could be raised in school and out, to identify children's gifts early and to nurture them throughout childhood; school hours could be reduced and student allowances provided to enable students to learn from compatible mentors in their area of interest, for educational credit.

APPRENTICESHIP TRAINING

The best learning environment, we discovered after my son refused to go to public school or do distance education, was an eco-school where he could learn academic subjects at his own pace, and gain practical skills through integrated activities like cooking for the class and doing outdoor work in exchange for certificates and work supplies. He completed grades nine, ten and eleven in one year and received mostly As. The program was cut the following year with the idea of reducing costs and integrating "poor learners" back into the public system, where they could learn more slowly, through endless repetition.

The opportunity for actual apprenticeships, for young people to explore their gifts under an advanced practitioner or Elder, is severely limited. It's rare that anyone has the time or interest to provide apprentice-ships in the old way, by making youth work for their training until they become competent practitioners, because knowledge holders are too busy making a living and youth often view conventional systems as the best op-tion. Within fifty years, society has transformed from a world where people learned their trades on the job and where recognition and pay was based on skill level and attitude, to a society where every job requires a certificate, and recognition and pay are based on that piece of paper and regular pro-motions. From my perspective, this has reduced access to employment (be-cause of the cost of training and licensing), job satisfaction, performance and competency across the employment world.

Contemporary options include entry into private lessons, trade appren-ticeships or, occasionally, practical college programs or cooperative univer-sity programs. Unless your family has the means, you've saved money, or have band funding, the only alternative is to work extra jobs or take out student loans. What many students don't realize (I learned the hard way) is that, if you have children and are also paying for childcare, student loans may be equivalent to the cost of a house by the time you're finished; this increases the pressure to take and keep the first work that comes along so you can repay your loans, which may reduce options for finding work or gaining experience in your area of training.

The low status given to apprenticeship programs needs to be addressed. Options for non-institutional-based apprenticeships—for those not pursu-ing regulated journeyman status—could be developed to increase options for training in the field, especially for unconventional trades like Indigenous health practitioner, herbalist, ceremonialist or knowledge holder. The de-mand and necessity for such unconventional trades is well established in Indigenous health literature. Ideally, Indigenous community-based trades can be subsidized by public funds, alongside trades currently entrenched within Euro-Canadian systems.

SELF-DETERMINATION

Based on what I was taught, personal self-determination is being aware, considering options and advice, and being able to make decisions based on an internal framework of living a good life. My father called this fierce in-dependence. I was raised to understand that it's everyone's obligation to be self-determining and speak when necessary, to keep society healthy. This is actually way harder than it sounds because being aware requires having a good understanding of family and societal pressures, knowledge, experience and a good understanding of the self. The more knowledge and awareness, the more choices a person has, the more self-determining a person can be. Fostering self-determination in children requires encouraging children to listen to their hearts, minds, bodies and spirits, and helping them to explore where their decisions are coming from. The only limitations to self-determination I made while parenting, was to do no harm to themselves, others, living things or property, and to be respectful and considerate in the process.

As an example, one of the earliest things I remember doing is telling my children to listen to their bodies and help them to interpret when they were hungry, thirsty or full, and to pay attention to what their body was craving, or what physical symptoms were telling them (like dehydration and headache). Another lesson was talking about the difference between wants and needs, how advertising makes you want something, then pointing out the connection later when they asked for the advertised product. Another way to mentor self-determination was to provide my kids with acceptable options, and later encouraging them to come up with their own options. If their choices didn't have the expected results, then I would brainstorm with them about the possible outcomes of other options. I hoped this would teach understanding and acceptance of consequences, that it's okay to make mistakes, and that with more information and experience they could make better choices. To support the growth of self-determination, I found it essential to answer every question my children had, however difficult; this included questions about death, the universe, sex, love, murder, good friendship, war and meaningful work. I soon found that they would tell me when it was too much information, and sometimes they'd ask more in-depth questions later.

When providing options, some of the strongest social sanctions came from family, friends and other parents. They would make jokes about my children "ruling the roost" and comment that they didn't want to spoil their child or that the parent was supposed to make the decisions. It was meant as kind advice, but felt like strong disapproval of my parenting style. My concern is that if we don't teach our children to make their own decisions at an early age, then, later in life, they will be less able to do so and will become unquestioning followers and vulnerable to peer pressure, rather than become self-determining individuals.

The difficulty of teaching self-determination to children is that they will get the hang of it pretty quick and start exercising their right, even if it's not convenient. Another belief some adults have shared was how damaging they felt providing information to children could be; they felt that some information would make their kids insecure when they should be allowed to be care-free. This caused a little friction in the early years, because my children's friends would go home with difficult questions. The skills that arise naturally from learning self-determination are the art of negotiation, critical thinking and self-assessments of integrity. This meant that sometimes my kids came up with more options if they could address the drawbacks, and taught skills in identifying barriers and developing compromises. The high school years were especially challenging as I continued to support my kids' decisions, with feedback and natural consequences. When they opted to go to public school for social reasons, I got on the wrong side of the school system when my children continued to be self-determining and go or not go, early or late, and dress or not dress, as they felt; at the same time, they also learned about the sanctions, stigmas and consequences of non-conformity. They learned about the direct link between doing the work and obtaining grades, but also about how some school staff can judge self-determination in education as laziness, stupidity, resistance (to what?), anti-social, damaging and as a precursor to a life of crime. Sometimes my children opted not to go to school late, because they could not face the mean looks, assumptions and comments of some of the office people. You can feel the disapproval and judgments of incompetence or even neglect.

Teaching self-determination to children also means modeling it; whenever conflict arose, I would offer to brainstorm or assist in resolving the issue. Being self-determining and choosing to address issues takes courage. If I was afraid to speak up, what chance did my children have? We learned together to choose when and how to resolve challenges. As my children got older, they relied less and less upon my assistance, and while I may have been frustrated, I feel good that they feel confident enough to make their own decisions. While many parents still believe that children should be seen and not heard, the school system and community institutions should still foster self-determination among children, who will learn when and where to assert themselves, and to assess natural and logical consequences for more critical engagement within society.

COMMUNAL FOOD AND WATER

Obtaining food and water was the central activity of our ancestors, yet it has been understated in the history books. The ability to share the food from hunting, fishing, gathering and farming demonstrated self-sufficiency and care, and created social cohesion and resilience through the efforts made, bonds created and knowledge shared. I experienced a similar lifestyle in my early childhood in Northern Manitoba when extended family would come together for months at a time in a small cabin on a lake. Trying to recreate this environment for my children, as a single parent, was challenging. One of the most enjoyable ways of doing this was by creating an "open-door" policy where family and friends could come and visit or stay over, by giving gifts of food and by hosting dinners where people could come and stay for days at a time. "Open door" also meant the fridge, so people could help themselves when they were thirsty or hungry. Rather than the "freeloaders" that some people assume, people would come and bring food or drink to share and/or help prepare and clean up after cooking and sleepovers. Hosting people in this way teaches children to be good hosts, to work with and care for the needs of others, to socialize with multiple age groups, to become aware of and accept idiosyncrasies, to enjoy companionship, to tolerate disturbance and to learn about life and relationships.

Sharing food and water in this way also increases respect and gratitude for the food species and water sources. In the old stories, the animals, fish and plants would hear our prayers for food, take pity on us, and present themselves to us so we could eat. We would accept these gifts and understood that they were giving their life to us, that life was sacred, that they would become part of us when we ate them and that with reverence, their lives would keep us healthy. In a similar way, the health of the water is reflected in the health of our bodies. To foster awareness of these relationships even more, I would use every opportunity to teach my children who their food was, and where it came from and what those species or water sources needed to be healthy. Hikes or walks are particularly good opportunities for passing this knowledge to children. We grew small gardens, shopped at farmers' markets and created a valley food cooperative with friends and family. This enabled us to buy in bulk and share sources of wild and organic meats, including buffalo, salmon, deer, moose, organic beef and turkeys. Buying in bulk makes local and organic foods more affordable and taught my children about the food they were eating. Meeting the hunters, fishers, farmers and gatherers made the concept of interconnectedness all the more real. By sharing food and knowledge, my children learned about the qualities and values of food security and food sovereignty and the need to protect the lands and waters that provide for us. Such personal relationships with food and water develop an appreciation and desire to protect, prepare and consume them in the healthiest form possible.

As healthy as Indigenous communal food and water relationships sound, I've been shocked to find some people react to gifts of fish and game with disgust. Conventional marketing systems have excluded fresh fish, game and vegetables to the point that they are often feared and rejected, even at regular farmers markets. There is an assumption that if food hasn't been inspected that it must be diseased, regardless of where it came from or how it was prepared..

While obtaining Indigenous foods—either directly or through trade— is affirmed in the Canadian Constitution, in reality, there's always the threat of fines, jail or even fights when those rights are exercised, and there are always people in the shadows ready to get in the way. If Indigenous foods were supported as much as Euro-Canadian agriculture, with funding, tools and facilities, we'd have greater food diversity, food security, food sovereignty and food safety, which would naturally improve the social cohesion of everyone involved. We'd have more hunters, fishers, farmers and gatherers around us, local lands and waters could be reserved and protected for those activities, and there'd be more opportunities for the food to be communally prepared, shared and traded. In the long run, these processes would improve nutritional wellbeing—especially for low income families like single parent families—by reducing the dependencies we have on less healthy, distant, non-fresh, prepackaged, high carbohydrate foods, without the need for questionable chemical preservatives, colourants, flavours and genetically modified species.

RELATIONSHIPS

In a world where everything is connected, it's critical to look at the quality of our relationships to ensure that everything is in balance and harmony. Nowhere is this more important than in the raising of children. The relationships we have with our children, and foster with other beings and the natural world create the foundations for living that our children need to thrive in healthy ways. This is one of the easiest principles to mentor because children are full of wonder and the opportunities for learning about relationships in the natural world are available on every walk or at every event. One of the sayings I passed on was that every being has a purpose and can teach us things. This concept was a little trickier to mentor as my children get older and were frustrated or bothered by other people; with patience and compassion, these issues became opportunities to learn about healthy boundaries.

One of the most profound teachings I was given is that our bodies are sacred, like all of creation, and no one is allowed to touch you or make you do anything without your permission. If they do, you have the right to protest or defend yourself. I taught my children this as soon as they were old enough to understand and encouraged them to learn self-defense. My children seemed to exercise this right the most when they were upset and wanted their space, which seemed in opposition to my urge as a mother to comfort with affection; they ended up teaching me that the best time for affection was when things were relaxed and going well. Teaching and respecting boundaries taught my children that they could control when, where, and if people could touch them, with implied or explicit consent, demonstrating self-respect and development of appropriate intimacy with others. In an authoritarian society where children are on the bottom of the pecking order, many people and strangers have assumed their right to touch children without consent, even in affection. While at first I would intervene, they learned to avoid and verbally reject such touch; not with fear, but with an awareness of the right not to be touched without consent.

After they got the concept physically, it was easy to extend the idea to their thoughts, emotions and spirit; they learned to recognize their own emotional, mental and spiritual states and triggers, and became aware of how and when they would allow people to interact with them, to protect their own wellbeing. The teachings that go with this are that no one can touch your spirit, even if boundaries are violated, and that how people treat you is a reflection of their health or lack of it, not your own. Just because someone wanted you to behave or speak in a certain way, didn't mean you had to; you had a choice. Engaging with other children, their parents, teachers and general public provided ample opportunities to explore, identify situations and practice these interpersonal boundaries. One example I remember was shopping in Winners. When my son was little, he was looking at toys and a store clerk was shadowing him with a sour look on her face. My nephew was close by and we were all keeping him in view. He came to show me a toy that he'd discovered broken but the clerk grabbed him and accused him of stealing; when he defended himself she accused him of lying and then of breaking the toy. My nephew confirmed my son's story and the clerk left with her sour look. When situations warranted it, I would offer suggestions for resolution, or offered to intervene on my children's behalf. In the scenario above, I offered to complain to the manager about the clerk, but my son opted to protect his emotional state from further assault. In a world full of racism and discrimination, you have to maintain your well-being and pick your battles. Combined, these teachings helped to develop a foundation for discernment and self-determination in personal relationships.

The biggest backlash for teaching good boundaries to my children was from parents and teachers who wanted children to do as they were told without question, or who were concerned that giving too much power to children would backfire, and that the children would become tyrants. Conversely, I watched on many occasions when parents and teachers would become tyrants or humiliate children in public, and wondered what impact this had on their self-esteem and future behaviour. If parents or teachers asked or complained about my children's assertiveness, I would sometimes share how respecting boundaries goes both ways and that children learn from us. My children learned quickly where my boundaries were, by being honest and expressing my frustrations or annoyance; this helped my children develop understandings that everyone in a relationship has thoughts and feelings to consider, which requires self-restraint and respect of other people's boundaries. It would be ideal if the concept of respecting personal boundaries was taught and reinforced in schools, but other than in a couple alternative schools, our experience was that most teachers and staff expected students to respect their mental, emotional and spiritual boundaries, and those of other students, but that such boundaries did not apply to what teachers could say to their students.

FREE TRADE AND GIFTING

I've heard lots of stories about how my aunties and father would make baskets and gather corn, fish and medicines and take them to markets that took a whole day of walking, or half a day with horse and buggy. These were opportunities for trade and conversation, meeting potential partners and deciding on common business; sometimes there'd be feasts, dances, music and lacrosse games. Over generations, people grew up knowing the people and their wares, and interfamily relationships were strengthened through good trades, intermarriages and generosity. Today, free trade means the import of foreign goods and services by big corporations and their employees who tend to be underpaid strangers and not interested or too busy making a living to develop long-term relationships with their customers. Imported trade undersells local craftspeople who must increase their prices to stay afloat, making good inexpensive local products and services out of reach for most community people. This serves to strengthen the power of corporations who can offer cheaper goods for cheaper prices.

One of the ways that I would foster awareness of the quality goods and services was to encourage my kids to explore diverse trades. They tried their hand making and even selling sculptures, artwork, lemonade, baking, wooden structures, making soap and paper, forts, clothing, knitting, etc. My oldest child organized events and flea market tables so he could buy, trade, provide services, and set up tournament websites to provide gaming and toy purchase advice to others. We also combed garage sales, markets and second hand stores to find the good quality items hidden within. Another way to teach about quality was by talking about the cotton, wool, silk, leather, wood and other natural fibers used for millennia, and which ones were good for different temperatures and weathers. This helps children to understand that, just because something is cheap, doesn't make it good quality and that good quality goods, made by specialized craftspeople, can last much longer. Conversely, they also learned that just because something had a designer label or was expensive doesn't make it better quality.

My dream is for our economies to move away from the import of foreign goods, to bolster local trade, craftwork and interest-free trade so that it strengthens communities and values individual gifts again, rather than fragmenting them. This bioregional ideal also extends to care of the natural world, since local acquisition of resources for craftwork tends to build stronger relationships with the environment. To foster free trade and gifting among my children I would talk about friends and family interests when we were out, and sometimes we'd pick them up a gift for giving at any time. My children and I found it strange when their friends' parents would rush out to buy something in return, at approximately the same value, as if trying to negate the gift we had just given. We have even heard their friends speak of how much anxiety gift giving would bring, even a plate of cookies. I tried to teach my children that gifts were supposed to be from the heart, with no strings attached and no obligation to give something in return. I also supported trade of toys, clothes and household items, and giving them away when they were outgrown or not being used, to discourage any fixation on material things. Moving a lot for work also helped with this process, because we would need to downsize for each move. Poverty is also a good teacher. With the confidence that circumstances are always changing and the Creator provides, and of course the fact that there is social assistance in Canada, learning to "make do" by being innovative can bring families together and identify strengths.

Community trade and gifting relationships can be supported by buying local craftwork and services, supporting local markets, organizing buying and sharing co-ops, and engaging in and encouraging free barter systems. While supporting free trade and gifting is best done in person, online trading sites are another way to locate and set up meetings with traders.

RESTORATIVE JUSTICE

Restorative justice refers to the concept of intervention when issues cannot be resolved interpersonally and begin to affect other people. In today's individualistic society, everyone is supposed to mind their own business and let the authorities deal with interpersonal transgressions. However, we have seen that the authorities do not have the knowledge or personnel to address interpersonal issues in a timely or appropriate manner. Restorative justice brings everyone together, the offenders, complainants, their families and representatives to discuss the causes and impacts of the offence, so that harmony can be restored for both the offender and complainant, through negotiation of reparations.

When raising children, most of the offences that people deal with are the hurts and insults of children, parents and teachers, and theft or damage of related toys, household items or school property. In trying to mentor courage and good relationships, I would invite meetings with parents, teachers and children, after something happened, to try and resolve the issue, either directly or through letters. Sometimes this was met with fear and defensiveness rather than the collaborative problem-solving that was intended. In some cases, the teachers would refer our issues to their principal, who would call me in for a nice meeting which seldom resulted in any action. On one occasion, when I broke up three boys who were kicking and punching a fourth boy in front of my grade one son, they wouldn't stop until I asked what their parents would say and said that I would report the incident to the principal. The principal listened politely, said that they were working on a bullying policy but that was the end of it and no policy emerged that year. On another occasion, when I challenged a teacher's assessment during a "student-led" interview, she had my child psychologically assessed without my permission. At home, restorative justice processes went a little more smoothly, where the perspective of everyone was invited and solutions were generated together. The wonder of children is that they can be fighting one day and playing the next. Some adults, on the other hand, meet any challenge to their behaviour with gossip, direct, lateral or passive attack, and long-term grudges.

The ones who are more open are rare, but refreshing to work with. In one alternative school my child attended, students led a weekly council meeting, where issues arising on the school grounds were dealt with using some restorative justice principles. Issues included the transgressions of staff, teachers, parents and students, which is unheard of in the public system. While this was a great innovation, it was connected to a punitive demerit system by vote, rather than reparations by agreement, which limited the potential for restoring relationships.

Restorative justice concepts and skills can easily be taught and mentored throughout the school system and in the wider community. Activities might be supported by a reduction in class size, inclusion as part of the curriculum, and through financial support, development and promotion of restorative justice facilities and services in the community.

PUBLIC RITES OF PASSAGE

Rites of passage are those rituals that assist people to make the transition from one state or status to another. In Indigenous communities this included birth, naming, first kill, puberty, marriage, rebirth, special recognition, death and more. During these rites, community members would instruct children in what they needed to know for their new roles, and the community would witness their milestones. This was important for developing self-esteem, a sense of belonging and purpose, mutual respect, meaningful relationships, cooperation and social cohesion. So many young people today do not have any of these things and wander aimless, hopeless, or depressed, into their thirties.

The question I heard from my own children was, "what's the point of living in a world where there is so much disharmony?" This is a natural question when the limits of material existence are realized, and is the root of youth despair today. The only answer I could give my own children was the teaching that we are spiritual beings on a physical journey and that life's purpose is to learn and grow from the challenges. I would add that my own goal was to be a good person and live a good life in the best way I could.

I had tentatively planned to prepare my son to go into a sweat lodge and spend time with respected men so they could provide him teachings about being a good man, followed by a coming of age ceremony, give-away and feast. With moving and time constraints, I wasn't able to get everyone together to organize a comprehensive event and, by the time he was fifteen, he was less interested in completing the process. In lieu, I called friends and family together for a graduation feast and invited them to provide advice for his new role as an adult. Even limited, the event was very moving in the acknowledgement of my son and his gifts, and in the advice, well wishes and offers of support for the rest of his life.

Coming of age ceremonies have been hosted by the Knowledgeable Aboriginal Youth Association (Vancouver, BC), Pacific Association of First Nations Women PAFNW (Vancouver, BC) and by the Turtle Lodge (Pine Falls, MB). Given the diversity of Indigenous cultural traditions involved in the Vancouver rites, it was an amazing and complex event to organize. Most of the first youth going through were in their late twenties and thirties; younger ones followed in the next years. Elders were brought together to give the young people teachings, hold pipe ceremonies and sweat lodges and put on public ceremonies and feast, with give-aways; some of the young people were stood up and given Indigenous names.

In any community, I'd recommend the development and hosting of rites of passage for friends and family, even if they're modified and not quite traditional. The more we reclaim these practices among our friends, family and community, the more they will be reintegrated into the rest of society.

CIRCLE TALK

I learned about circle talk when I went to full moon ceremonies, and in teaching circles at university. I later used it as a research method and as a teleconference method. Essentially, talking circles involve inviting people to leave the world behind, to sit in a circle and express themselves in uninterrupted turns, about the topic, issue or decision being discussed. The facilitator discusses what the circle is about and after each person has an opportunity to talk, might comment, summarize and introduce the next (go) round. The principle of circle talk is that everyone who attends has the right to speak, or just listen, which provides accountability and thoughts from diverse angles, and empowers and heals the participants.

In a family of three, the circle is small and the principle can still be applied to discussing a topic or issue, or to making a decision that is acceptable for everyone. Circle talk obligates people to be self-determining and considerate, and know their own minds, when using their voices. Circle talk is also used with principles of restorative justice, to provide an equitable and organized process for everyone to be heard. At home, sometimes the circle would be widened to include friends and family members. While circle talk principles became part of our way of dialoguing with each other, it wasn't a scheduled activity. During family crisis, I suggested healing circles with healer-facilitators but the issues were usually resolved without such formality. We also extended the concept of circle talk to use of the TV and car radio, where we would take turns choosing the show or song of our choice. Circle talk teaches inclusivity and mutual respect, the benefit of diverse perspectives and fosters healing, self-esteem and synchronicity in decision-making. The skills learned in circle talk at home can improve engagement in other situations, by increasing the ability to critically access how fair, relevant and inclusive the relationships are.

CONSENSUS

According to Indigenous stories, people used to sit in council and talk about an issue until everyone agreed about how to address that issue, for as long as it took, for hours or weeks. If people disagreed with the direction of the consensus, they could—as self-determining individuals—state their disagreement and remove themselves from further discussion and any benefits and consequences, without community alienation. I was happy to be witness to several consensus processes; one at an Elder's gathering and the other at the Victoria Native Friendship Centre (BC). The latter council was called to address an inter-Nation issue; the talks went on for over three days, into the early morning hours, and community members brought food, prepared it, entertained the children, and went in and out of the talks; people would take breaks when they could. The consensus created by that council strengthened the whole community.

In a single parent household, away from community, consensus is easier to build, but does not provide the same rigor or supports as traditional councils. When attending meetings for work or school in the mainstream community, the process is entirely different, very brief and not very hospitable or caring. It's no wonder that people get aggravated if they have to sit for more than a couple of hours. The expectation is that decisions will be made within that time period, usually by the loudest and most dominating people, regardless of whether all the appropriate people are at the table or whether everyone gets to speak. Children are usually considered annoyances and rarely invited to speak unless to prove an adult's point. I brought my children to many gatherings, meetings and conferences, with both Indigenous and non-Indigenous people and processes. The effect of witnessing consensus processes was shown in my children's increased respect for diverse opinions at public gatherings, and when my children invited the opinions of their friends during discussions and decision-making, so that everyone felt included. I noticed this benefit was challenged more as the children got older and more exclusionary processes were adopted, especially in the school system, where the governance structure was authoritarian and where student decisions could be ignored. In a society where consensus is not the norm, people who try and accommodate everyone end up losing out or even being ridiculed. Competition, even in decision-making, is the norm, and, as in other forms of war, the spoils go to the victors.

The benefit of learning consensus building, even in a competitive and aggressive society, is that it's easier to discern people's agendas and motivations. Those who work for the greater good, who are good team players, are easier to identify, which makes choosing friends and allies more conscious and strategic. Consequently, my children can work well in groups and also recognize when their ideas are being trampled on, even when it's observing the methods of teachers.

LEADERSHIP FROM BELOW

Leadership from below was the dominant form of governance for Indigenous communities. What this meant was that with everyone exercising their self-determination, representatives were limited to representing only what individuals had actually agreed to. The deficits and benefits, in turn, only applied to those that had agreed to them. In theory, Canadian society is supposed to have this process and laws are made with the supposed agreement of the majority. In practice, it's leadership from above where the loudest and most dominating people at the top end up making the decisions, in hierarchies of influence, for the good of certain groups, to the detriment of individuals without influence, other species and the natural world. To many Indigenous people I've spoken to, this is insanity, and can only lead to ruin.

When fostering self-determination in my children, I told them to think about what was beneficial, detrimental, or both, and to make their own decisions. Following rules or people blindly, I told them, was for people who couldn't, or wouldn't, think for themselves, and reminded them that rules were supposed to be in the best interest of all people. Following rules implies agreement, but most people—in my experience—aren't aware that they have free will and choice, or are too afraid to voice or act upon anything outside of the law, unless they are feeling restless or destructive. I cautioned my kids to be aware of the potential attacks or consequences if they decided not to play by the rules, and pointed out how people have ended up in jail, kicked out of groups, losing their jobs, or even murdered. The issue of self-determination, especially by children, was met with the most fear and anger, both in and out of the public school system, as if we were personally attacking people by questioning the rules and processes. As my children got older, they became very aware of the punishment that would follow if we spoke up, so they began to ask that I not intervene. Deference to authority figures and to official reasonableness—right or wrong—is the norm in Canadian society, and a difficult habit to avoid or break. I watched this in Ottawa as the staff around me deferred to the perspectives of those in power, especially to those with budget influences. Closer to home, my son was asked to profile a political party in Canada and did a brilliant essay on the Rhino Party but failed his assignment because the teacher thought he was being disrespectful by choosing that party to write about. Upon protest that it was a legitimate party, the second reader gave him a pass. Fostering self-determination and true democracy at home, in school programs and processes, and in the wider community, is integral to becoming an adult and having free will. By educating our children about their personal right to be self-determining, and included in governance and law-making, we can only improve our society, even if there are backlashes against unconventional worldviews. The more our leaders actually represent what we say and assert, the more socially and environmentally responsive our societies will be. Hence, it's the responsibility of every man, woman and child to select the right people to speak for us, and to hold them accountable to that task.

CONCLUSIONS

Indigenous principles for environmental sustainability and social cohesion are as relevant today as they have been for thousands of years, but are severely challenged by the dominant (western) worldview that reinforces hierarchies of competition, usury, oppression and privileged access to power, influence, resources and material possessions. This clash of worldviews is not just a theory, it has real interpersonal impacts upon mothering, and the wellbeing of our children, when we are trying to pass on teachings and live according to Indigenous principles. I'd like to think that passing on Indigenous ways is easier in Indigenous communities, but I know through experience, discussions, travel and research that Indigenous worldviews are under siege everywhere. I would like to re-pose a question made by an Indigenous friend in New Zealand: why not invite non-Indigenous people—who are really just environmentally-disconnected people—to become grounded again in the natural world, and return together to the loving and fulfilling communities we once had? The recommendations made under each Indigenous principle provide a pathway for reconnecting all Canadians to the processes that have sustained and could still sustain our relations for millennia. The children are our future, and mothers are the literal bearers and nurturers of that future. *Gitche Miigwetch,* thank you for listening.

16.

Growing Up

A Dialogue between Kim Anderson and Dawn
Memee Lavell-Harvard on Personal and
Professional Evolutions in Indigenous Mothering

KIM ANDERSON AND DAWN MEMEE LAVELL-HARVARD

Kim: For starters, let me ask you, Memee; why do you think it is important to produce a book on Indigenous mothering, and, in particular, why now?

Memee: After the first volume on Aboriginal mothering (Lavell-Harvard and Corbiere Lavell), there were so many people who immediately wanted to know when we were going to create another one. Some had missed the opportunity to contribute the first time, but there were also those who simply found that the stories personalized the experience of Indigenous women, and they felt that was critical: to put an identity and a humanity to what can be some very disheartening statistics about the crises that a lot of our women are facing in their day-to-day lives. So, month after month, and year after year, everywhere we went, there were always people asking when we going to be starting our next volume, and so it seemed that the time had come. Those are the voices from the community that guide us, they tell us what we should be doing.

Kim: I think the inclusion of voices from around the world is interesting, and perhaps reflective of where we are going as Indigenous peoples. Of course, I know there were articles from outside of Canada the last time as well. But do you see a shift?

Memee: Well, international connections have come out of my work with the Ontario Native Women's Association and the Native Women's Association of Canada. I have seen that, as Aboriginal women become more politically active and evolve beyond the grassroots level community organizations, it is only natural that we start networking and dialoguing on international levels, recognizing those commonalities. There is a very strong network, globally, and interestingly enough, Aboriginal women in Canada are politically organized in a way that is just starting to happen for some of the Indigenous peoples around the world. Unfortunately, in Canada, we've also seen that, in order to make the changes we need, we have had to look for support outside our borders (UN Committee on the Elimination of Discrimination Against Women); it wasn't until Canada was shamed on the international level that some of those major foundational changes were made.

Kim: That's true; the activism did start from a global place early on—but it's all of that really significant work that happens at the grass roots that makes it possible. It's an ongoing interaction between the local and the global that we can work with in terms of the literature now as well.

Memee: Exactly. That's what I find one of the most interesting things about Indigenous peoples' organizing at a global level, is that the work is populated by Indigenous mothers who are really very grassroots, very down to earth. That's different from the political leadership that we typically interact with, the big movers and shakers in the non-Aboriginal world.

Kim: I'm interested in this question that you were writing about in your chapter in the last book, about the "commonality of difference" (Silver). You know, it's hard to articulate such a thing as "Indigenous mothering," but what about this commonality of difference? Where are we at now as opposed to where you might have been in 2006 when you published *Until our Hearts are on the Ground*?

Memee: That's a really good question...I think I am even further from any sort of solid definition of Aboriginal mothering now! As I go through the stages of my own mothering, I realize that defining mothering is more complex than I had originally thought, which was based on my naiveté and lack of experience as a mother. A lot of the literature, images, media, and so on are focused on the diapers and bottles generation, but now I'm progressing with my own children—I have one who is now seventeen, but also one who's still in Kindergarten. I'm covering both fields that way, but also entering that stage in my life where I realize that mothering isn't just about taking care of children. My parents are reaching the generation where that relationship is turning around now—so I am in what everybody talks about as the "sandwich generation."

Kim: Yes, and I would say that double caregiving role is a similar experience that cuts across many cultures. Do you think that there's anything in terms of Indigenous mothering practices that might be distinct within that role? *Memee*: I believe it's the role that we see for our mothers and our grandmothers, once they have moved beyond the physicality of caregiving; you know, the day-to-day needs, the cooking, the cleaning. I think within Indigenous traditions there is more respect for grandmothers' wisdom and knowledge based caregiving. This is different from some non-Aboriginal families or cultures, where the elders are sometimes seen as having lived past their usefulness. In Indigenous communities they are still caregivers, but just in a more knowledge-oriented, spiritual way.

Kim: Yeah, I think it's a question of continuing to have responsibility. In Indigenous communities that I know, elders have responsibility to younger generations—it's about fulfilling your life stage responsibility. Even though you aren't always able to do some of the physical caregiving, you still have caregiving responsibilities to be a mentor, a teacher—contributing in some way to the wellbeing of the collective. You're not a burden to the collective; but, rather, you continue to maintain responsibility to it. So, I think that's something that's distinct. I don't know if we've had a lot of theoretical writing around that, although this is something I was trying to get at in terms of the governing role of the "old ladies" in my Life Stages book (Anderson *Life Stages and Native Women*). So it's interesting that you pointed that out; that, yeah, a lot of the literature starts from the space of pregnancy, and the early years, and the caregiving, and the profound physical connection and nature of that role. That's where I was at and writing from when the first book Indigenous Mothering anthology was published as well! And now I'm personally moving into new stages of mothering; trying to think about what that means in terms of ongoing mothering practices.

Memee: That's something that we need to explore more in the future, and specifically from an Aboriginal perspective. There is such a wealth of knowledge within that role of the grandmother, of reaching that stage in life. When you are involved in the daily grind of the physical caregiving of young children, you are less reflective and more likely to be caught up in trying to stay one step ahead of the laundry piles and the dishes!

Kim: Yeah—that's a good way of putting it. If we think about it from the medicine wheel model of life being comprised of the physical, mental, emotional, and spiritual, maybe you're more on the physical side in those earlier years. But as you progress through the life stages, you move more into the mental and the spiritual components of the wheel—in terms of responsibility and in terms of practice. In my case, as an educator and a researcher, it's questions of "how do I mentor people who want to do what I do?" "how do I work with younger people?"

Memee: That's actually something I wanted to ask you about, because I still don't even have five minutes to stop and think about what is the difference, because I'm still doing Kindergarten!

Kim: Well, I guess I am getting more time to focus and think, and hopefully that means I'm starting to take responsibility for keeping an eye on the bigger picture—not just for my own kids, but for younger people overall. In the work I do as a professor, this translates into a responsibility to students: to mentor them, to look out for them, to seek opportunities, do training, and all that kind of stuff. This is part of the job of being an educator, of course. But it's also just part of being an older person in Indian country. I see it as an Indigenous mothering practice—you're automatically an educator if you are taking up your life stage responsibilities. I'm also lucky to have Elders who are role models to me. They aren't professors, but they work with people all over the place in that educating and support role. These are the grandmothers who are really "mothering the nation."

Memee: I know, with my own research (Lavell-Harvard) the women talked about the importance of those other mothers, those older women who were there to act in the role of a mother and a grandmother when they were in the urban communities, away from their Aboriginal communities.

Kim: Yeah, so mothering as a practice never really ends for Indigenous women, right? I think whether you choose it or not, it's just part of Indigenous cultures—in all the variations that we have, and of all the different types of communities we find ourselves in. So, if we're working in a university, there's like a mini-Indigenous culture going on within that. You find yourself in that mothering/auntie role with students, or with younger scholars or whatever. Of course, in that case, there's literature that documents the added workload that represents for Indigenous scholars, and I would say, in particular, for Indigenous women.

Memee: So can you say anything more about how being an Indigenous woman has informed your practice as a mother?

Kim: I think that one informs the other; it was mothering that first led me to thinking about what it means to be an Indigenous woman, and then thinking about what it means to be an Indigenous woman shaped my mothering practice!

I often talk about how I started researching and thinking about Indigenous womanhood after I had my first child, who's now nineteen, because this caused me to reflect on the sacredness of womanhood (see, for example, McKegney). My experience of that intense physicality of pregnancy, birth, and early years taught me the sacred feminine—and then I started looking for Indigenous cultural practices that validate that sacredness. It was part of developing a gendered identity—thinking about what Indigenous womanhood means in the big picture—and then thinking about what kind of mother I was going to be, as an Indigenous woman. So I looked for ways to celebrate their developmental milestones and life stages with ceremony. I tried to include my children in the adult environments that I belonged to—so dragged them around with me to meetings, research trips, conferences, and so on, as I knew that making space for children in these environments has always been part of an Indigenous education. I tried to teach them that they have roles and responsibilities to the collective-whatever that collective is and however it looks, right? It's been a process of recovery for me, especially having not grown up in an Indigenous community. But you didn't either, right? What about you?

Memee: Actually, it is kind of hard to describe; because my mom lost her Indian status when she married, we didn't actually live right on the reserve. But she was still a teacher there, so we lived just down the road. According to my father, we might as well have been on the rez since we were over at my grandparents, or they were over at our house, almost every day. Looking back, I realize that I've probably always led a double life. I grew up in a family that was always full of outlaws and rule-breakers. You know, the babies slept in the bed, we did ceremonies out under the full moon, we had feasts for the ancestors, and I think one of my uncles was growing pot in the garden out back. But we learned to hide it—we bought a baby crib and we planted rosebushes out front so that when the in-laws came around, or the local church ladies—whoever it was, you maintained appearances. You had to make it look like you were engaged in appropriate practices. My brothers and I used to joke about the fact that if we had ever let anything slip, man, the CAS[1] would have been over there so fast...

But it's interesting now to see how the wider community has come around on a lot of things that we never really gave up. Those traditional mothering practices had just gone underground, like a lot of our traditional practices. Now it's nice to be more out in the open. I've even noticed a difference between my oldest, who is seventeen, and the little one, who is now in Kindergarten—just how much society has changed; not having to constantly be surreptitious and furtive about hiding our Aboriginal practices. But I look at my grandmothers and my great grandmothers and their survival strategies. They knew how to make it look like they were going along with the Indian agent or the local church priest. You had to do enough work to maintain appearances so that you weren't openly defying these people, because that would bring wrath down on your head and on your family. It's nice to have more acceptance of traditional ways, of being grounded, of recognizing ourselves as human beings, as part of nature, as part of this larger natural force, so that birthing and breastfeeding and attachment and parenting is all part of a biological, natural process, and not a scientific experiment.

Kim: It's interesting for me to hear you talk about the difference between how you experienced parenting with your seventeen year old, as opposed to your five year old. My youngest is seventeen, and I remember still feeling kind of defensive about practices like home birth, the family bed, taking them with me as I went to work and school, or breastfeeding on demand. But in terms of the next generation, I work with young mothers who are still getting backlash for those things—I think it depends on which circles you are in. So, now, that's one support role I play in terms of saying, "Oh yeah, I did that however many years ago, and my kids turned out okay..." And, luckily, I am able to speak, not just to my own personal practice, but now, also from my research of Indigenous mothering practices, historically, and across Turtle Island.[2] Attacking these mothering practices was a huge part of the colonial project. I think this is why it's important to have the literature too, because then you can begin to see the commonality of difference in Indigenous mothering and the common and widespread assault on it.

Memee: Seeing this commonality is so important for these new generations—to recognize that Indigenous mothering is part of a long-standing historical legacy of strength and bonding; it isn't just some crazy notion or fly-by-night practice that, in a few years, will be completely debunked—this isn't radical. It may feel radical to those who have been raised in different ways. When you look at the mother outlaws literature (O'Reilly 59-74) you realize that we aren't the only ones who resisted mainstream practices. This gives you a certain amount of freedom to embrace your mothering, and not feel the guilt that you're somehow damaging your children by not complying with what is generally deemed to be correct. I'm grateful for the work of non-Aboriginal mother outlaws, because they were able to crack open spaces for these practices—and that would not have been possible for underprivileged or racialized women. There are those of us who would have been much more easily dismissed as just crazy uneducated Indians. In the end, I think that ability to survive despite all of the interference is the most common experience.

Kim: Can you think of some of these so-called "radical" practices for parenting kids beyond the early years—so, school age children, teens, young adults, or even middle-aged people—mothering in those stages?

Memee: Well, here's an example: I got a text from the mother of one of my daughter's friends saying "Oh, my God, it's ten o'clock and I'm running back down to the Walmart to buy this for junior's project that's due tomorrow…" And then asking me "What are you doing for this project?" My response was, "I don't know…we used whatever cornflakes boxes we had in the house and I didn't worry about it." I think this is part of our traditional Ojibway ethic of non-interference—of treating even the smallest members of our household as having their own will and their own self-determination. An important part of that is they also have to experience the natural consequences of their own lack of responsibility. For young children, obviously, school is one of the most important responsibilities that they have, so I think it's important to stop saving them. But they look at me like I'm the worst parent in the world. They're all sitting there in the playground the next morning, everybody's got bags under their eyes because this project was due and I think, "First of all, some of these kids are in *Kindergarten*—I mean, let's face it, one C on a project in Kindergarten is not going to affect their chances of getting into Harvard!" But there is such a competition, and such an importance placed on how well your kid does, because that reflects on you as a mother. I'm not suggesting that I let my children step out in front of a car—obviously we have some safety parameters here, but I'm constantly being judged as the worst mom on the block because I don't do my kids' projects for them. I let them go to the teacher and say "I forgot." Let the teacher get upset with them, let them get a C. I'd rather they experience that in grade two, than when it comes up and bites you in your first job or in university, or even in high school where these things actually start to matter. So, I think that's a good example, that ethic of non-interference, of letting our children experience the natural consequences of their decisions, because they truly do learn from that.

Another example was when I let my other child go to school without her gloves. She was resisting it, so I let her make her own decision. When they called up from the school to tell me my daughter was really cold, I said, "No, tell her I'm busy and that she should remember to wear her gloves tomorrow." I mean, she wasn't in danger of frostbite; we're not talking minus 20 degrees. I'm not cruel—she was a little bit uncomfortable and I let her be uncomfortable for a whole day. I didn't have one argument over gloves for the rest of the year. But, by God, I'm sure the principal, and the secretary, and everyone who was trying to help save her, they were all looking at me like I'm the worst parent in the world.

Kim: Well, I can't say I have been the best at non-interference, but I do remember those battles during the school years of both trying to resist my own impulses to control things, and resisting the culture of control that my kids experienced in the mainstream system. I am also well aware of this "helicopter parenting" generation we find ourselves in—and having to check myself about doing too much for them. I reflect a lot on stories I have heard from elders about how independent and at the same time interdependent they were as kids—like my friend/teacher Rene Meshake, who told me if he was hungry, he knew it was time for him to go snare a rabbit! (see Anderson). In looking at these histories of childrearing, I can see why, so often, outsiders would confuse the culture of non-interference with neglect. And it's still happening today—look at the story you just told!

Of course, in the urban contexts we live in, pressures to conform are influenced by class and whatever school you find yourself in, too. But when it comes to newer generations of Indigenous mothering, there's something I heard from the Anishnaabe psychologist Jane Middleton Moz that really struck me. Jane told me in an interview one time that we can produce shame in our kids by doing too much for them. She pointed out that, for those who grew up in environments of addiction, or who were deprived of material and other supports, it's easy to fall into this new culture of giving too much. We might think we are doing better, but in trying to make up for the past, it's possible that we take away responsibility and accountability in our children (see Anderson, 171).

I worry about that in terms of parenting my own kids, but I also think about how I can apply traditional Indigenous principles to encourage my students to take responsibility. So, I think there, again, there's an example of the wisdom of Indigenous parenting practice; this principal of non-interference and of encouraging responsibility, independence, and interdependence at the same time.

Memee: Yes, and sometimes a little hardship is good for them, because then they learn for themselves how to solve problems, and how to prevent it from happening next time. My aunt and I joke about it, we call it the Ojibway way.

Kim: From what I've seen, taking responsibility happens early on for Indigenous children. Especially historically and in land-based communities, young children were understood to be responsible for their own destiny and wellbeing, and for that of the collective! My friend Gertie Beaucage told me it was her job to set the fishing nets—and that no one ever had to remind her—she was well aware that the family wouldn't eat if she didn't (Anderson, 80). Maybe if we reflect on stories and practices like this—and try to build on that strong tradition of childrearing it will help to alleviate what Jane Middleton-Moz calls the "learned helplessness" that feeds into the crises we have in our communities (Anderson, 171).

So, we have lots of work to do, but lots of stuff to work with. It's still hard, though, to think about the critical situation for Indigenous women—as we can see in some of the articles in this book. As I was editing and looking at the statistics from your book chapter in the 2006 anthology (Lavell-Harvard and Corbiere Lavell, 184-194), I was wondering how much has changed. The fact exists that too many of our mothers remain in crisis, struggling with poverty, violence, child welfare. Where do we find our way forward in all of this?

Memee: Well, I think it's good for starters to recognize that Indigenous mothers around the world have had to struggle against violence for a very long time. I agree, it's very hard to tell sometimes whether we are making any progress, because it seems the more we work on this...the rates almost seem to be going up. The violence, the stories we hear, seem to be getting worse. But one of the perspectives that we've taken on this—and that does help to give us hope—is that the violence against our women has been there all along. Now we are finally actually talking openly about it. We're not sweeping it under the rug; we are starting to track it. Look at the Sisters in Spirit (NWAC), and Stolen Sisters (Amnesty International) reports, and even the latest RCMP report (RCMP, see also Pearce). Perhaps that's actually a sign that people are starting to disclose, starting to understand and name it: it is domestic violence; it is spousal rape; it is racial and gender violence. It is not normal day-to-day stuff, or that's "just the way life is." So, I do think we are making progress, even if only in terms of increasing awareness, and that's what is ultimately going to lead people to make the changes we need to protect our women. The silence is our biggest enemy.

Kim: I'm glad you said that. I hope that in publishing some of the articles in this volume, we are participating in that process that will ultimately lead to more change.

Memee: I have noticed, in the work we are doing on missing and murdered Aboriginal women, that, once again, it is mothers who are driving the change.[3] The mothers are out there voicing concern, keeping those memories alive, and honouring those women. The mothers are out there, still looking for their daughters. The mothers are leading vigils, keeping the fight for justice alive, and getting the word out there. They are the ones who have made the difference in terms of not allowing this to be just cast aside anymore; not allowing people to forget, and that's really critically important for the work that we do, when we're talking about the violence against Aboriginal women in Canada, specifically, but also around the world. It's very easy to get desensitized or to brush aside numbers, such as almost twelve hundred missing Aboriginal women in Canada. If they are nameless, faceless, that is something that people can easily ignore or forget about. But we know that was somebody's mother—or daughter. And that is the fundamental relationship that comes out again and again, in the vigils and in the work that we're doing. It's the mothers who are keeping it alive. And many children are left behind, because of violence against our women around the world, often the grandmothers find themselves taking care of children once again.

Kim: Yeah, for sure. As you were talking, I was thinking about the work that I've been involved in with Walking With Our Sisters and Christi Belcourt.[4] Christi put out this call for beaded moccasin vamps and there was a tremendous outpouring of support. And then we did a call for writing about missing and murdered women, and were astonished at the number of people who are out there, either doing research in this area, or with the capacity to do so. I was really heartened to find such a large community of people beginning to coalesce around making change, all this since ONWA did the *Breaking Free Report* in 1989.

Memee: I think it is directly connected to Indigenous women who are doing that mentoring, who are providing that mothering, that support within the institutions that have been so alienating and so oppressive in the past. Also, in the institutions, there are now more non-Indigenous allies—like the mother outlaws I referred to before, who helped create a space for alternative mothering practices thereby allowing Indigenous mothering practices to gain acceptance.

So, we need to continue to talk and write about Indigenous mothering experiences and practices. In terms of struggle, it's important to bring attention to the fact that, after centuries of colonization, Indigenous women are still being judged, we continue to be viewed as negligent, unfit mothers. But it's not that Junior is going to school without lunch because he has a bad mom; Junior is going without lunch because mom probably didn't eat last week either. It's a poverty issue in the whole household, in the whole community, and it has been for generations now. Junior's clothes aren't clean because the family lives in a shack with no water and no electricity, or worse yet, maybe they are homeless. How are you going to make sure Junior is clean, and his clothes are well-pressed for school, when the family is living in the car?

Kim: So there remains much work to be done in terms of acknowledging the legacy of colonization—and hopefully, now we are in positions to make all of the experiences of Indigenous mothering better known.

Memee: And that converts to, again, a sense of responsibility for mothering to the whole community. When you get into those positions, you do feel that additional responsibility to give back, to contribute, to pave the way and support the others who are not in that position yet.

Kim: An Indigenous woman's work is truly never done, Memee—that's certainly true in your case, I know. So thanks for the talk, and the work together on this book!

NOTES

[1] Children s Aid Society
[2] North America
[3] Memee is referring to the work that she does as the President of the Ontario Native Women's Association.
[4] Walking with our Sisters is an art installation project by Métis artist Christi Belcourt. Its intention is to commemorate the Missing and Murdered Indigenous Women of Canada and the United States. It is estimated that 600+ Native women have gone missing or have been murdered in the last twenty years. The installation is made up of 1,700 + pairs of moccasin vamps (tops) created and donated by individuals worldwide to draw attention to this injustice. It is touring thirty cities in Canada and the United States between 2013 and 2019.

WORKS CITED

Amnesty International Canada. *No More Stolen Sisters: The Need for a Comprehensive Response to Discrimination and Violence Against Indigenous Women in Canada.* 2009. Web. June 21, 2014.

Anderson, Kim. *Life Stages and Native Women: Memory, Teachings and Story Medicine.* Winnipeg: University of Manitoba Press, 2011. Print.

UN Committee on the Elimination of Discrimination Against Women. *Concluding observations of the Committee on the Elimination of Discrimination against Women : Canada.* 2008. Web. June 21, 2014.

Lavell-Harvard, Dawn Memee. The Power Of Silence and The Price of Success: Academic Achievement as Transformational Resistance for Aboriginal Women. 2012. Unpublished Doctoral Dissertation. University of Western Ontario. Web. June 21, 2014.

Lavell-Harvard, Dawn Memee and Jeannette Corbiere Lavell. Eds. *Until our Hearts are on the Ground: Aboriginal Mothering: Oppression, Resistance and Transformation.* Toronto: Demeter Press, 2006. Print.

Lavell-Harvard, Dawn Memee and Jeannette Corbiere-Lavell. "Aboriginal Women vs Canada: The Struggle for Our Mothers to Remain Aboriginal." *Until our Hearts are on the Ground: Aboriginal Mothering: Oppression, Resistance and Transformation.* Eds. Dawn Memee Lavell-Harvard and Jeannette Corbiere-Lavell. Toronto: Demeter Press, 2006. 184–195. Print.

McKegney, Sam. *Masculindians: Conversations about Indigenous Manhood.* Winnipeg: University of Manitoba Press, 2014. Print.

Native Women's Association of Canada. *What Their Stories Tell Us: Research Findings from the Sisters in Spirit Initiative.* 2010. Print.

Ontario Native Women's Association. Breaking Free: A Proposal For Change to Aboriginal Family Violence. Thunder Bay: ONWA. 1989. Print.

O'Reilly, Andrea. " 'We Were Conspirators, Outlaws From the Institution of Motherhood': Mothering Against Motherhood and the Possibility of Empowered Maternity for Mothers and Their Children." *Mother Outlaws: Theories and Practices of Empowered Mothering.* Ed. Andrea O'Reilly. Toronto, Women's Press. 59–74. Print.

Pearce, Maryann. *An Awkward Silence: Missing and Murdered Vulnerable Women and the Canadian Justice System.* Dissertation: University of Ottawa. 2013. Web. June 21, 2014.

Royal Canadian Mounted Police. *Missing and Murdered Aboriginal Women: A National Operational Overview.* 2014. Web. June 21, 2014.

Silver Cynthia. "Being There: The Time Dual-earner Couples Spend With Their Children." *Canadian Social Trends* (Statistics Canada catalogue no. 11-008-XPE) 57 (2000). 26–29. Web. 21 June 2014.

About the Contributors

Kim Anderson is a Métis writer, researcher and educator and an Associate Professor teaching Indigenous Studies at Wilfrid Laurier University in Brantford, Ontario. Her single-authored books are *A Recognition of Being: Reconstructing Native Womanhood* (revised edition forthcoming with Canadian Scholars' Press) and *Life Stages and Native Women: Memory, Teachings and Story Medicine* (University of Manitoba Press, 2011). She has a PhD in history, and has published over thirty peer-reviewed book chapters and journal articles on subjects including Indigenous mothering, Indigenous feminism, Indigenous masculinities, Indigenous child and family well-being, and Indigenous research methods. Kim lives with her partner and their two teenage children in Guelph, Ontario.

Mary Anderson has received a BA from the University of Saskatchewan, a BFA from Ryerson University, and an MA from York University. She has had an extensive history with the community-based sector in Saskatoon, and has held various researching roles in both Toronto and Saskatoon that have focused on community activism and cultural significance. Mary continues to play an active role as an emerging artist; much of her work focuses on socio-political subject matter, such as Aboriginal motherhood, Toronto sexual assaults, and the marginalization within her nearby St. James community. She is currently working on a cultural project with the University of Toronto's Factor-Inwentash Faculty of Social Work that focuses on early 20th century representations of women and children in Toronto's core neighborhoods.

Cyndy Baskin, PhD, is of Mi'kmaq and Celtic descent, originally from New Brunswick, who has been living in Toronto for many years. She belongs to the Fish Clan and her traditional name translates into English as something like "The Woman Who Passes on the Teachings." She is an Associate Professor in the School of Social Work at Ryerson University and a prolific writer with three books and numerous journal articles to date. Cyndy has also worked as a social worker and continues to assist agencies and communities in developing culturally-based programming for Aboriginal people.

Genevieve Blais is a young Oneida woman with a background in Biology and Biochemistry at the University of Toronto. She is currently pursuing a degree in Medicine with a strong desire to understand Indigenous Health in Canada. She also works closely with Traditional Healers and Elders as an Osh-Ka-Be-Wis at Anishnawbe Health Toronto.

Jennifer Brant, Mohawk woman and mother of two boys, is completing her PhD in educational studies at Brock University. Jennifer is the recipient of a Doctoral Fellowship from the Social Sciences and Humanities Research Council. Jennifer teaches in the Aboriginal Studies program and is currently employed as the Program Coordinator for the Gidayaamin Aboriginal Women's Certificate Program, Brock University. Her work is driven by her passion to contribute to Indigenous community well-being. Her research interests include: Indigenous maternal pedagogy, Indigenous women's literature as a source of empowerment, cultural identity formation, and the advancement of ethical space for Indigenous scholarship.

Leslie Brown is a researcher, grandmother, motorcyclist and currently the Director of the Institute for Studies and Innovation in Community University Engagement at the University of Victoria. She is the co-chair of the Pacific Housing Research Network and Principal Investigator of Siem Smun'eem, the Indigenous Child Well-being Research and Training Network. Her research and practice interests include Indigenous child, family and community welfare, community development and community-engaged research. Her connection to sex work is through family.

Sohki Aski Esquao (Jeannine Carrière) is Métis from the Red River area of southern Manitoba. She teaches Social Work at the University of Victoria. Her research interests include Aboriginal adoptions and identity, advancing Indigenous knowledges and the rights of sex workers and their families. She has a number of publications including the manuscript *Aski Awasis Children of the Earth: First Peoples Speaking on Adoption* (2010). Her connection to sex work is through personal experience and through T.E.R.F. Winnipeg.

Sinéad Charbonneau is a Métis community organizer around issues of violence against Indigenous women, access to human rights, and sex work. Her Métis family comes from Haudenosaunee territory and she was raised by her mother on Lekwungen land. She works on the Someone's Project as well as on a national study of managers in the sex industry. Her connection to sex work research is through friends in the industry and activism with sex workers.

Helene Connor is of Māori, Irish and English descent. She has whakapapa (genealogy) links to Te Atiawa and Ngati Ruanui iwi (tribes) and Ngati Rahiri and Ngati Te Whiti hapu (sub-tribes). She has one daughter. Helene's research interests include: utilizing a Māori feminist standpoint to research issues of relevance and interest to wahine Māori (Māori women); the intersections between gender and ethnicity and cultural representation; personal narratives and biographical research; mothers and mothering. Helene is a Senior Lecturer in the Department of Social Practice, Unitec, Auckland, Aotearoa/New Zealand.

Lorena Fontaine is Cree/Anishnabe from the Sagkeeng First Nation in Fort Alexander and the Opaskwayak First Nation in The Pas. Her mother attended St. Alban's and All Saints residential schools in Prince Albert and Elkorn residential school. Lorena is a professor of Indigenous Studies at the University of Winnipeg, Manitoba.

Lisa Forbes' roots are Cree, Métis, Scottish, and English. Her right to Indian Status was restored in 1987. A member of Peguis First Nation, Lisa works in community economic development with SEED Winnipeg and is a long-time human rights activist and member of Amnesty International. Her mother attended Birtle residential school.

Malika Grasshoff An anthropologist and historian, Makilam received her Ph.D. in history and ethnography from the University of Bremen, Germany. She is an indigenous Kabyle and was raised in a Berber village in northern Algeria until she was seventeen. Although she has since lived in Europe, she remains very close to her roots, and her testimony, interspersed with personal experiences, sheds new light on the rituals and myths of this vanishing society.

Caitlin Janzen is a Ph.D student in the Graduate Program in Sociology at York University. Her past research work has been in the area of violence against women, sexual exploitation of children, and sex work. Her doctoral research will focus on the role of women as spectators and witnesses in representations of violence against other women. Caitlin is involved in activism in the areas of violence against women and rights and services for sex workers.

Kirthi Jayakumar is a Writer and Legal Researcher with a background in Peace and Conflict, Human Rights and Public International Law. She runs The Red Elephant Foundation, a civilian peacebuilding initiative; and A38, an academic foundation for Public International Law.

Paul Kadetz is Director of the undergraduate program in Public Health and lecturer at Xi'an Jiaotong-Liverpool University in Suzhou, China. He is also a research associate of The Refugee Studies Centre, University of Oxford and an associate of the China Centre for Health and Humanity at University College London. He has conducted extensive research concerning local level healthcare systems and healthcare access in multiple contexts. His co-edited volume, *The Handbook of Welfare in China*, is forthcoming.

Dawn Memee Lavell-Harvard, PhD, is a member of the Wikwemikong First Nation, the first Aboriginal Trudeau Scholar, President of the Ontario Native Women's Association (ONWA), Vice-president of the Native Women's Association of Canada, Adjunct Faculty at Queen's University and full time mother to Autumn Sky, Eva, and Brianna. Since joining the ONWA as a youth director in 1994, Ms. Harvard has been working to break the cycles of poverty and violence, and empower Aboriginal women, for which she received the Queen's Diamond Jubilee medal in 2012. She was co-editor of *Until Our Hearts Are on the Ground: Aboriginal Mothering, Oppression, Resistance and Rebirth* (Demeter Press, 2006).

Dawn Marsden is Anishnaabe, French, a mother of two children, and lives in Coast Salish territory. She has training and experience in fine arts, public health, Indigenous knowledge, environmental issues, counselling, education, health and research. Her graduate and post-doctoral work focused on Indigenous identity, supporting Indigenous health practices, and community-based research. Since 2005, she has worked as a contract researcher doing participatory health research and evaluations, strategic planning, course and program design, teaching, knowledge translation and applications of IK to health, food sovereignty, and eco-social strategies for local, global and space development.

Wendy McNab is Cree/Saulteaux from Treaty 4 Area (Gordon's/Cowessess/Peepeekiss First Nations). Her mother, Pete, attended the Marieval and Qu'Appelle Indian Residential Schools in Lebret, Saskatchewan. Wendy works with First Nation Health & Social Secretariat of Manitoba.

Bela McPherson, MSW, RSW, is of Haudenosaunee (Mohawk), French and Scottish decent and is a member of Turtle clan. She grew up in the United States and moved to Toronto in 1995. She has a private psychotherapy practice in Toronto. Additionally she teaches part-time in the Faculty of Social Work at Ryerson University and as a Sociology instructor at Mothercraft College. She currently specializes with individuals who have experienced childhood traumas, addictions and violence/trauma. She assists on community research projects locally, provincially and nationally. Her current areas of interest are: children and families, Aboriginal health and well-being and youth homelessness.

Lisa Murdock is an off-reserve member of the K'atl'odeeche First Nation, located in the Northwest Territories. Lisa was born and raised in Winnipeg, Manitoba, where she continues to reside with her husband and three children. Lisa's mother survived St. Henry's Mission in Fort Vermillion and St. Joseph's Roman Catholic Residential School in Fort Resolution. Lisa's professional background includes social research, policy development and program administration aimed at improving life outcomes for Aboriginal children and families. She currently works as a consultant for the Province of Manitoba.

Hannah Tait Neufeld has worked for 20 years with Indigenous women and children globally on the revitalization of traditional foods and medicines, beginning in northeastern Brazil and central Java, Indonesia. At the University of Manitoba, she went on to study generational changes in food acquisition patterns during pregnancy in a First Nation community. Her dissertation explored urban First Nations and Métis women's experiences GDM through their relationships with food. Currently, as a Banting Postdoctoral Research Fellow in the Indigenous Health Lab at Western University she is studying how processes of environmental dispossession may have impacted the transference of traditional food knowledge.

Wendy Proverbs is Kaska-Dena and lives in Victoria, BC. She has a Master's degree in anthropology and is currently working on her aunt's memoir of her time at Lejac residential school as well as researching birch-bark basketry. She is mother to a son and daughter.

Stephanie A. Sellers holds a doctoral degree in Native American Studies with an emphasis on Women of the Eastern Woodlands. She is on the faculty at Gettysburg College. Her poetry and coyote stories have been published in journals such as *Calyx, American Indian Quarterly, American Indian Culture and Research Journal,* and *Native Literatures: Generations,* among others. Her most recent book from Peter Lang USA is *Native American Women's Studies: A Primer.* Dr. Sellers is a native Pennsylvanian who lives on a working homestead in the northern range of the Appalachians and is a mixed-blood woman of Cherokee, Shawnee, Jewish, and European immigrant lineages.

Laura Campbell Senese grew up in southern Ontario and traces her family roots back mostly to Italy and Scotland. Her longstanding interests in health and the environment led her to pursue a BSc in Biology, followed later by an MA in Health Geography, which explored relationships between urbanization, Indigenous rights, and health. Since then, she has had the opportunity to work on a number of community-based Indigenous health research projects. In the process, she has had the great privilege of learning from and working alongside many Indigenous health researchers, knowledge keepers, and other community members; she endeavours to respect and honour the stories and knowledge they have generously shared with her.

Dr. Janet Smylie is a Métis woman, mother of six, family physician and health researcher. She currently works as the director of the Well Living House Action Research Centre for Indigenous Infant, Child, and Family Wellbeing at St. Michael's Hospital and is an Associate Professor in the Dalla Lana School of Public Health, University of Toronto. She maintains a part-time clinical practice at Seventh Generation Midwives Toronto. She is a member of the Métis Nation of Ontario, with Métis roots in Saskatchewan. Her research interests focus on contributing to thriving Indigenous communities by applying Indigenous ways of knowing and doing to health services and programs.

Roberta Stout is Cree and a member of the Kehewin First Nation in Alberta. Her mother, Madeleine Dion Stout, is a survivor of Blue Quills residential school. Roberta works as an independent researcher and consultant.

Susan Strega is a Professor in the School of Social Work, University of Victoria. She is the co-editor, with Leslie Brown, of *Research as Resistance: Critical, Indigenous and Anti-oppressive Approaches* (Canadian Scholars Press, 2005) and the co-editor, with Sohki Aski Esquao of *Walking this path together: Anti-racist and anti-oppressive child welfare practice* (Fernwood, 2009). Her connection to sex work is through personal experience and through PEERS Victoria.

Rebeka Tabonbodung is the Founder and Editor-in-Chief of *MUSKRAT Magazine*, an on-line national Indigenous arts and culture magazine. Rebeka is a documentary filmmaker, poet and Indigenous knowledge and oral history researcher. Her documentary work has screened at festivals across Canada and internationally, while her written works have been published in numerous journals and anthologies. Rebeka is an M.A. graduate in Sociology & Equity Studies in Education, and her latest research and film work documents traditional birth knowledge from Wasauksing First Nation where she is also a member. Rebeka is the Research Coordinator of the Indigenous Knowledge Network for Infant, Child, and Family Health at St. Michael's Hospital.

Qwul'sih'yah'maht (Robina Thomas) is a member of Lyackson First Nation (Coast Salish). She is an Associate Professor in the School of Social Work at the University of Victoria. Robina is committed to Indigenous education and her research interests include Storytelling, Residential Schools, Indigenous women, Indigenous child safety and Uy'skwuluwun (Being of a good mind and spirit). She is committed to understanding anti-racism and anti-colonialism and how these can be "lived." Her connection to sex work is through family.

Samaya Van Tyler was born and raised in England. After moving to Canada, she taught in northern Saskatchewan, Alberta, and British Columbia. The University of Victoria in British Columbia, Canada, home for her undergraduate and graduate studies, is where she found her own voice among the storied voices of women moving in and out of margins to disturb academic border lines around the globe. She is the President of *Common Voice: Supporting Widows with HIV/AIDS*, a society in its infancy, which was conceived in the wake of her personal experience regarding the death of Loise, one of the women in her study.

Sara Wolfe is Ojibwe with family ties to Brunswick House First Nation. She began her career in healthcare with a focus on Aboriginal and maternal-child health in 1997. She completed her midwifery training in the International Midwifery Preregistration Program, Ryerson University and Thames Valley University, UK. Sara is a founding partner of Seventh Generation Midwives Toronto and was a co-lead on the newly established, Midwifery-led and Indigenous governed, Toronto Birth Centre.